GOVERNING THROUGH CRIME IN SOUTH AFRICA

Advances in Criminology

Series Editor: David Nelken

Recent titles in the series

Transitional Justice
Images and Memories
Edited by Chrisje Brants, Ton Hol and Dina Siegel

Racialized Correctional Governance
The Mutual Constructions of Race and Criminal Justice
Claire Spivakovsky

The Arts of Imprisonment
Control, Resistance and Empowerment
Edited by Leonidas K. Cheliotis

The Hidden Order of Corruption
An Institutional Approach
Donatella della Porta and Alberto Vannucci

Comparative Criminal Justice and Globalization
Edited by David Nelken

Racial Criminalization of Migrants in the 21st Century
Edited by Salvatore Palidda

Pervasive Prevention
A Feminist Reading of the Rise of the Security Society
Tamar Pitch

Children's Rights and the Minimum Age of Criminal Responsibility
A Global Perspective
Don Cipriani

Hate on the Net
Extremist Sites, Neo-fascism On-line, Electronic Jihad
Antonio Roversi

Decisions to Imprison:
Court Decision-Making Inside and Outside the Law
Rasmus H. Wandall

The full list of series titles can be found at the back of the book.

Governing through Crime in South Africa

The Politics of Race and Class in Neoliberalizing Regimes

GAIL SUPER
University of Cape Town, South Africa

Routledge
Taylor & Francis Group
LONDON AND NEW YORK

First published 2013 by Ashgate Publishing

2 Park Square, Milton Park, Abingdon, Oxon OX14 4RN
711 Third Avenue, New York, NY 10017, USA

Routledge is an imprint of the Taylor & Francis Group, an informa business

First issued in paperback 2016

British Library Cataloguing in Publication Data
A catalogue record for this book is available from the British Library

The Library of Congress has cataloged the printed edition as follows:
Super, Gail.
Governing through crime in South Africa : the politics of race and class in neoliberalizing regimes / by Gail Super.
pages cm. -- (Advances in criminology)
Includes bibliographical references and index.
ISBN 978-1-4094-4474-9 (hardback)
1. Crime--Political aspects--South Africa. 2. South Africa--Politics and government. 3. Neoliberalism--South Africa. I Title.
HV7150.5.S87 2013
364.968--dc23

2013011981

ISBN 978-1-4094-4474-9 (hbk)
ISBN 978-1-138-26696-4 (pbk)

Contents

Acknowledgements

This work is based upon research supported by the South African Research Chairs Initiative of the Department of Science and Technology and National Research Foundation. I would like to thank the staff at the University of Cape Town's Centre of Criminology for hosting me during the project. I benefitted tremendously from the warm atmosphere at the Centre. Particular thanks are due to Elaine Atkins and Professor Clifford Shearing. I would also like to thank Professor Monique Marks for her helpful comments, Professor David Garland for his support and critique and my editor Alison Kirk.

For those friends and family in my life who saw me through the process – you are many and I will name only a few: my guru and yoga teacher, Sri Dharma Mittra, you were thousands of miles away but were with me throughout the process; Eric, also thousands of miles away but a light in my life; Gideon, Mark, Mike, Rene and Kirsten, for putting up with my angst, of which there was plenty. During the last stages of writing Tudo, a rescue dog, entered my life – our walks resulted in a few epiphanies and lots of love. Finally, thanks and love go out to the rest of my family – my father who is a pillar of support in my life, my mother for seeing the other 'real' side, my sister for being such a great listener and last but not least, my beautiful daughter Maya: you have put up with a lot from me and I am truly blessed to be able to share my life with you.

Prologue

The *Cape Times* on Monday 21 November 2011 contained the following two front page articles: 'Mountain Knife Attack' and 'Children die in Desparate Search for Food'. The former was headline news whilst the second, off to the side – with less visual impact – was substantially shorter. I am using them to launch this book because they highlight two major problems that characterize South African society: the threat of crime and the images of heartbreaking poverty that weave their way through the everyday landscape of our urban consciousness.

> **Mountain Knife Attack**
>
> A Hiker has described how he fell off a ledge, broke a leg and bruised his ribs while running away from three muggers armed with a knife on the Karbonkel Mountain in Hout Bay. Despite his injuries, the three men then threatened JJ Badenhorst, 33, a businessman from Greenpoint, with the knife and stole his belongings.
>
> While this was happening, Badenhorst's friend, Thea Burger, managed to run away and escaped with a few cuts and bruises.
>
> The attack on Saturday, the latest in a string of incidents, occurred three days after a group of tourists was attacked and a woman mugged in Cecilia Forest near Constantia. Two men were arrested for that incident. Yesterday, law enforcement authorities and volunteers patrolled Table Mountain as part of a safety initiative.
>
> Marc Truss chairman of the Table Mountain Forum, said there had been a big turnout, with many volunteers taking to the mountain.
>
> Badenhorst, speaking by telephone from Constantiaberg, said he had fractured his left leg during the incident and doctors planned to operate on it.
>
> He said he and Burger had started hiking up the Karbonkel Mountain, keen to have a quiet walk.
>
> "While we were walking, we saw three men behind us. They looked suspicious and we felt unsafe. We started walking through the bushes, not on the normal route, to try and get away.
>
> "Suddenly the three men were just behind us. We started running downhill," Badenhorst said.
>
> … "We fell from one section onto a hiking trail. I could feel I broke my leg. I shouted to Thea to run. The three men were definitely chasing us. They wanted to run after Thea, but saw I couldn't go anywhere and stole the stuff I had. They are definitely professionals. They knew what they were doing," he said.
>
> Badenhorst said the mugger who threatened him with a knife had scars on his face and his eyes squinted. He could not immediately recall finer details or how the other two looked …

> The incident had not deterred him from using the mountain. "But next time I'll go in a bigger group, " Badenhorst said … Police spokesman November Filander said no one was arrested.
>
> Following Saturday's mugging, the Twitter account @TableMntnWatch, run by the Table Mountain Safety Action Group (TMSAG), listed the Karbonkel Mountain trail along with Cecilia Forest and Noordhoek Beach as crime hot spots. (Dolley 2011)
>
> **Children die in Desperate Search for Food**
> The four Mmupele children had not had a decent meal in weeks when they set out from home in the sweltering North West heat to find their mother and food. The children, aged two, six, seven and nine, were found dead in the veld. They apparently died of hunger and dehydration.
>
> The bodies of the two younger children were found dead about three days after the children left the Verdwaal, Itoseng, settlement, about 25 km from Lichtenburg. Those of the older children were found more than two weeks later.
>
> The four – three boys and a girl – had tried to follow their mother, a pregnant Kedibone Mmupele, 27, who had walked to the farm of Kobus Pretorius an 18 km walk away where her own mother, Martha Mmupele, was visiting. She hoped to return home with mealie meal and chicken for the children.
>
> Verdwaal – about 25 km outside Lichtenburg – was established fairly recently for former farm dwellers, some of whom continue to work on the farms. The residents are largely reliant on the farms for food, and the ration of mealie meal and chicken from Pretorius's farm, given to Martha Mmupele's boyfriend – an employee – often fed the family.
>
> "We were all very hungry because there hadn't been much food in the house for weeks, so by seven that morning I was already on my way to the farm, knowing I would be back by that evening" Kedibone Mmupele said. She left her sons – Onkarabile, 2, and Nkume, 6 – brother Sebengu, 9 and sister Mapule, 7, in the care of her 15-year-old brother, telling him to take them to a relative's house before he went to school.
>
> Itoseng police officer Johannes Mashaba said the four children followed their mother's route. They had walked about 7 km when they met a neighbor … who joined them for about 5 km. They told her they were hungry and thirsty … She eventually left them [after having tried to] "convince them to turn back or come with me because they could be kidnapped". (Makhubu 2011)

These articles tell archetypal stories about life in South Africa. The first one has numerous subtexts. The ugly face of crime that threatens an otherwise idyllic South African dream – intruding even on the perceived right to enjoy a walk in the pristine beauty of Karbonkel Mountain. Another theme is that of the expert victim hero who, despite the attack still tries to protect his woman friend and thereafter relates his ordeal from the sanitized safety of Constantiaberg, a private medical clinic which caters for the well-off.[1] Thus quite clearly the victim of this crime must be one of South Africa's well-off/cushioned classes, certainly if he lives in Greenpoint, one of Cape Town's recently gentrified trendy urban neighbourhoods, and can afford treatment at a private clinic. This is, after all, part of the reason why the article made the front pages. Despite the fact that violent crime and the fear of it is part of the fabric of the everyday life of all who live in South Africa – evidenced by the numerous coping devices deployed to deal with it – much of it does not make the front pages of the newspapers. It is simply not newsworthy. Cape Town's natural beauty, the mountains and oceans, are its claim to fame – these are what make the city special. The fact that peace-loving people, searching for some calmness amidst the chaos of everyday life, should be violently attacked in such a setting induces outrage in the minds of the 'reasonable citizen' subject. Why isn't the government doing more to combat crime? Why do 'criminals' act with impunity? Why aren't more of them arrested and imprisoned? The subtext of seeing 'three men behind us' implies that it was three 'non-white'[2] men. The victim describes his attackers in stereotypical terms – the scar-faced gangster mugger with squinty eyes. He must be coloured[3] because the attack has taken place near a 'coloured' township. At the same time his description of the attack as having been perpetrated by 'professionals' is reflective of the discursive shift which characterizes the post-apartheid period. This depiction of the criminal as being a 'professional' – not sick or in need of help but as highly organized and effective, part of an organized crime syndicate that needs to be stamped out, like a cancer (Standing 2006) – is part of mainstream discourse in South Africa today. On the other hand the police are represented as totally ineffective and this is juxtaposed with an active Table Mountain Watch. The new struggle to reclaim cities and mountains is one that has emerged in the post-apartheid era and is alluded to in the article's reference to the Table Mountain Watch and Table Mountain Safety Action Group. This says much about the perceived ineffectiveness and impotence of the state to do anything about crime, resulting in citizens having to protect themselves. These self-protection initiatives range from private sector activities, gated communities, booming private security guard businesses to vigilantism and xenophobic outbursts.

1 My interpretation is based on the manner in which the incident was framed in the newspaper article. I certainly do not intend to be disparaging of Mr Badenhorst, nor to imply any wrongdoing on his part.

2 Given that the attack took place near a 'coloured' township – Karbonkelberg is situated just behind the coloured township of Hangberg – and that the muggers are described as appearing to be 'professional', in the context of the racial stereotyping associated with non-white criminality in South Africa, the racial implications are obvious.

3 Where I use inverted commas around the words 'Native', 'Bantu', 'Non-White', 'Black', 'White', 'Coloured', 'Asiatic' or 'Indian' it is to indicate that I am dealing with a category of official discourse. When referring to 'people categorized by these labels but alluding to realities beyond official classification' (Ashworth 1990: 12) I use the term black, coloured, etcetera without inverted commas.

The second piece tells a much more mundane and quotidian story about the everyday poverty that engulfs a substantial proportion of South Africa's population. Taking place in 'Verdwaal', the settlement for former farm dwellers, which literally means 'lost', the fear of crime – in this instance in the form of kidnapping – that is very much present in the minds of both poor and rich, and the subtext about the politics of farm labour – farmworkers are a traditionally exploited bloc of workers – are all themes that underpin this text.

Not only does South Africa have one of the highest rates of inequality in the world, with many black people still living in poverty and income concentrated in the top decile of earners, but intra-race inequality and poverty levels have actually increased in the post-apartheid era (Leibbrandt et al. 2010). In fact almost half of South Africa's population live in poverty (Marais 2011: 203), with blacks being much poorer than coloureds, who are much poorer than Asians, who are poorer than whites – thus, the between-race inequality, which characterized apartheid, is still high, and falling only slowly (Leibbrandt et al. 2010). Due to job losses, blacks have became poorer after the end of apartheid and less than 1 in 10 (9 per cent) had a total monthly income of R7500[4] in 2005–2006 (Marais 2011).

Although this book is not about the government's neglect of the poor, the poverty and inequality that characterize South African society does, as I argue in the book, have a fundamental role to play in the way that crime policies have been developed and implemented. The emergence of neoliberal economic policies and punitive penal policies are part of a political field in which the poor are not well represented (Garland 2010) and punishment is somehow absurd because of efforts to present as just the enforcement of laws that emerge out of unequal social relations (Carlen 2010). The 'semi-peripheralized' (Cheliotis and Xenakis 2010: 366) nature of South African society, with its endemic poverty and inequality, results in 'tensions' (Cheliotis and Xenakis 2010: 367) that manifest as lower and middle class anxieties. As such, the 'police mentality' (Dubber, cited in Lacey 2008: 100) that characterized apartheid and focused on governance of the lower classes, is still noticeable. These tensions have played out in unique ways in South Africa – with violent vigilante attacks taking place in poorer townships where outraged community members, in Durkheimian collective outbursts, have taken the law into their own hands and murdered alleged criminals, prior to the police getting involved or, even with police complicity. This is often done via necklacing – where a tyre is placed around the person's neck and set alight – a technique that was used by political activists, against those alleged to be police spies, during the struggle against apartheid. This resonates with the official discourse of an ANC government that once called for ungovernability in the townships, accusing the apartheid government of criminalizing all forms of political resistance, but now as a government accuses criminals of being the biggest threat to the new democracy, completely stripping their actions of all political overtones and divorcing them from a socio-economic context.

---

4 US$844.

Chapter 1
Starting the Conversation

This book is an exploration of how crime and government intersect in post-apartheid South Africa. The main question that I ask is how the transition to democracy in South Africa has affected government discourse, perceptions and treatment of 'criminals'. One of my goals is to encourage recognition of the deeply political nature of crime policies and how they both reflect and distribute power in society (Gottschalk 2006: 254). Normatively we might have expected the African National Congress (ANC) to be against the prison and in favour of an approach to crime which actively seeks to do something about structural causes. We might have expected it to be reintegrative and inclusive in its choice of criminal justice policies. Yet this has not been the case and, in South Africa today, imprisonment comprises a central plank of the government's crime policies. The fact that the ANC has adopted punitive penal policies alongside neoliberal economic and social policies is at odds with what it promised and what was expected from a socialist-orientated revolutionary organization with precursors, roots and connections to grassroots democratic movements.

By way of a historical case study, from 1976 to 2004, the book examines how the problem of crime has emerged as a major issue to be governed in post-apartheid South Africa. Having undergone a dramatic transition from authoritarianism to democracy, from a white minority Nationalist Party (NP) government to a black majority ANC one, South Africa provides rich material on the role that political authority, and challenges to it, play in the construction of crime and criminality. The book is not about what causes crime or how to control it but is about its socio-cultural and political significance. Looking at this in the context of a change in regime is immensely productive and it is hoped that adding a perspective from a freshly democratized country will provide some interesting and illuminating empirical material to the broader debate on crime control in post-welfare/neoliberalizing/post-transition polities (Bright 1996, Cohen 1985, De Georgi 2006, Dixon 2000, 2004a, 2004b, 2004c, Feeley and Simon 1992, Garland 1996, 2001, Gordon 2001, 2006, Hannah-Moffat 2000, 2005, Lacey and Zedner 1995, O'Malley 1992, 1996, 1999, 2004a, 2004b, Nelken 2010, Parenti 1999, Pratt 2000, Rose 2001, Samara 2003, 2005, 2011, Simon 2001, 2007, Sparks 2000, 2003, Wacquant 2001a, 2001b, 2007, 2009, Van Zyl Smit and Van Der Spuy 2004, Young 1999).

Official Criminology

The empirical focus of the book is on state discourse about crime and criminality ('official criminology') within the context of social, political and economic shifts. I treat official discourse about crime – Commissions of Inquiry, statements by politicians, political party manifestos, white papers, laws and annual departmental reports from the Justice, Prisons, Welfare and Police departments, as well as parliamentary debates on crime and other policies (economic, social, budgetary) – as a type of political text designed to shape governmental practice and its public perception. I used police reports to ascertain whether and how the perceived, officially reported crime rates and patterns were changing. These crime rates, together with the moral panics precipitated by their release (or non-release), have influenced the government to adopt certain crime policies, as I discuss in Chapter 2.

Since official criminology does not arise in a vacuum, and being cognizant of the danger of overprivileging governing authorities and giving an overly smooth and coherent account of what is in fact contested, my analysis includes the policy positions of relevant think tanks, such as the Human Sciences Research Council and the Institute for Security Studies, articles in criminal justice journals, newspaper articles and secondary literature. I have also conducted selective in-depth interviews with certain key people[1] and I researched the policy papers of the ANC prior to its assuming the mantle of government.

These texts serve as my portal – to analyse how things have changed or not, and to see how policy-makers construct subject populations (such as the pass law offender, the parole violator, the supercriminal, the illegal immigrant) and the causes of crime. This is part of the larger story that I am telling, about the politics of crime, the politics of rhetoric, in the context of the politics of change from apartheid to post-apartheid, from white minority to black majority rule, from authoritarianism to democracy. Being a 'law and society' project this book uses the study of society to understand official criminology, and also uses official criminology to understand society (Garland 2010: 16). As Garland (2010: 16) states, it 'works in both directions – studying a social context to better understand a legal institution, but also using a legal institution to better understand a society'. Thus, running alongside the study of official criminology is a sub-theme about South African society, which seeks to use crime, and what the state says and does about it, as a lens through which to view South Africa and the unequal social relations that are still very much a part it.

In tracing how various political rationalities intersect with, configure and reconfigure penal policies, the book analyses the ways in which crime policies are based on certain political assumptions, use racial or class categories and are linked to specific political projects. Two of the themes that emerge in Chapter 2 are the changing relationship between crime and politics as the ANC went from being a

1 See Appendix 1 for a list of people that I interviewed.

resistance organization to becoming the government, and the changing relationship between crime and race as blacks went from being the oppressed group to being the governing group. A large part of what I set out to do here is to trace the ironies and hypocrisies involved and how these relationships changed over time.

Revealing of more than just rhetoric, official discourse is not a mere empty gesture but a form of communication and as such is performative (Singh 2005a, 2005b, 2008, Garland 2010). As a rationality of rule, it is inextricably linked with broader issues of political authority. Thus, for example, in Chapter 6 I discuss the way that the ANC government justifies its existence in terms of a nationalist discourse that is rooted in its liberation struggle credentials. This also doubles up as a call to all morally upright South African citizens to take up the new struggle against criminals, discussed in Chapter 5. As such, official criminology functions as a technique of political and ideological hegemony and plays a symbolic and instrumental role that goes well beyond its actual effect on crime rates or its ability to prevent crime (if this could be measured) (Garland 1990, Melossi and Pavarini 1981, Foucault 1977).

'Political Criminology'[2]

Politics and crime are connected on many levels. The most obvious connections lie in the political appointments of criminal justice officials, the politicization of crime policies and prosecutorial decisions based on overtly political considerations. In a context where patronage and corruption are very present, politics and power enter into the very act of deciding what and who to prosecute, particularly when public figures such as the Commissioner of Police are charged with fraud, sentenced to a term of imprisonment after a protracted trial (with his legal defence being paid for by the state), only to be released on medical parole after serving only a year, most of it in the prison hospital (to which most ordinary prisoners do not have access, due to massive overcrowding); where the current President, after being acquitted in a rape trial, was charged with fraud, only to have the charges withdrawn by the National Prosecuting Authority in a highly controversial decision; and where criminal prosecutions are interwoven with national intelligence and political power struggles between various high-level ANC politicians.[3]

In addition, shifting definitions of crime and punishment are both shaping of, and shaped by, political developments, which are in turn rooted in the microcosms of societal power structures (Bright 1996, Davis and Slabbert 1985, Foucault 1977, 1982, 1991, Hay 1976, Thompson 1975, Tonry 2009, Wacquant 2001, 2007, 2009). Indeed, the perception of crime is as much about 'cultural politics' (Garland 2010: 7) as about crime, and crime itself is a fluid, mutating concept dependent on cultural norms (Durkheim 1982). In post-apartheid South Africa

2 Scheingold (1998) uses the term.

3 I return to these issues in the Epilogue.

miscegenation and homosexuality are no longer criminal offences and black people are free to live and move where they like yet prison sentences lengthened with the dismantling of apartheid and have continued to do so in the 'new' South Africa. Thanks to mandatory minimum sentencing and other non-discretionary sentencing laws, overcrowding has worsened and the ratio of social workers and psychologists to prisoners is woefully inadequate to address even basic needs. I discuss this in Chapter 6.

As discussed in Chapter 2, police annual reports still refer to 'unrest' as a veiled acknowledgement of the intersections between crime control policies and political legitimacy. This chapter also tracks how the Nationalist Party government portrayed political opponents as ordinary criminals and how the ANC government has decoupled crime from politics – no longer recognizing political justifications for committing crimes – whilst the problem of crime has itself become an intensely politicized issue, playing out in election campaigns and parliamentary debates. These linkages between 'political authority and crime control policy' (Scheingold 1998: 875) are often sublimated and not discussed in mainstream criminology.

Time Frame

I start in 1976 because at this point the South African government experienced crises in both the political and economic spheres and it started to deploy different techniques of rule. The political and economic reforms embarked upon by the South African government during this period represented an attempt by the Nationalist Party to create a compliant black middle and working class with changes in the production of knowledge about crime, the move towards technical approaches and a greater emphasis on science both reinforcing and reflective of this shift (Marais 2001, Tikly 2003).

No doubt influenced by the anti-communist rhetoric percolating in the USA, the fear of the black masses embracing communism was fierce and the 16 June 1976 uprising was seen as the start of a 'revolution … being led by young Black militants who are socialists and communists' (*Hansard* 1977a col: 806). By 1977, apartheid, and particularly the heavy state regulation of the South African economy, started to be criticized by both English and Afrikaner capital. The official opposition United Party accused the NP government of practising a type of socialism and there was much parliamentary debate about a 'free economy' and what this meant for South Africa. The NP claimed that it was free whereas the United Party, which equated capitalism with freedom, stated that it was not and that South Africa needed a 'responsible body of people among those Black people who [would] stand up for the private enterprise system' (*Hansard* 1977a: col: 806). It accused the NP of being a party that 'stands for the big state, the big tax, the big operation by the state at the cost of the individual' (*Hansard* 1977a col: 801).

From the early 1980s the Nationalist Party government implemented certain neoliberal reforms. These reforms were aimed at repairing a faltering hegemony without actually changing the racialized class structure of South African society. They included the privatization of public transport and housing in black townships and the recognition of a limited form of black self-government. These specific South African reforms occurred within the context of 'transnationally networked neoliberalization projects' (Brenner et al. 2010a: 212). The latter included an ideological assault against the British and US style welfare states and anti-communist rhetoric that was fast attaining hegemony in the West. Initially based on a critique of Keynesianism, they resulted in a series of 'market-centric' commodifying reforms (Brenner et al. 2010a: 210) in the specific contexts of countries such as West Germany, Chile, the UK and the USA. As Brenner et al. (2010a: 212) describe them, these projects were 'an intellectual amalgam' and 'unevenly developed ideological form' precisely because they drew on an 'eclectic, uneven, net-worked and historically specific intellectual-political legacy'. Thus it is important to see how the mid-1970s crisis of apartheid rule in South Africa, which resulted in a shift away from 'racial Fordism'[4] towards privatization, coalesced very well with transnationally percolating neoliberalized discourse within a specific South African context. Neoliberalization processes in South Africa have been directly shaped by racist ideologies, such as the '*rooi gevaar*' (red/communist danger) and '*swart gevaar*' (black nationalist danger), and this was part of the institutional landscape inherited by the post-apartheid government.

The research for the book ends in 2004 but I bring my story up to date in the Epilogue. I chose 2004 as a cut-off date because this was ten years after the first democratic elections and Mbeki, Mandela's successor, had just completed his first term of office. By this stage the various figures of the criminal: the drug addict, pass law offender, *rondloper* (street walker), vagrant and 'idle and undesirable', which used to be important discursive categories, had become decentred by the notions of 'organized crime', the 'supercriminal' and the 'corporatized' (Standing 2006: 57) street gang, in terms of a discourse which wore the double-breasted mantle of both managerialism and punitivism. I discuss this in Chapter 4. It was also the time at which, with the appointment of the Jali Commission of Inquiry Into Alleged Incidents of Corruption, Maladministration, Violence or Intimidation in the Department of Correctional Services, a glaring disjuncture became apparent between the ideals and visions of the 'new' South Africa and the very disappointing (and corrupt) reality of what was happening in practice. Like Singh (2008: 4) I do not use the term 'post-apartheid' in the sense of the 'end of apartheid and beginning of a new liberal democratic era' but as being indicative of the emergence of a new political rationality, in a governmentalizing South Africa. My use of the

4 Marais (2001: 11) uses this term to describe the Nationalist Party project of extending the benefits of a social welfare state to whites only.

terms 'new' and 'post' is with a sense of irony in view of the continuities between apartheid and post-apartheid rule.

By 2004 it was very clear that certain powerful blocs within a deeply fractured ANC were sympathetic to market-based policies, with almost one-third of its National Executive Committee members serving as directors of Black Economic Empowerment (BEE) companies and social justice being 'peripheralized' (Marais 2011: 5, Bond 2000, McCord 2007, Peet 2002, Terreblanche 2012). The idea was that BEE would create a 'black capitalist class' that would operate together with the state to create a developmental state (Marais 2011: 142). Despite improved access to schools, water, health care, sanitation, electricity and housing subsidies, the proportion of households living in informal settlements is still high, urbanization has increased and there has been an increase in the 'scale of need' (Marais 2011: 213). Not all local authorities provide free water, and registering as an indigent is a time-consuming and bureaucratic process. Social welfare is targeted and means-tested, and aimed mainly at children, the disabled and the elderly, i.e. it is not universal (Marais 2011: 242). According to Marais the reason that many households are ineligible is because the grants were not intended to combat poverty but are instead based on the assumption that all healthy adults should be able to earn a living through working (Marais 2011: 243). Yet labour market inequality has risen in the post-apartheid era – due to rising unemployment and increasing earnings inequality (Leibbrandt et al. 2010, Everett 2010). Between 1970 and 1995 South Africa's labour force grew by almost 4 million but only 1 million jobs were created. Yet the South African government has adopted a narrow definition of unemployment inasmuch as it does not count anyone who has not 'taken active steps' to find employment in the four weeks prior to being surveyed and also not people who report earning from 'begging', 'hunting' or growing their own food (Marais 2011: 176). Even using a narrow definition of unemployment, one in four working-age South Africans are not employed. If one counts workers who have given up looking for jobs then by the 2000s unemployment ranged from to 34 per cent to 40 per cent (Marais 2011: 177). Public Works Programmes (PWPs) are meant to serve as 'ways into formal employment' yet the jobs are temporary and as such do not address the 'crisis of the labour market' (Marais 2011: 192, Phillips 2004).

At the same time the ANC government has actively sought to build a 'new' South Africa along nationalist lines, incorporating the formerly politically excluded black masses. Part of this has entailed a punitive crackdown approach to crime couched in the rhetoric of the liberation struggle. This has occurred alongside the incorporation of blacks into a rampant consumer culture. Coupled with unemployment and inequality the tensions and contradictions in South African society are plain to see – ranging from the Gucci Black Economic Empowerment millionaires, the old white money associated with the mansions in the leafy suburbs, through to the vendors of the *Big Issue* and ubiquitous beggars who populate the traffic lights in the central urban and affluent suburban areas.

Shifts and Continuities

Whilst one way of characterizing official criminology in South Africa is in terms of a shift from 'community based crime prevention'/'social crime prevention' in the early heydays of the democratic transition to 'crime control' and a 'getting tough' approach from 1998 on (Rauch 2007, Van Zyl Smit and Van der Spuy 2004), this book is concerned with overlaps and how different discourses can in fact coexist quite 'peacefully'. Highlighting the contingent nature of the discourse on crime and punishment in terms of an analysis which is centred on the interconnectedness of discourses avoids the risk of linearity inherent in viewing the penal complex in terms of stages and phases, as opposed to linkages, points of intersections, messiness and recursivity. The book questions those accounts (Rauch 2002, 2007, Van Zyl Smit and Van der Spuy 2004, Samara 2003, 2005, 2011) which divide the South African penal field into phases of rainbow nation style restorative justice immediately post-1994, followed by a punitive period from 1998 on. In fact, as I discuss in Chapter 5 it is interesting how restorative justice has been lauded by parties on both the right and the left, for different reasons. Even in the immediate pre- and post-1994 days of rainbow nation discourse criminals were excluded from the polity and regarded as a threat to democracy. The fact that the ANC deployed the death penalty against those found guilty of treason against the movement, not to mention its punitive treatment of cannabis smokers in the training camps – discussed in Chapter 6 – shows how a punitive approach to 'deviance' was already built into ANC policies prior to it assuming the role of governing party.

Following Buur and Jensen (2007: 33), who point to the danger of 'othering'[5] apartheid because it prevents an identification of the politics underpinning the production of subjectivities in both the apartheid regime *and* in democratic South Africa, I offer a critical account of the politicized 'progress'/evolutionary perspectives[6] on South Africa's transformation from white minority rule to democracy. These perspectives present the 'new' South Africa as being radically different from the old. Apartheid policing is generally identified with the 'suppression of opposition to apartheid' (Nathan and Colin 1993: 1), the Nationalist Party approach to managing crime as a 'counter-discourse of repressive crime control' (Van der Spuy et al. 2004: 167) and, the 'government's counter-

---

5 Via the political perspective that 'apartheid … [is] the benchmark of evil that a truly democratic South Africa must distance herself from'.

6 See Mabin (1998: 1), who refers to 'discourses of progressive change' being accepted across the political spectrum. Gordon (2006: 245) refers to the 'triumph of South Africa's rejection of apartheid and embrace of non-racial democracy' and to South Africa being regarded as a 'beacon of democratic transformation at the end of the twentieth century' and the transition to democracy has been referred to as a miracle (see Waldmeir: *Anatomy of a Miracle*, Sparks: *Beyond the Miracle*; Friedman and Atkinson: *The Small Miracle* – cited in Gordon 2006). Du Plessis and Louw (2005: 428) refer to South Africa's transition to democracy as being a 'remarkable success'.

insurgency strategy 'as leading to an overall increase in the prison population and a proliferation of political trials' (Fillipi 2011: 630). I argue that the picture is somewhat more complex than depicted by these authors and that the apartheid government had embarked on certain reforms which had their own consequences. Although official criminology in the 'new' South Africa has jettisoned NP rule as simply being hardline, rightwing and conservative, things were not so simple, nor were they static and unchanging. For example, in February 1981 the daily average number of detainees was more than 104,622 – the highest ever in South Africa's history. One might have expected a repressive regime to call for the building of more prisons yet the Department of Justice admitted that the provision of additional cells would not 'in itself solve the problem' and that steps had therefore been taken to 'reduce the influx into prisons' (Department of Justice 1982a para 7.1:2). A departmental working group, the Krugel committee, was thus established to deal with the problem. In Chapter 6 I discuss my finding that in the 1980s the NP government declared an intention to do more about rehabilitating black and coloured prisoners. Thus, for example, Skelton's perspective that when Western countries were carrying out their important work on alternatives to punitive measures, 'South Africa was in the grip of a harsh law and order regime' (Skelton 2005: 153) not only romanticizes Western reforms but also tends to overlook the fact that apartheid was not a static form of rule but was reforming and changing in its quest for narrative coherence.

Politically provocative as it may be, my argument is that penality under apartheid was complex and that crime and punishment policies underwent a process of reform during the period of my research. Many elements, such as the turn to community, that we associate with post-apartheid discourse on crime, were present in the policies adopted in the previous period and furthermore these also represent breaks with that of classical Verwoerdian[7] apartheid. In Chapter 5 I argue that the period from 1976 to 1989 was not solely based on the exercise of sovereign power, that the apartheid state embraced some of the tenets of liberalism and was *also* concerned with governing through the black community. As Tikly (2003: 14) argues, the apartheid state was both a 'liberal' and 'illiberal' state – although full citizenship was only granted to whites, blacks were not treated by illiberal means alone, and the courts in particular often strove to operate within a liberal framework.

This book argues that the apartheid regime contained elements of sovereign, disciplinary and governmental power as does liberalizing/constitutional rule in the 'new' South Africa. It is the conditions under which one comes to prominence over the others, and how they are configured in relation to each other, which are interesting. Similarly I argue that one should not overplay the coherence of modern punishment and that in fact it is characterized by unevenness. To argue that apartheid was punitivist misses the point that it was also reforming. As King

---

7 The ultimate aim of Verwoerdian apartheid was to have no black citizens and no black people with the right to reside in white cities (Budlender and Davis 1984: 161).

(1999) points out, liberal states engage in illiberal practices and illiberal states engage in liberal practices. Hutchison (2006: 444) argues that 'punishment and reform have always been braided together in modern liberal penality' and punitive techniques have a history of being deployed in a variety of locations and across a wide period of the modern era (Brown 2002). In Chapter 6 I show how the prison, reinvented as a restorative prison in the 'new' South Africa, is integral, rather than antithetical to, the new democracy because it is a symbol of how things have changed.

One of the central arguments in this book is that crime and punishment issues present opportunities to engage in state-building (Gottschalk 2010: 41–2).[8] Just as the emergence of the penitentiary was a 'project *constitutive* of liberal democracy' (Dumm 1987: 6) in the early USA, so too has the prison in South Africa, reinvented (discursively at least) as the reintegrative prison, played a central role in the constituting of the newly democratizing and liberalizing South Africa.

Unevenness

Despite the continuities between crime and punishment policies in the 'old' and 'new' South Africa it would be grossly simplistic to argue that crime control in the 'new' South Africa is merely a continuation of the old. Instead I show how official criminology has been remade and adapted to the post-apartheid South African environment; how new forms, such as the restorative prison, the maximum security prison and the private prison have emerged; how the discourse now functions as a mode of uniting South Africans around the problem of crime and the criminal 'other'; how crime prevention has taken on new social meanings, producing a responsibilized ethical South African citizen; how the criminal figure has emerged as one of the main threats to human rights in the post-apartheid polity; and how the victim-expert has assumed a central role in policy-making.

The book analyses the mixed messages given off by the South African government insofar as it embraces human rights, social crime prevention and restorative justice (Skelton 2005, Gould and Bruce 2009) together with a punitive discourse on crime and criminality. Are the competing penal discourses (restorative justice, 'lock 'em up and leave 'em' style punitivity, community crime prevention,

8 According to Gottschalk (2006: 236) the carceral state was an important chapter in American state-building and not just a manifestation of a successful political whim by strategic conservative politicians in the last 30 years. Similarly, Dumm (1987: 5) argues that the prison in particular plays a central and constitutive role in the shaping of 'legitimate order'. Hirsch (1992) ties the birth of prison directly to the birth of the new Republic and Meranze, too, points out that the penitentiary was complementary to and indeed integral to liberalism and enlightenment ideas and not antithetical to them, because it was seen as restraining the 'directly violent power' of the state (Gottschalk 2010: 46).

community policing, human rights, managerialism) and the confusing array of contradictory penal policies (Gould and Bruce 2009, Skelton 2005, Marais 2001, Frank 2007, Schonteich 1999a, Schonteich and Louw 2001) due to a weak state and a ruling party that was fractured and unprepared for governing (Bruce and Gould 2009: 16, Marais 2001, Johnson 2009)? Are they attributable to an ANC that had no clear guiding ethos when it became the governing party – other than the idea of the 'struggle' and the vaguely socialist parameters of the Freedom Charter, which gave it credibility as a nationalist organization (Marais 2011)? Perhaps. Yet this eclecticism is not something that is unique to the South African penal field and the co-existence of discourses – the turn to managerialism alongside community crime prevention initiatives and a harsher punitive discourse on how to solve the crime problem of the 'late modern' or 'post-modern' state – has been the subject of much academic debate in the West (Bright 1996, Cohen 1985, Feeley and Simon 1992, Garland 1996, 2001, 2003, Gray 2005, O'Malley 1996, 1999, 2004, Rose 2000, Sparks 2003, Wacquant 2001, 2007, 2009, Pratt 2000, Shearing 2001, King 1989, Lacey 2008, Stenson 1993).

Conceptual Frameworks

The book draws on two sets of literature or conceptual frameworks – governmentality and 'variegated neoliberalization' (Brenner et al. 2010a) – to explain the puzzle of the eclectic, yet patterned, South African penal field.

Governmentality

The governmentality literature asks what the systems of thought were that supplied the authorities with the knowledge, objects and images to enable particular forms of action. Seeing government as being not so much a matter of the 'realization of a programme' as a series of 'assemblages' that link up 'general ethical rationalities to specific, local and technical devices' (Rose 1999: 190) is useful for analysing the various forms and techniques of crime prevention and control in South Africa, some initiated by government and others by citizens.

Technologies spread because of their appropriateness to particular political ends and are often the outcomes of political struggles to put them onto the agenda (O'Malley 1992). Thus the technology of the National Crime Prevention Strategy (NCPS), discussed in Chapter 5, developed in relation to its role in the political programme of the new ANC government – to prevent crime in a paradigmatically different way to that of the apartheid government. This entailed a shift from a 'crime control' to a 'crime prevention' approach. The process of drafting and reaching agreement on the final version of the NCPS was a contested one – with left wing activist consultants, themselves very influenced by Jock Young's left realist criminology, having to modify their ideas in response to input and objections from the powerful Business Against Crime lobby group and government ministers, including President Mbeki himself. The political programme of a transformational form of crime prevention was thus only partially implemented, which in turn resulted in the 'partial implementation' (O'Malley 1992: 259) of the technology contained therein. Those initiatives which had the support of Business Against Crime received funding whereas the less politically sellable socio-economic interventions got scant support and were ultimately marginalized. The political programme of crime prevention was in turn influenced by broader governmental strategies, such as the South African government's 1996 macro-economic Growth Employment and Redistribution (GEAR) strategy, which contained some distinctively neoliberal elements, such as the claim that job creation through labour market flexibility is the most sustainable way to reduce inequality (Nattrass 1999).

The techniques of restorative justice, moral regeneration and familialization that I discuss in Chapter 5 are all techniques of crime prevention, where the targets of governance are both the individual offender and the community in the 'new' South Africa. The offender must be acted upon before s/he reaches the point of no return – this is premised on taking responsibility via the language of empowerment and as such underpins a neoliberal, what Rose would call an 'advanced liberal' rationality. To give another example, shortly after the 1994 elections, opposition parties accused the government of being soft on criminals and on crime. In order to prove that it is in control of the problem and address populist concerns, the South African government has adopted both the technology of long-term imprisonment as well as that of restorative justice – to suit its particular political ends. They may well be contradictory discourses but the book examines how they have been melded together. In looking at the overlaps and articulations between practices such as restorative justice and responsibilizing risk techniques it becomes possible to see how conflicting ideologies can underpin the same policy document.

Neoliberalization Processes

The unevenness and messiness which characterizes the South African penal field can also be analysed in terms of the outcome of 'neoliberalization processes' which intensify the uneven development of 'regulatory forms' (Brenner et al. 2010a: 207), such as the criminal justice system. The term 'variegated neoliberalism' (Brenner et al. 2010) entails positioning 'variegation' (Brenner et al. 2010a: 207), at the centre of neoliberalization.

'Neoliberalization' – a 'tendency of regulatory change' that started in the 1970s – entailed a drive to commodify social life and deploy speculative financial instruments with the 'market' presented as the way to respond to regulatory problems (Brenner et al. 2010b: 2). Since variation is an integral part of neoliberalization there is no 'pure form of neoliberalization' (Brenner et al. 2010b: 2–3), even in the face of the patterning fundamentals of 'market logics' (Brenner et al. 2010a: 202), private property and commodification. The book demonstrates how the South African government has made similar policy choices (managerialism, situational crime prevention, restorative justice, the Prevention of Organized Crime Act, zero tolerance policing, targeted policing, the harsh treatment of undocumented migrants) to that of other neoliberal governments. Despite these similarities and patterns these experimental regulatory forms are implemented differently, within different historical contexts, in terms of particular forms of path-dependent developments and institutional reforms (Brenner et al. 2010a). In other words, they manifest in a South African way.

Brenner et al. (2010a: 215) refer to 'globally neoliberalized rule regimes' which are implemented in terms of restructuring strategies. There are patterns but because these forms are instituted in different institutional terrains, are path-dependent and blended with non-neoliberal elements, the restructuring always results in further differentiation. Thus neoliberal reforms are never complete (Larner 2009, Peck et al. 2009, Brenner et al. 2010a) and 'institutional polymorphism' (Brenner et al. 2010a: 215–16), along with 'endemic regulatory failure' (Brenner et al. 2010a: 215–16) is par for the course. Neoliberalization therefore entails an unevenly developed pattern of restructuring which is 'deeply dysfunctional [and] extraordinarily malleable' (Brenner and Theodore 2002: 345). This malleability and ability to reinvent itself via reconfiguration and remoulding is, for me, one of the defining characteristics of penality in South Africa and I have put it at the centre of my analytical framework. Variegated neoliberalization resonates with a governmentality approach which also emphasizes messiness and contingency; however, 'the former, rooted as it is in a geographical political economy approach, recognizes that the unevenness of neoliberalization processes results from *patterned and patterning processes*' (Brenner et al. 2010a: 202) and not from a mere random collection of marketization projects.

To put it crudely: neoliberalization results in unevenness and unevenness results in further neoliberalization. This unevenness is the point of departure in the book. Neoliberal ideology is particularly adept at melding different discourses since it is so uneven and flexible as to not have a core (Bourdieu 1998). The black box of 'neoliberalism' is often used uncritically by authors such as Wacquant (2001, 2007, 2009), Parenti (1999), De Giorgi (2006), in the sense that its many contradictions are not unpacked. Instead, it is presented as a fully realized project of capitalist oppression. In a South African context Gordon (1998, 2001, 2006) and Samara (2003, 2011), adopting a political economic approach, argue that criminal justice policy in South Africa has followed macroeconomic policy – just after the government adopted its neoliberal GEAR policy in 1996 there was an almost simultaneous shift to a more punitive criminal justice policy (Gordon 2006, Samara 2003). This neoliberal turn explains the similarities between South African and American crime policies (Gordon 1998, 2001, 2006, Samara 2003, Standing 2003, Dixon 2000). These authors are not very clear about what they mean by neoliberalism and equate it with punitive crime policies, whereas in this book I argue that it is in fact too reductionist to equate neoliberalism with punitive penal policies since it also has a 'benign', softer side. Simon's (2007) work on 'governing through crime', which emphasizes not only the repressive side of punishment and crime control but also its enabling, productive and empowering side (Simon 2007: 191), is useful in analysing the turn to community alongside neoliberal reforms that started in the late 1970s and became entrenched in post-apartheid South Africa. For all of these reasons I have opted for an analytical framework that combines the literature on governmentality and crime with its emphasis on messiness and contingencies, together with a more macro-political economic approach that emphasizes global patterning processes as well as unevenness and malleability.

Chapter 2
The Spectacle of Crime in the 'New' South Africa[1]

> At one stage, right after our first democratic elections, we were the envy of the world … if you have been following the Crime Line stories this week you will know that people are being raped, mugged, murdered, hijacked and burgled. They are screaming for the death penalty to be reinstated and some have even suggested resorting to more old-fashioned methods, such as hanging, drawing and quartering and whipping with the cat o' nine tails … As the country descends into barbarism, so the people call for barbaric solutions … The streets are filthy, transport is dodgy, many areas are not safe to go to at all, people are ripped off by business as a matter of course, even before the muggers can get to them, the unemployed and homeless have taken over public areas and people are taking the law into their own hands in the absence of justice. Our peacekeepers are demotivated because as soon as they arrest someone he or she is out on bail. (Cassere 1996)

Introduction

There is no doubt that the ante about crime, as a problem to be addressed, has been upped dramatically in post-apartheid South Africa. However, crime has always played a major role in governance here, whether through techniques which focus on exclusion and repression or through more inclusive, responsibilizing techniques. In this chapter I look at the spectacle of crime in post-apartheid South Africa and how it has become a major problem to be governed. Yet crime is not an unproblematic pre-existing objective entity, which is static and unchanging over time. How it is constructed and controversies over its nature and extent (i.e. how to measure it) are constituted by and constitutive of power relations within society.

Apartheid statistics excluded the bantustans (black homelands), thus resulting in a substantial 'dark figure' of unrecorded crime and, given the dearth of policing resources in the townships, crime in these locations was also vastly undercounted (Shaw 1997, Scharf 1990, Dixon 2004a, Steinberg 2012, Kynoch 2005). Because the apartheid regime never kept adequate statistics the question of whether crime increased or decreased with the demise of apartheid is not a simple 'yes'. Whilst I

1 A version of this article was published in the *British Journal of Criminology* (Super 2010).

do not attempt to answer the question of whether crime has increased in the 'new' South Africa I do question the 'transition leads to more crime' account and offer a more grounded sociological explanation for why crime plays such an important role in governance in post-apartheid South Africa. The themes that I explore here are the changing relationship between crime and politics as the ANC went from being a resistance organization to being the governing party and the changing relationship between crime and race. I start by looking at the problem of crime during the period 1976–89.

1976–89 (Reform of Verwoerdian Apartheid)

The Role of Race

Crime is always newsworthy when there is not something else, like an aeroplane crash for example, to occupy the front pages of the dailies. In South Africa the race and class of the victim play a crucial role in the interest factor. Before the dismantling of apartheid started in the late 1970s, the brutal murders of whites were deemed newsworthy, probably because of their infrequent occurrence, whereas crime in black townships was not reported. Victimization is the flipside of criminalization: just as coloured and black men were disproportionately criminalized under apartheid so too were coloured and black crime victims largely ignored by white South Africans. In general, except to the extent of reporting on faction fighting,[2] the media did not report on crime in black communities.

The techniques used by the South African Police for policing black areas were those of crime blitzes, raids and swoops. (They were criticized for netting only technical – i.e. pass law[3] – offenders and for driving others underground.) Because the focus of policing was on keeping blacks out of white areas, and the threat of being overrun by a marauding black mob was dominant in the post-Soweto era, there was much concern about attacks on elderly white females – the image of the black male raping or assaulting the white elderly woman in the enclave of her home in the suburbs was dominant. In 1976 white women were 'living in fear of their lives', threatened by outsider 'vagrants and other undesirables' (*Cape Times*, 18 October 1976). Thus the 'year marred by a rash of lawlessness' included:

> The brutal hammer death of schoolgirl Cathee Harries … the baffling murder of Miss Nikki Baker in her Gardens Flat … the death by strangulation of Mrs Gwen O'Leary in her Seapoint home … the recent slaying of Mrs Miriam Kraitzick in her Bantry Bay mansion. (*Cape Times*, 30 December 1976)

---

2 See for example *Cape Times*, 29 December 1976: '46 Blacks die in Natal violence'.

3 In terms of Influx Control legislation, black people had to carry passes in order to legally work in white areas. See Chapter 4 where these laws are discussed in greater detail.

Not only was policing racially differentiated – for example in 1976, of the 34 police stations in the Cape Peninsula only four were in coloured residential areas (*Cape Times*, 19 June 1976) – but so were the subsequent crime statistics. The crime of 'public violence' included 'White on non-White and Non-White on White' (Department of Justice, Police and Prisons 1977) as well as a separate category which included 'faction fighting where only Bantu are involved'. Rape and attempted rape were divided into 'White female by White male, Coloured or Asian female by White male, Bantu female by White male, White female by Bantu male, Non-White female by Non-White male'. Murder was divided in terms of 'White by White, White by Coloured or Asian, White by Bantu, Coloured or Asian by White, Bantu by White, and Non-White by Non-White'. Burglaries were divided into 'White' and 'Non-White residential premises'. This continued until 1982, when the mode of presenting statistics changed and the race of offenders was no longer included in the statistics.[4] The victims of rape and murder were, however, still divided into 'White and Non-White' victims and this continued until 1993. The statistics that were produced were thus related to political changes: categorizing on the basis of race did not contribute to the attempt by the state to create a compliant black middle class and the ideological shift from explaining criminality on the basis of race alone.[5]

Despite fears of the archetypal black criminal attacking the helpless white victim, in fact between 1976 and 1977 only 220 murders were committed across racial lines whereas 7,122 blacks were murdered by other blacks and 136 whites by whites. Similar patterns were followed for other violent crimes: 101,916 blacks were assaulted by other blacks, 12,244 whites by whites and 8,245 assaults across racial lines (*Financial Mail*, 26 May 1978). Violent deaths in coloured and black communities never had much of an impact, in the sense of being construed as a crime problem, because they never affected whites.

Crime and 'Unrest'

As popular resistance to minority rule intensified after 16 June 1976, and the hegemony of Afrikaner nationalist ideology started to crack, the ability of the state to keep control was increasingly questioned by opposition parties and the media. This politicization of law and order in the 1970s was accompanied by a fundamental shift in the political economy and a definitive shift on the part of the state to the embracing of free-market principles concomitant with the reassessment of the functionality of apartheid to capitalism.

The police used 'clean-up' operations as excuses to combat political dissent, thus a Pretoria 'clean-up' in November 1977 entailed the police arresting 626 people after a six-hour 'clearing-up operation' in which they cordoned off the black township. This resulted in the arrest of not only 410 people for reference book

4 See Department of Law and Order, 1989.

5 I discuss this shift in greater detail in Chapter 4.

offences[6] but also 198 school children, arrested allegedly to determine whether they were 'children in need of care'. The police emphasized that the operation had nothing to do with 'black unrest' despite the fact that school pupils in that township were at the time engaged in an examination boycott to protest against 'Bantu education' (*Cape Times*, 11 November 1977).

By the mid-1980s, with the struggle against apartheid intensifying, crimes such as public violence showed steep increases, from 164 in 1983–84 to 4,408 in 1984–85. The 1984–85 Police Annual Report had an index for the first time and the 'Introduction' referred to the fact that: 'in addition to combating crime, [the police] had to contend with the first large-scale outbreak of politically inspired violence since 1976' (Department of Law and Order 1986: 1). There was a section on 'Internal Security' which included statistics on

> unrest (petrol bomb incidents; arson; fire damage; looting; hand grenade incidents; persons killed by others; injured by others; killed by security forces; injured by security forces; killed by development board officials; injured by development board officials…); unrest at and the boycott of teaching institutions; events in the field of labour; acts of terrorism. (Department of Law and Order 1986: 1)

From 1985 onwards, as resistance against the apartheid regime increased, and there was a broad call on the side of the liberation movement to make the townships ungovernable, the annual police reports started to get longer and more attention was devoted to the 'political unrest situation' (Department of Law and Order 1986: 1). The state justified the imposition of successive States of Emergency as crime prevention devices, the claim being that there were criminal thugs in the townships who were stoking the fires of 'unrest' and that due to 'greater cooperation between the police and members of the public since the introduction of the emergency' crime had declined dramatically (*Cape Times*, 7 July 1987). This was part of an overall ideological thrust which attempted to criminalize political protest. The term 'unrest' was the official euphemism for a range of activities, many of which were ANC-led struggles, against the apartheid regime. Internal unrest included 'strikes, tribal clashes [and]; student unrest' (Department of Justice, Police and Prisons 1977). These actions were criminalized and 'thousands of man hours … spent' (Department of Justice, Police and Prisons 1978a: 1) on combating them.

As the townships erupted, the police embarked on more 'crime blitzes' and 'clean up operations' in black and coloured areas, indicating a shift from a policy of benign neglect of illegalities in townships to one of law enforcement, on the basis of political expedience, as well as the need to impose 'law and order'. The South African Police (SAP) conflated preventive action with riot policing, euphemistically referred to as the 'maintenance of law and order'. Raids were often accompanied by pamphlets which stated: 'We rely on you, the concerned citizen, to help us identify suspected arsonists, petrol bombers and stone throwers'

6 Failure to carry a pass book.

(*Cape Times*, 14 May 1986). They would seal off townships under the pretext of conducting 'crime prevention exercises', wearing riot gear and firing tear gas into homes, justifying their actions by claiming that a 'crime prevention exercise had taken place as criminal elements have been exploiting the sporadic unrest situation in the townships' (*Cape Times*, 14 May 1986). The swoops were also justified on the basis of intervening in 'black on black' violence. As this extract from the November 1985 SAP newsletter, *Servamus*, put it:

> Widely ignored in the current township riots is the S.A. Police's protection role for African residents. Time and time again they have plunged through violent mobs to rescue African victims. Said one resident, 'The police appeared as knights in shining armour, to stop Black destroying Black'. (Toups 1985)

In typical cases arrests were made for possession of cannabis and mandrax, public violence, car theft and murder. Suspected stolen goods were also confiscated. One of the reasons given for the need for the community to be directly involved in combating crime was because political offenders tried to 'poison' the community's mind against the '*handhawers*' (bearers) of law and order (Williamson 1984: 152). The 'Leninist strategies' of the ANC and SACP included using 'common crime as revolutionary tactic' with 'criminal elements ... used to do dirty work for revolution' (Williamson 1984: 152).

Detention and 'unrest related' statistics increased hugely after the State of Emergency was declared in 1985 and by 1986, 7,777 people had been arrested in terms of the emergency regulations (Department of Law and Order 1987: 11). For the first time articles about incidents of unrest over a 24 hour period were appearing in the newspapers, based on information released by the Bureau for Information. By 1989 the liberal press reported that whereas 'a political rally quickly draws enough police to the scene ... there is far less evidence of a police presence in the face of daily criminal behavior' and that the Democratic Party was correct to insist that 'a bigger police force is essential for the state to fulfill its obligation to protect all citizens' (*Cape Times*, 2 August 1989).

The maintenance of 'law and order' was distinguished from 'combating crime' and the state attempted to distinguish between using the 'ordinary criminal law' to counter 'normal, ordinary criminal activities' versus 'terrorist onslaughts' (*Hansard* 1987a, col: 2754). Thus, according to Justice Minister Kruger the 'Black Power gangs of today' were 'criminals ... mafia type gangs' and their activities were 'thuggery' (*Hansard* 1977b, col: 4243). But this dichotomy was a largely spurious one – it all depended on who was doing the defining. Just as the state depicted township activists as criminals and terrorists,[7] stripping their acts of a political

7 Thus in regard to the 16 June 1976 protests the Cape Times reported the police as saying that: 'Incidents of violence and vandalism in Black Peninsula Townships since the first Soweto riots two weeks ago have been the work of tsotsis with no political motives – and not local "sympathy points" for rioters in the Transvaal, the police believe. It was certain

dimension, so too did 'comrades' – the colloquial term for left wing township struggle activists – commit criminal acts in the name of politics. In this sense the state, in eliding the distinction between crime and politics, produced its counterpart in the ability of the 'comrades' to politicize crime (even against black victims) and try to legitimate it. Thus the ANC/United Democratic Front[8]/Pan African Congress[9] claimed that their acts which had been designated as criminal/terrorist by the apartheid government were in fact politically motivated and justified by the fact that they were fighting a just war against an unjust state. The 'comrades' accused the South African government officials, and their lackeys, of being the true criminals. When gangs looted trucks driving into the townships some political activists presented this as part of the struggle (Jensen 2008). Similarly, what might be regarded as gratuitous acts of violence, such as 'necklacing' – the setting alight of a tyre doused with petrol which had been placed around the neck of the victim – assumed some kind of political salience due to the fact that the targets of these acts were accused of being spies or apartheid collaborators, and thus on the wrong side of the just war. However, this did not entail a simple inversion of what the state claimed was crime on the one hand and what the left claimed was justifiable political action on the other.

In the carnivalesque 'free for all' (Glaser 1998) atmosphere of political protest, where looting and robbery were also present, political and criminal activity often became difficult to distinguish, as did gang elements from legitimate protesters. What might have started with criminal youth often did not end with them. As Glaser (1998: 316), writing in the context of the Soweto Riots, states: 'The usual spatial separation broke down once the students were on boycott.' Similarly in the 1980s, the usual separation between comrades and gangsters broke down in the face of spiralling unrest – what started as political protest often degenerated into criminal activities/gratuitous violence-containing elements of both. As Marais (2011: 26 quoting Morris) observes: in an era of racial and political polarization an 'all or nothing approach', with a tendency to equate 'armed struggle with revolution and legal struggle with reformism', generated calls for a 'people's war'. In this context theft against collaborators and whites did not have much criminal stigma and violence 'was almost seen as a public act of symbolic revenge' (Glaser 1998). Simpson (2001: 121) states that the counterculture inherent in the violent nature of youth politics of the 1980s 'lent itself as easily to criminal organisation

that these incidents [arson] and other isolated outbreaks of rock-throwing and vandalism in peninsula townships since Soweto, had nothing to do with "politically inspired rioting", Captain Right said. "By and large the townships had remained peaceful and the decent folk who form the majority of the populace have stood behind us…" he said' (*Cape Times*, 1 July 1976).

8 A broad coalition of organizations formed in South Africa in 1983 to protest apartheid.

9 A liberation party that was left of the ANC, founded in 1959, after a number of members broke away from the ANC.

as it did to political organisation – and indeed even to a gravitation between the two'. To add more complexity, gang participation in political protest was not always opportunistic – often they *were* acting out of a shared sense of rage against the establishment and gangs would engage in 'spontaneous political sympathy' actions (Glaser 1998: 317). Given the informal and spontaneous nature of the links between gangs and protesters the boundaries were constantly shifting The term 'comtsotsi'[10] that arose in the 1980s is indicative of this ambiguity (Glaser 1998).

The Recognition and Politicization of the Crime Problem

The Progressive Federal Party called for an 'urgent inquiry into the crime rate' (*Cape Times*, 5 April 1976) in 1976. In 1977 the director of the Institute of Criminology at the University of Cape Town expressed the opinion there had been a marked increase in crime but he conceded that this could not be adequately measured (Katzin 1977). Although the 1978 police statistics revealed that there had been no 'unusual' increase in crime this did not appease an uneasy public and a critical press and, as is the case today, the statistics were not necessarily regarded as a correct indication of the 'real' crime situation. There were complaints about too few police and a consistent call for 'bobbies on the beat', which was mixed in with a discernible discourse on the need to alleviate socio-economic circumstances (as a crime prevention device) to quell the 'alarming urban crime wave' (*Financial Mail*, 26 May 1978).

Whatever the statistics indicated there was a clear concern on the side of the public that the rate of serious crime had 'reached epidemic proportions' (*Financial Mail*, 26 May 1978) and that the government was not doing enough to solve the problem. 'Adequate policing' did not mean 'occasional and well publicised raids, which merely drive criminals to ground for a few days, but round the clock vigilance ... building more police stations ... employing more policemen' (*Financial Mail*, 26 May, 1978). The 'black townships' in particular were seen to be in need of more policing.

Although overall prosecutions fell between 1968 and 1978, the fact that drunkenness was reclassified from recordable 'offence' to a non-recordable technical 'infringement' might have caused this decrease. It was the rate of violent crime (which made up nearly one third of all offences prosecuted) that caused concern in certain quarters, the fact that the South African rate of violence was out of all proportion to the incidence of violent crime in other societies (Midgley 1977). Yet in true denialist fashion, the Minister of Justice, Police and Prisons criticized those who stated that South Africa had one of the most violent societies in the world as 'doing the country a great disservice' (*Cape Times*, 6 June 1977). According to him the fact that fewer people were being prosecuted indicated a drop in crime rates.

10 An amalgamation of the word 'comrade' with 'tsotsi', the latter meaning gangster.

Official statistics show that in fact crimes such as murder, robbery and housebreaking had been increasing from the mid-1980s, with a dramatic increase in official crime statistics in the 1980s (Shaw 1995). Bearing in mind that most police stations were situated in white areas, the official crime statistics were almost certainly biased to collecting information about those crimes which affected whites: as such the increase would certainly have been an indication that more whites were now being targeted by black criminals. By way of example, in 1987 'theft out of vehicles' (Department of Law and Order 1989) was separated from 'theft in general', an indication of the increasing concern with the type of offence that affected mainly whites. This would also explain why more attention started to be paid to the question of crime in parliamentary debates in the 1980s. Whereas in the past the Progressive Federal Party (PFP) had been accused of mollycoddling criminals, now the PFP accused the government of not doing enough to combat crime. Ironically, a Nationalist Party MP, in lamenting the 'alarming increase of rape across the colour line' stated that it appears as if 'it is a new form of terrorism' (*Hansard* 1981a, col: 3952).

Despite denials to the contrary the 1981 Bloomberg Commission of Inquiry to Investigate Crime on the Cape Flats was evidence that the government was taking the crime problem seriously enough to institute a formal investigation. Yet in 1983, La Grange, the then Minister of Law and Order, dismissed the research findings of the UCT Institute of Criminology that Cape Town had one of the highest crime rates in the 'western world', maintaining that 'crime was well under control and was being contained at a satisfactory level' (*Cape Times*, 21 May 1983). He also refused to furnish Parliament with statistics on violent crime in the Cape for the preceding year because it would 'involve too much time and effort' (*Cape Times*, 3 March 1983). With embargoes and disinvestment looming in the 1980s the government restricted information flow via press censorship and released less information – the annual reports of the SAP shrank to a few pages (Edwards and Hecht 2010: 632).

The shift to calling for prevention, which I discuss in Chapter 5, was linked in with a clear perception that crime was increasing and by 1986 the fact that the police were fighting 'unrest' was regarded as a cause of the 'soaring' crime rate (*Cape Times*, 22 September 1986). This fighting of 'unrest', coupled with the 1986 Abolition of Influx Control Act, which repealed the pass laws, engendered the perception that the crime rate had 'reached the same pitch of viciousness and menace in affluent residential areas at which it has operated for some time in the poorer townships of the Cape Flats' (*Cape Times*, 1 November 1986).

Private security firms reported that business was 'booming' as increasing numbers lost 'faith in the police and turned elsewhere for protection' (*Cape Times*, 1 November 1986). The Progressive Federal Party blamed the government's 'political failure to secure the peace by negotiating with blacks' (*Cape Times*, 4 April 1987) for the increase in crime. According to them the fact that large numbers of police were 'allocated to deal with political unrest rather than undertake crime prevention duties' led to 'under policing of the suburbs' (*Cape*

Times, 4 April 1987) and this favoured the growth of crime. Despite ascribing the crime phenomenon to a variety of causes – for example forced removals and discrimination – the proposed solution, from the liberal opposition, was always a call for a more visible police presence and a greatly expanded police force. On the other hand the Conservative Party blamed increased crime on the repeal of the Pass Laws. It claimed that:

> From the suburbs in Pretoria we are getting feedback which amounts to the fact that crime is increasing at an alarming rate. The people there say the hands of the police are … tied. In the past they could use the pass laws to get at vagabonds at night and at least check to see that crime did not increase unhindered. (*Hansard* 1986a, col: 7922)

This conservative Afrikaans backlash should be seen in the context of increasing resistance to apartheid by more enlightened ('verligte') Afrikaners, as evidenced by the July 1986 visit to Dakar by 61 Afrikaners to meet ANC leaders. The three days of meetings resulted in a declaration of commitment to ending apartheid and the building of a united, democratic and non-racial South Africa (Ngculu 2009).

1989–94 (Transitioning into the 'New' South Africa)

Crime, Political Violence and 'Unrest'

Police annual reports during the transition period reflected a shift in the patterns of victimization: there was a dramatic increase in the number of attacks on 'civilians in their own homes'[11] (i.e. white victims of crime) and attacks on police. The (white) senior citizen victim, over 50 years old, emerged as a distinct category. The 'hijacking of trucks (and cargoes) and passenger vehicles' emerged as a new crime in 1992 and Ak47s, the Russian-made Kalashikov rifle which *Umkonto We Sizwe* cadres had used in the armed struggle, were increasingly reflected as being used in robberies, with robbers having shifted from targeting banks to 'security firms conveying cash' (Department of Law and Order 1994: 104). These later became known as 'cash-in-transit heists'. 5,457 passenger vehicles were hijacked in 1992 and 7,208 in 1993, representing an increase of 32.09 per cent. According to Shubane (2001: 198) it was 'comtsotsis' who first used car hijacking in the 1980s – arguing that they were advancing the goals of struggle.

There was a lot more written on crime in the police reports and a new section on 'The Crime Situation in the RSA' was added. Thus for example, the 1991 Police Annual Report noted that there had been a 'progressive increase in crime' since the beginning of the 1980s. This increase was attributed to the 'unrest situation'

11 The 1992 Annual Report reflected an increase of 48.98 per cent.

which had, since September 1984, 'increased in intensity' (Department of Law and Order 1992: 2) and 'unrest' was regarded as a 'strong stimulant for crime' (*Hansard* 1990a: col: 738).

Although there was much angst about crime during this period, so much so that by 1994 the police annual report had jumped from nine pages (in 1977) to 142 pages, as has always been the case in South Africa, the geographical and racial distribution of crime was very uneven. Between 1990 and 1991 there were only 453 white murder victims and 14,656 black victims. On the other hand, 108,828 house-breakings were at 'white residential premises' (Department of Law and Order 1991) and only 50,575 at black ones. This spate of burglaries was referred to as the 'siege of the suburbs' (Kneen 1991). Given that the murder rate was almost 37 times as high in the case of black victims – a figure that far exceeded the 5:1 ratio (Le Roux 1996) of blacks to whites in South Africa – these statistics are telling, and a shocking indictment of the underpolicing and high rate of violent crime in black townships.

During this period there was a clear concern with political/'unrest' related violence such as taxi wars, hostel wars and people being thrown off trains. The Unrest and Violent Crime Investigation Unit, established in September 1991, investigated high profile politically motivated crimes such as the murder of Amy Biehl[12] and the St James Church Massacre.[13] But statistically, political crimes accounted for very little of the violent crime. Although 'politically inspired violent crime' rose by 51.85 per cent it still comprised less than 1 per cent of the reported serious crime figure. Political violence constituted 0.72 per cent of the total crime statistics in 1992, with murder committed with a political motive constituting 12.67 per cent of the number of violent deaths (Department of Law and Order 1993: 101). Yet between '30 per cent and 40 per cent of the manpower of the SAP' was used to 'stabilize' and prevent 'unrest' (Department of Law and Order 1993: 101). This was justified by 'the potentially explosive effect and seriousness of political violence' (Department of Law and Order 1993: 101).

The government sought to actively criminalize and thereby depoliticize the 'unrest' in the townships. It was standard to claim that the politically neutral police were trying to 'maintain law and order' in the face of attacks by 'the comrades', with the result being 'unrest' (Ndabandaba 1990a: 350). It was the comrades who 'molested the out group, burnt their houses, looted their cars and victimised them in a number of ways such as petrol bombs and kangaroo courts'. The 'out group' were the 'progressive residents who owned property, businesses and good cars' (Ndabandaba 1990a: 351).

The ANC, on the other hand, adopted the opposite perspective. It perceived the violence as part of an 'overall state strategy', the aim being to weaken and

12 An American exchange student who had been murdered in 1993 by a group of Pan African Congress youth.

13 In 1993 11 members of the congregation were killed and 58 injured by four cadres of the Azanian People's Liberation Army.

discredit it as an organization (ANC 1990a: 4). It identified a sinister 'third force', to which the police, at best, turned a blind eye and, at worst, were actively involved in fomenting the 'black on black' violence.[14] At the same time, however, in an attempt to claim the moral highground, the ANC acknowledged cases of recruitment of *criminal* elements from the ANC and *Umkhonto we Sizwe* (MK), the ANC's armed wing, into the police hit squads 'in order to portray the ANC as being involved in the violence' (ANC 1992c: 4). This was to counter the claim by the state that the ANC Self Defence Units (SDUs) were involved in crimes of violence and other criminal actions (Department of Law and Order 1993: 59). It insisted that MK was observing the ceasefire and denied the allegation that the SDUs were in fact MK units. It (ANC 1990a: 4) instead claimed the deliberate state subversion of SDUs, which were 'under the control of communities' in order to discredit it. This talk of *criminal elements* prefigured the divide between politics and criminality which would come to figure strongly in ANC discourse, when as government, it was no longer fighting the struggle against the apartheid state but against a new enemy – the figure of the criminal, now stripped of any claim to political justification.

The 1990s were also all about the negotiated handover of government to the ANC, the suspension of its armed struggle and the Convention for a Democratic South Africa (CODESA). As political parties were decriminalized and political prisoners released, so too did the concept of 'transitional justice' (Simpson 2004: 2) emerge and become distinguished from criminal justice. A distinct debate about the criteria for indemnity emerged, where the lines between what was political and hence justifiable action – deserving of indemnity – and common (unjustifiable) crime, were drawn and redrawn.

The Separation of Crime and Politics

1990 represented the start of the official transition to democracy – it was the year in which the ANC was unbanned, a moratorium was placed on the death penalty and Nelson Mandela released from prison. It was also the year in which the State President declared that 'apartheid' was a

> purely political concept which neither appears nor is defined anywhere in our legislation. If it means discrimination on the basis of race or colour, the government's declared policy is that it is unacceptable and has to be eliminated in an orderly manner. (*Hansard* 1990a, question 1, col: 676)

---

14 See for example *The Star*, 9 April 1991: 'Open letter to State President de Klerk and his Cabinet from the National Executive Committee of the ANC'. The ANC was of the opinion that 'the Government's equivocal attitude to the cycle of violence reflects either an attitude of cynical irresponsibility or is evidence of connivance at acts organised terror in the hope that they will succeed in destroying or seriously crippling the ANC' (ANC 1992c).

The February 1990 unbanning of the ANC and the South African Communist Party led to discussions between the government and the ANC, and the signing of the Groote Schuur and Pretoria Minutes in May and August respectively. These agreements resulted in the drafting of indemnity legislation. It now became important to distinguish between political and non-political offences in order to decide who would receive indemnity and which 'security and security-related prisoners' (*Hansard* 1991a, col: 1826, question 2) would be released. This was not that easy. The concept of what constituted a political offence or a 'security' prisoner was not cut and dried and release decisions were controversially received, both outside and within the prison walls. Although certain offences, such as 'treason directed solely against the state and not involving a common or ordinary crime such as murder' were regarded as 'purely political', according to the Minister of Correctional Services in certain circumstances, even a 'common law' crime such as murder could be regarded as a political offence (*Hansard* 1991a, question 2, col: 1826).

The shadowy intersecting of political and common crime was exemplified in the 'unrealistic expectations' (Department of Law and Order 1993) of those prisoners who had envisaged a mass release taking place with the transition to democracy. They blamed the apartheid regime for causing them to commit crimes and claimed to be in prison 'because of apartheid' (Steinberg 2004: 247). Steinberg (2004: 272) poignantly quotes a prisoner as lamenting the fact that:

> The ANC came home and started preaching high words of forgiveness and reconciliation. But they meant forgiveness for their own people and for right wing murderers. We are the ones who fought the *boere* in prison; but as far as the ANC was concerned we could rot in hell.

There was also a shift in the ideological justifications underpinning policing. Whereas before 1990 the emphasis was on 'the revolutionary role of organisations' after 1990 it shifted to 'the primary role of the individual' (Department of Law and Order 1993: 51). This was attributed to 'a change in the occurrence of violence' and the new 'de-politicising approach of the Force' (ibid). As such: 'the actions of people ... would now be judged from a political-ideological point of view' (ibid).

Because 'crimes of violence' had both a 'political and criminal dimension' it was necessary to distinguish between crime due to 'political motives' and due to 'economic strains'. 'Taxi violence', for example, was attributed to 'economic strains' and not 'political motives' (Department of Law and Order 1994: 102). Yet Dugard's research has shown how taxi violence both influenced, and was influenced by, political violence. She (2001: 132) attributes the violence to the 'acute and unregulated competition' that characterized the taxi industry, one of the first institutional forms to emerge out of the neoliberal reforms implemented by the NP. Taxi associations armed drivers, and eventually specific associations began to be associated with particular political movements (Dugard 2001). Yet as was the case for other forms of political violence, in the immediate post-1994 period taxi violence continued, albeit in a different form (Dugard 2001). The term 'unrest' did not disappear from state discourse about crime in the 'new' South Africa and the uncoupling of crime and politics, which started during the transition period, continued.

1994–2004 (Consolidating the 'New' South Africa)

Crime's 'New Visibility'[15]

Although, as Durkheim (1982) pointed out, crime is a 'normal' sociological fact, and fear of crime did not suddenly arise in post-apartheid South Africa, it is a highly charged and politicized issue and the way in which it emerged as a 'key governance issue' in the post-apartheid era has been referred to as 'striking' (Humphries 2000: 1). Whether or not one accepts the mainstream argument, with all its variants, that the transition to the 'new' South Africa caused the crime rate to increase, there is no denying that it has been accompanied by a change in the demographics of victimization and criminalization. This has occurred together with a change in the types of crime that 'make up the numbers' – i.e. what is recorded in official statistics.

Whilst crime's new visibility in democratic South Africa is not just because of an increase in crime, the extent of which is in any event debatable and unevenly distributed, it has certainly changed its patterns, locations and targets – in a sense, crime has became democratized. This is not to say that crime and violence assume the same forms in poorer communities or manifest in the same way as in middle-class/wealthier communities (Bruce 2007). The point is that middle class whites are more victimized than before (given that crime now moved into areas that had previously been cordoned off from the social problems of poor blacks). Also, thanks to Black Economic Empowerment[16] (BEE) policies and the emergence of a black middle class, whose members also constitute attractive crime targets, the black elite are a new constituency whose voices are heard in the crime debate and, due to the change of regime, poorer blacks are now also prepared to lay criminal charges, without the fear of being labeled an *impimpi* (police agent/spy). As a report by the UN Office on Drugs and Crime (2005: 53) states:

> The South African government has made great efforts to repair the relationship between the police and the public, and if they have been successful, an increase in the rate of reporting would be expected. In other words, it is impossible to tell

15 Los (2002: 168) uses the term in the context of former Eastern Europe.

16 A form of affirmative action that was aggressively (and controversially) implemented during Mbeki's presidency.

> whether more people are being robbed or whether more people are reporting the robberies they experience to the police.

Whereas in the late 1970s and early 1980s most references were to the police speeding to crime scenes and murder and robbery squad detectives arresting people within weeks/hours of the murders (*Cape Times*, 30 December 1976) police in the new democracy were regarded as unable to quell what was regarded as a crime epidemic, so much so that in 1997 a State of Emergency was contemplated to deal with the problem.

Human Sciences Research Surveys revealed that, whereas in 1995 only 10 per cent of respondents viewed crime as the most pressing concern, this figure had almost doubled by early 1997. In November 1998, more than 20 per cent of the respondents ranked crime as their top concern, just behind service delivery (24 per cent) and jobs (23 per cent). The increase in the fear of crime was directly proportionate to the decline in the belief in the state's ability to deal with it and although in 1994 76 per cent of the sample believed that the government was to some extent in control of the crime situation, by 1995 83 per cent believed that it had little or no control (Alence and Pimstone 1999). The emergence of the vigilante group PAGAD (People against Gangsterism and Drugs) was blamed on the state's failure to 'remedy the situation of lawlessness' (*Cape Times*, 19 August 1996). There were many newspaper articles about how ineffective the police were and their inability to do anything about 'urban terror' (*Cape Times*, 12 August 1996). There was thus a major shift in the public's perception between 1994 and 1995. A press which had previously called for socio-economic upliftment and more bobbies on the beat now complained about 'too much liberty' and called for more efficient, intelligence-driven policing and harsher punishment (*Cape Times*, 19 September 1994).

In 1999, the Nedbank ISS Crime Index found that, between 1992 and 1998, there was a decline in the percentage who reported feeling unsafe, from 56 per cent in early 1992 to 49 per cent in late 1998, and that this was due to a 'reduction in the number of black South Africans who feel unsafe, from 62 per cent to 44 per cent'. However, the percentage of white South Africans who felt unsafe increased from 55 per cent to 63 per cent. This was a change from 1992 when 'whites generally felt safer than blacks' (Alence 1999). This shift in perceptions was probably due to the fact that whereas political 'unrest' was far more likely to affect blacks than whites, the advent of democracy also brought about a shift in crime and victimization patterns because there was a dramatic increase in the amount of crime that moved into the formerly protected white middle class suburbs (Shaw 1996). According to Simpson (2001, 2004), South Africans interpreted the violence which preceded the election as political in nature and described most of what followed as criminal in nature. He (2001: 116) ironically refers to the '"miraculous" political transition, of which reborn South African democrats became so proud'.

The transition from one government administration to another not only exacerbated pre-existing bureaucratic problems but also created new ones. Thus, for example, the effect of the 1995 ruling of the Constitutional Court,[17] that the accused in a criminal trial was entitled to all written statements in the police docket, resulted in prosecutors now having to spend much of their time making photocopies of dockets, due to a lack of administrative support (Schonteich 2001a). White prosecutors became dissatisfied with the Department of Justice's affirmative action policy and low salaries and between 1994 and 1998 546 prosecutors resigned – out of total of less than 2,000. This resulted in a decline in the average level of prosecutarial experience (Schonteich 2001a). The result was that the number of prosecutions and convictions continued the decline which had started in the 1970s, when the state increasingly focused on prosecuting people for violent and property crimes whilst ignoring the easily solvable less serious offences (Schonteich 2001a: 158). Whereas between 1991 and 1992 485,000 cases were prosecuted, resulting in 373,600 convictions, between 1995 and 1996 this had declined to 291,000 prosecutions and 218,000 convictions (Schonteich 2001a: 171).

The extent of public concern with crime is evident in the numerous 'private' initiatives that South African citizens have deployed in the fight against crime in the 'new' South Africa. These include vigilante activities in the poorer communities, neighbourhood watches, private security, road closures, gated communities, City Improvement Districts and the ubiquitous car guards in the more affluent and commercial areas. The fact that in 2000 there were 216,000 security guards (compared with 105,000 police), of whom, according to Schonteich (1999a), a quarter were 'functionally illiterate,' did not inspire public confidence. High levels of guard labour are, according to Lacey (2008: 136)[18] 'strongly associated with high levels of social and economic polarization, political conflict, low levels of political legitimacy and social sector and welfare spending'.

The Politics of Crime in the 'New' South Africa

Along with the ratchetting up of anxiety about crime, it also became politicized and a convenient anchor on which to attack the post-apartheid ANC government. What Los (2002: 168) refers to as 'crime's new visibility' resulted in images of a system bordering on chaos and collapse becoming entrenched in both the political discourse of opposition parties and also in the type of articles that surfaced in the media.

The fact that crime policies have figured strongly in all post-1994 elections is indicative of its importance. One only has to look at parliamentary debates and the election manifestos of political parties from 1996 on to see how the discourse of crime has entered the political arena. Its politicization also entails a broad consensus about the need for a punitive approach to combating crime and

17 Shabalala and Others v Attorney-General of the Transvaal and Another (CCT23/94) [1995] ZACC 12; 1995 (12) BCLR 1593; 1996 (1) SA 725 (29 November 1995).

18 Citing Bowles and Jayadev 2006.

a jockeying by political parties, to claim credit for each other's punitive criminal justice policies.

The government narratives included the 'crime is normal' and/or not as big a problem as the fearmongers make out, that it was 'stabilizing' and/improving, that it was a symbol of white fears of the 'black man' and that in fact it was doing a lot more to combat crime than the apartheid government did. On the other hand the discourse of opposition parties was moored to narratives of things falling apart, that the ANC was ignoring the crime problem, covering things up and should have been doing a lot more.

In August 1997 Meyer Khan, the executive chair of South African Breweries, a private company, was appointed as police chief executive officer. This was part of a 'political strategy' (Laufer 2001: 18) to address the perception of declining criminal justice system efficiency, especially as it concerned the white community. During that same year a Committee of Inquiry, appointed by the Minister of Safety and Security, spent more than six months analysing weaknesses in the gathering and processing of crime statistics (Louw and Schonteich 2001: 43). A few months later, Bulelani Ngcuka became the National Director of Public Prosecutions (a newly created post), Steve Tshwete the new Mininster of Safety and Security, Jackie Selebi the National Police Commissioner, Willie Hofmeyer head of the new Asset Forfeiture Unit, and Frank Dutton head of the Scorpions[19] (Laufer 2001). In November 1999 Selebi announced to Parliament that by April 2000 there would be a marked drop in violent serious crime. According to Louw and Schonteich (2001: 42), Selebi's confidence was 'mind-boggling', given that

> crime increased by 15 per cent between 1994 and 1999, and that on a yearly basis levels of recorded crime increased at a faster rate between 1998/99 than at any other time since 1994.

As crime became a political football, central to election campaigns, so too was it uncoupled from politics, thus giving rise to an approach which presented criminals as being a threat to the new human rights culture which symbolized the young democracy. It was almost as if there was an inverse relationship between public concern about crime and the disappearance of a discourse which grounded an offender within his/her structural context. This was to be expected given the cheap points which could be gained by appeasing an angry and insecure public.

Pure Evil

In pre-democratic South Africa politics was criminalized in the sense that political organizations, such as the ANC, were banned, and political actions, such as

19 The Scorpions is the colloquial term for the first organized crime unit in the South African Police. See Chapter 4 where I discuss this development in greater detail.

strikes, were too. The ANC, however, largely ignored crime in pre-democratic South Africa: on the one hand it overly politicized and thereby justified violence, and on the other, it largely ignored the fact that violent and petty crime had always been everyday issues faced by township residents – its discourse (and practice) was focused on the struggle against apartheid.

Once in government the ANC embraced the fiction of a simple binary between politics and crime. This became especially apparent in the amnesty process. Thus, amnesty would not be granted in respect of someone who, having been subjected to the invidious and unjust forced removals, stole in order to relieve him/herself of the abject poverty consequent upon such removals.[20] As Fillipi (2011: 642) states:

> the process of selecting applicants for amnesty, with its dismissal of criminal convicts still held in prison skewed a potential finding that criminal actions were more intertwined with political actions than is generally recognized.

It is ironic that the ANC should separate crime and politics so clearly, having been the victims of such a dichotomy previously.

Development in the 'new' South Africa was now threatened by the ugly face of criminal violence and the ANC invested the fight against crime with the struggle narrative. For example in 2004, President Mbeki stated that

> To make a real difference ... we must engage in the kind of popular mobilisation we undertook during the struggle against apartheid ... as communities we need to create widespread awareness of how complicity with crime and criminal behaviour promotes crime (Mbeki 2004).

Whereas, prior to 1994, ungovernability had been a part of the struggle against apartheid, there was now, according to Dullah Omar, the first minister of Justice, a need to inculcate respect for an objectified, reified concept of 'the law' and 'civilised societies' based on a consensual model of penality and crime control (*Hansard*, 1994, col: 2061). Yet even during the struggle there had been a concerted attempt to separate crime from politics, in a manner that was somewhat Stalinistic at times. The ANC had always been at pains to distinguish its own lawbreaking from that of ordinary criminality, and political prisoners had distanced themselves from common criminals, even though they often engaged in tacit alliances within the prison (Filllipi 2011, Glaser 1998, Alexander and Kynoch 2011, Ngculu 2008). I discuss this in greater detail in Chapter 6.

In post-apartheid South Africa police and private security have been increasingly called on to quell increasing 'unrest' incidents such as organized

---

20 Others have written on the Truth and Reconciliation Commission and I do not intend to scrutinize it here; suffice to say that in adopting a narrow view of reparations and crime and politics it did not deal with the complex nature of criminality in South Africa (See Simpson 2004, Fillipi 2011,Gillespie 2007).

resistance to water and electricity cutoffs, housing evictions, the demolition of informal settlements, service delivery protests and strikes. It is ironic that even in 2002 the SAP Annual Report still had a section on 'unrest incidents'. These comprise 'various types of actions such as shooting, the detonation of explosive devices, stone throwing, petrol bomb attacks, arson and malicious damage to property' (Department of Safety and Security 2002: 51). The continuities with apartheid rule, in terms of which organized resistance was criminalized and subjected to public order policing, are plain to see.

Along with the simultaneous depoliticization and repoliticization of crime, so too came an increased concern with measuring.

Measuring Crime in the New South Africa

The measuring of crime has been prioritized in the new South Africa along with the turn to managerialism, which applies endless logframes, calculations and quantifications to the business of government. What it is that we count and the questions that we ask are fundamentally important to the structure of the truth that emerges from the quantification exercises, and it is important to note that this truth is contingent, contested and negotiated.

Although a concern with victims was around in the old South Africa, the post-apartheid victim has a much stronger presence. This may well be because the patterns of victimhood have shifted: there are now far more white middle class victims of crime and additionally, with the state having invested the fight against crime with a moralized struggle nuance, having likened it to a fight to entrench human rights, the narratives of poorer black victims are now also heard in popular discourse. The emergence of a powerful black middle class adds another angle to the category of victimhood.

The first national victim survey was conducted by the Department of Safety and Security in 1998 and the second one by the Institute for Security Studies (ISS) in 2003.[21] Other specialist research institutions that have been involved in these 'scientific victim surveys'[22] include Statistics South Africa (SSA) and the Human Sciences Research Council (HSRC). The knowledge produced by these studies, shapes, forms and structures both the public discourse and also official criminology. In this sense, then, the truths about victimhood emerged together with the category itself (Hacking 1986, 1999).[23]

---

21 Subsequent surveys were conducted in 2007, also by the ISS, and in 2011, by Statistics South Africa.

22 The 2002 Annual Report of the National Commissioner of the South African Police Service uses this term (Department of Safety and Security 2003: 36).

23 Hacking (1999: 104) refers to 'interactive classifications,' which can change the way people perceive of themselves, and 'dynamic nominalism', whereby different types of people come into being at the same time as the type is being created (Hacking 1985: 228).

Just as victim surveys both produce and measure victimhood, so too has the new technology for producing data – the ability to correlate crime rates with prosecution and conviction rates – resulted in the realization that prosecution systems are inefficient. Similarly, the Geographical Information System (GIS),[24] part of the 'National Spatial Development Perspective',[25] is invoked as an administrative technique[26] to map crime but the information and maps that it produces have a direct impact on where police resources are directed and which communities get policed. As Comaroff and Comaroff (2006) point out, this technique invokes space as a tool for 'mapping disorder' yet, like the criminal, space is also a product of apartheid history and is heavily invested with materiality and meaning. The GIS maps crime and produces 'hotspots' but ignores the racial and class elements that invest and underpin these 'zones of disorder'. In this way, then, it produces that which becomes the subject of the state's gaze, recriminalizing and resubjectifying its citizens.

While the state claims that crime rates have stabilized and in fact Annual Reports do show that they have dropped substantially since 2001, most people, especially whites, do not believe the official statistics (Department of Safety and Security 2004, Du Plessis and Louw 2005, Schonteich 2001, Shaw and Gastrow 2001). What is abundantly clear is that with democracy has come a shift in public perception about crime: not only does the public see it as escalating but popular discourse generally presents the government as being both unable and unwilling to do anything about it. Yet murder, the most reliable indicator, declined from 68 murders per 100,000, in 1995–96 to 43 murders per 100,000 in 2003–4 (United Nations Office on Drugs and Crime, 2005).[27] The 2011–12 statistics, to which I return in the Epilogue, show an even greater decrease. Vehicle theft also declined from a peak of over 107,000 incidents in 1998–99 to just over 88,000 in 2003–4

He gives the example of multiple personalities which are 'more like gloves than like horses. The category and the people in it emerged hand in hand.'

24 Implemented as a pilot project at five stations in Johannesburg in 2001 and thereafter rolled out to 340 priority stations.

25 It focuses on 'map searches and crime pattern analyses of plotted crimes, crime return statistics, time analyses of plotted crimes and grid analyses of plotted crimes' (Department of Safety and Security 2003: 13).

26 The 2002–3 Annual Report includes it under the 'administration' section.

27 This substantial decrease means that South Africa is no longer the 'murder capital of the world' (Du Plessis and Louw, 2005) but, at 20,000 murders per year, it is still unacceptably high and victims are disproportionately young black and coloured working-class men (Silber and Geffen 2009). Black and coloured women are also disproportionately victimized by violent crime. According to an investigation by the Medical Research Council in 2004, whereas 2.8 of every 100,000 white women die of murder, 8.9 black and 18.3 coloured women do (cited in Silber and Geffen 2009:40) Although reported rape decreased from 225.7 per 100,000 in 1994 to 113.7 in 2004, this, too, is a disturbingly high figure. Indeed, much of the concern about crime in South Africa seems to be over its frighteningly violent nature.

(Department of Safety and Security, 2004: 19).[28] However, robbery, and particularly violent robbery, continued to climb, so much so that a special category of crime called 'robbery with aggravating circumstances' was created.[29] This 'reassurance gap' (Gilling 2010: 1145) between 'public perceptions that crime was rising and the statistical "reality" of falling crime rates' may indeed have been due to the violent 'signal crimes', such as public muggings, rapes and house-breakings, that generated a social reaction of fear and anxiety, not necessarily in proportion to the actual incidence of such crimes (Gilling 2010: 1146).

Attacks against people living on farms and smallholdings have attracted significant attention since the police first started recording them as separate incidents in 1997. Whereas official discourse attributed the acts of violence against the farming community to robberies (because 90 per cent involved a robbery), the white farming community regarded them as 'terror attacks aimed at driving them from their land' (Department of Safety and Security 2003: 47). The victims claimed an ominous political agenda on the side of the violator, whereas the state offered a more sanitized rational choice-type explanation for the transgressions. The murder of Eugene Terreblanche, former leader of the far right Afrikaner Weerstand Beweging (AWB) on his farm on 3 April 2010, by two of his employees, is a case in point. AWB supporters claimed that the murder was politically motivated, especially in light of controversies around the singing of militant struggle songs – with lyrics containing the words 'Kill the Boers' by the then ANC Youth League leader, Julius Malema. The government was, however, quick to issue a statement that attributed the murder to purely criminal motives.

In July 2000 the then Minister of Safety and Security, Steve Tshwete, announced a moratorium on the public release of crime statistics, because they were supposedly inaccurate. This followed a 1994 disagreement between then deputy President Mbeki and senior (white) police officers: the latter argued that crime was 'spiralling out of control' (*Cape Times*, 2 November 1994) whereas Mbeki denied this, stating that those who argued thus drove away investors and dented the image of country (Shaw 1995: 38). The ban on the release of crime

28 House-breaking at non-residential (i.e. business) premises decreased from 225.7 per 100,000 in 1994 to 139.3 in 2004. On the other hand, house-breaking at residential premises increased since 1994, from 596.2 to 645.2 per 100,000 in 2004 (Department of Safety and Security 2004: 19).

29 'Robbery with aggravating circumstances' increased from 218.5 in 1994 to 288.1 per 100,000 in 2004 (Department of Safety and Security, 2004: 19). This represented a 31 per cent increase (Du Plessis and Louw 2005). Although 'robbery with aggravating circumstances' included the 'high profile' crimes of 'carjacking', 'highjacking of trucks', 'robbery of cash in transit' and 'bank robbery', these crimes in fact *decreased* substantially and, because 25–50 per cent of all 'aggravated robberies' involved cellular telephones, the increase was attributed to the robbery of cellular telephones (Department of Safety and Security 2003: 41). It may also be the case that part of the increase was caused by higher rates of reporting. (See, however, Du Plessis and Louw (2005), who argue that the increase is too high to attribute it all to increased reporting and that this represented a real increase.)

statistics specified that no information could be given to anyone outside the South African Police Service. According to the government there was no point in releasing incorrect statistics. At the time Tshwete lambasted those who blew the crime problem out of proportion. The ban lasted almost a year, until 31 May 2001.

In 2004 the ANC claimed that the perception that crime had increased was one that was held by whites and was in fact wrong since 'various surveys confirm that it has stabilized and in some instances has dropped dramatically' (*Hansard* 2004a, col: 2476). In this way the ANC government used denial and refusal to divulge information as a tactic of rule – just as the NP government had done before it.

Because of the dearth of statistics pre-1994 it is impossible to start determining when South Africa began to experience a crime increase, although 1986 seems to have been a watershed year in which there was a noticeable increase in official crime statistics. In this chapter I have not sought to give a 'true' picture of the crime situation in South Africa; instead I have shown how the act of measuring came to assume greater importance than before and how the numbers engendered controversy. Because the veracity and accuracy of this statistical narrative are subject to resistance and struggle, there is always a call for more and better numbers. Like the prison, which continues despite the endless litany of problems associated with it, allegations about inaccurate or at worst lying numbers only result in more of the same, affirming an 'underlying faith in their revelatory potential, intensifying the quest for ever more rigorous uncorrupted statistics' (Comaroff and Comaroff 2006: 224). Ironically, race still plays a key role in state discourse about crime.

Conclusion

Just as conservative commentators blamed the repeal of Influx Control legislation for an increase in crime, so, too, has the transition to democracy been blamed for an increase in the crime rate in post-apartheid South Africa.

As apartheid started to be dismantled in the 1980s, the fairly low rate of crime in the cities and white neighbourhoods started to increase. Concerns about the growth of crime and the government's ability to successfully deal with it increased exponentially, with opposition parties blaming the government's focus on quelling political unrest and the repeal of petty apartheid legislation as the reason for a burgeoning crime rate. This was because the pattern of exclusion and segregation, based on apartheid principles, of separating likely victims (whites) from likely offenders (poor blacks) had, until this point, been a primary method of crime control. This method of segregation was perceived to be effective insofar as whites were concerned.

A number of consequences followed the transition. There was a rise in the actual victimization rates in previously white neighbourhoods. There was a rise in the fear levels of new victims, whose physical security was now much more at risk. This was not limited to whites only, since BEE policies put into place by the new ANC government meant that a substantial black middle class started to emerge who also became the victims of crimes, and the voices of poor blacks whose victimization had, under the apartheid government, been largely ignored now started to be heard. As a government professing to represent the masses, the ANC had to be seen to be listening to this constituency.

Whereas the apartheid government criminalized political resistance, the ANC government has stripped crime of a political and social context, leaving behind the unadulterated criminal, the evil 'other'. This discursive attempt to separate crime from politics was particularly relevant to the indemnity debates, in terms of who would and wouldn't be granted immunity from prosecution for crimes committed during the apartheid era. Yet because of the blurriness of the distinction between 'pure' crime and crimes committed with a political motive, the line between the two was revisited and redrawn on many occasions. There is certainly no objective truth about what constitutes political crime and what does not. Yet on many levels, crime and politics are inseparable: Did the criminal have a political motive? What was the politics behind the criminalization of particular acts/omissions? What is the socio-political context within which a particular crime is committed? Who gets policed? What types of offences are policed?

More often than not, when a government faces political challenges and perceives a threat to its power and capacity to govern, then it will deploy force and the tactics of criminalization. It governs through coercion in order to contain the dissent and to impose control. Categorizing activities as criminal that, in ordinary circumstances, should be legitimate, such as peaceful protests, is one thing, but in instances in which protests turn violent, where there is 'unrest', then the waters become murkier and there is slippage and overlap.

As crime has become subjected to ever better and more intensive measurement in the new South Africa, so, too, has it become an object to be governed and through which governing occurs. However, techniques of measuring crime are not 'pure science' and are not the bearers of some objective truth. The truth produced by the numbers is constructive and productive of other truths and the apolitical facade of numbering masks a deeper politics. The changes in the way that crime is measured, such as through the GIS and Victim Surveys, are not purely technical, but highly productive.

In post-apartheid South Africa, it is now criminals and no longer the apartheid police whom the ANC regards as the destroyers of human rights. Yet race has continued to play a crucial role in terms of newsworthiness, criminalization, victimization, feelings of safety, allocation of state and non-state policing resources, political discourse and interpretation of crime statistics. Thus although the concern about crime did not suddenly emerge with the transition to democracy in 1994, its form and content have changed sharply over the years.

Chapter 3
Explanations for Crime

> Crime control strategies and criminological ideas are not adopted because they are known to solve problems but rather because they characterize problems and identify solutions in ways that fit with the dominant culture and the power structure on which it rests (Garland 2001: 26).

Introduction

This chapter discusses official explanations for the causes of crime in South Africa and how these have changed over the years. I also track changes in how the ANC explained crime prior to becoming the ruling party. For each period that I describe I set out the main criminological ideas and explain the changes that occurred between and within different periods. Since I am not doing an analysis of the production of criminological ideas, or a sociology of knowledge of the South African criminological field, I do not discuss the rapidly expanding literature by non-state criminologists/sociologists, particularly those who write about what causes the particularly violent nature of crime in South Africa.[1] Where I do refer to sources other than state documents, it is to show who the major influences were and to identify the ideas on which state produced texts are based, in order to give a sense of the context within which official ideas have emerged.

Criminology is a relatively new field in South Africa and the first criminology society, The Criminological Society of South Africa, was established only in 1986. The discipline was introduced as an independent university subject in 1949, a year after the Nationalist Party was voted into government (Van Zyl Smit, 1989). Cronje is regarded as the founder of 'Afrikaner Nationalist Criminology' (Van Zyl Smit 1990: 4, Dubow 1995, Van der Walt 1975, Van Der Walt et al. 1982). Afrikaner Nationalist Criminology was based on the essentializing theory that racial segregation was a means of preventing crime.

I argue that during the 1970s essentializing racist explanations, although still present, were decentred in official criminology. Instead, the social and economic conditions within which the offender found him/herself were increasingly regarded as having a negative influence. By 2004, although the socio-economic explanation was still used as an explanation for crime it had been displaced (and thereby somewhat muted and/or deprioritized) by, and at the same time melded

1 See Bruce 2007, Dugard 2001, Foster et al. 1998, Kynoch 2005, 2008, 2011, Steinberg 2001, 2008, 2012, for an introduction to this literature.

with, other explanations, such as 'transition theory'. This has taken place in terms of an overall framework which seeks not so much to explain crime as to make practical suggestions for making the criminal justice system more effective.

The theme of employment is presented as key to preventing crime, and unemployment as being linked to criminality underpins official explanations for crime in both the 'old' and the 'new' South Africa. In the 'new' South Africa 'relative deprivation' (Department of Safety and Security 1996a: 2.21: 7) is said to have been heightened by the transition to democracy, and unemployment is regarded as one of the primary causes of crime. I argue that official criminology deploys the unemployment argument as a means of explaining why the police cannot solve the crime problem, rather than as an entry point into dealing with South Africa's poverty and inequality. The fiction at the heart of the argument that unemployment causes crime is that work is in fact unattainable for many people in South Africa, given the high unemployment rates. As such, work is not a way to bring people out of poverty, yet social inclusion is based on waged employment, despite the fact that wages are the main source of income for only 57 per cent of black households, with 38 per cent relying on pensions and grants (Marais 2011: 193). The unemployment argument also does not acknowledge the growth of casualization and subcontracting and the decline of formal employment (Barchiesi 2010, Marais 2011). Casualization is, as we know, one of the characteristics of global neoliberalization processes (Brenner et al. 2010a, 2010b, Bosworth and Guild 2008).

1976–89 Reform of Verwoerdian Apartheid

The Field

The two-volume publication *Misdaad in die Gemeenskap/Crime and Society* (1975) is an example of orthodox criminology in South Africa at the start of the period under discussion. Its contributors were largely white Afrikaans males, such as Van der Walt, Louw, Benususan, Freed, Retief and Duwenange. Ndabandaba was the only black author. Many were based at the University of South Africa (UNISA), which established an Institute of Criminology in 1973, and the University of Pretoria, where Cronje, Venter and Van der Walt were all employed, at various points in their careers. In the late 1970s these Afrikaans universities were closely associated with the production of state policies (Ashworth 1990) and were major producers of PhD theses on criminology.[2]

Between 1975 and 1979 there was a series of state-appointed Commissions of Inquiry which played both justificatory and reformist roles (Gelb 1991: 25). The most important ones, for the purposes of this book, were the Commission of Inquiry into the Penal System of the Republic of South Africa (Viljoen Commission), the

2 Personal communication from Dr Linda Chisholm of the HSRC in July 2005.

Commission of Inquiry into Labour Legislation (Wiehahn Commission) and the Commission of Inquiry into Legislation affecting the Utilization of Manpower (the 'Riekert' Commission).

The then state run Human Sciences Research Council (HSRC) was also an important player in the production of research on crime. In the 1980s there was an overall scientification drive, which saw the state-funded HSRC being substantially reorganized, expanded, producing more research and publishing the 1980 South African Plan for the Human Sciences (Marais 2001: 275). There was also a shift in regard to the production of criminological knowledge with state departments ratcheting up their research capacity. The 1980 National Symposium on Crimes of Violence in South Africa was the outcome of greater co-operation between security forces and criminologists (Van Zyl Smit 1990: 8–9) and the 1982–83 Department of Justice Annual Report referred to the need for a more intensified, co-ordinated and practically orientated crime research programme in regard to the causes of crime (Department of Justice 1984a: 61). This 'reformist' language espoused 'technocratic rationality' and assigned powers to 'experts' to develop scientific and 'objective' solutions to 'national' problems (Posel 1984: 2). As such there was a drive to engage with science, as opposed to ideology, to develop and drive policies.

The merger of the English-speaking National Institute for Personnel Research (NIPR) with the Afrikaner-dominated HSRC in 1985 resulted in a strengthening of the HSRC. It also represented a turn towards 'science' through the greater use of statistics and empirical research about non-white 'population groups' (Tikly 2003, Marais 2001, 2011). In terms of this new inclusiveness, which reflected and structured the ideology of 'multi-racialism', the 1985 Human Sciences Research Amendment Act changed the definition of 'research': it was no longer research in the field of the human sciences for all 'national groups' but the words 'national groups' were now omitted – so as to confirm the 'universality of the research activities of the HSRC and of science' (*Hansard* 1985a, col: 4055). In a 1986 HSRC publication Schurink and Kerr (1986) refer to a shift, since 1977, from a 'consensus/conservative or positivistic approach dominated by the 'use of quantitative methodology in studying the crime phenomenon … [with] qualitative studies … nearly non-existent' to a more qualitative approach. Instead of gleaning information about black criminals from official statistics, researchers from the HSRC now started to study black subjects via qualitative methods, and Lotter and Schurink's (1986) study on prison gangs is an example of this. The fact that those criminologists who were associated with the state received access to institutions, such as the prisons, that were closed to other researchers, obviously influenced the nature of the criminological knowledge that was produced. In 1989 the HSRC established a Centre for Criminological Research and Glanz (1989: 1) identified a shift in focus from offender to victim, due to the failure of programmes that had tried to reduce crime by 'trying to change the offender and improve his/her environment'. This shift towards the foregrounding of victims was apparent as early as 1984 when the Annual Report for the Department of Health and Welfare mentioned victims for the first time. The First Child Protection Unit in the South African Police was established in 1986.

Critical criminologists, on the other hand, emphasized the role of state policies, particularly apartheid laws, in explaining crime. As Sumner (1982: 23) pointed out, orthodox criminology's support for indigenous institutions and values had to be situated in the context of the needs of the South African government to sustain the rural economy and homeland system, in the context of an overall political project that sought to grant qualified citizenship rights to certain blacks and to exclude others. Conservative criminologists critiqued 'critical' criminology for being a 'politicizing' rather than a 'behavioralist' (Theron 1979) approach, because it emphasized the role of politics in causing crime instead of looking at individual behaviour. The University of Cape Town's Institute of Criminology, situated in the law faculty, and founded in 1977, was at the forefront of this critical approach. Academics such as Haysom, Slabbert, Davis, Sandler and Pinnock sought to uncover the way in which policing was used to 'stigmatise and control ... curb and repress action which threaten[ed] dominant social relationships' (Davis 1985: 11). Their studies examined security legislation, the Group Areas Act and labour controls (Davis 1985: 11). Davis, in 1985, described 'orthodox criminology' as a criminology which failed to analyse the role of law in the 'coerced growth of capitalist domination' and which was 'ahistorical and pro-state' based as it was on the 'economic theory of modernization'(Davis 1985: 10).

Critical criminology sought to uncover how changes and developments in categories of crime were related to 'changes in social structure, particularly the mode of production' and the way categories of crime 'become units of a dominant moral ideology' (Davis 1985: 11). Whereas orthodox criminologists attributed gang formation to urbanization and 'denormation' resulting in loss of social control, critical criminologists explicitly blamed the state for causing this loss of community and broken social cohesion due to the forced removals in terms of the Group Areas Act (Pinnock, cited in Van der Spuy et al. 2004: 170). From the mid-1980s critical criminology concerned itself with studies of the conditions of children in prison and 'rights based studies' (Mclachlan 1984, Van der Spuy et al. 2004). This should be seen in the context of the increasingly authoritarian manner of the 1980s state crackdown on political activists, as resistance to the apartheid regime intensified and successive states of emergency were imposed.

In a sense critical criminologists in South Africa made the same mistakes as the critical criminologists of the 1970s in the USA and UK – in that they neglected to focus on crime in the townships, on the very real fact that crime was a problem in South Africa and that it affected mainly poor people. Even in the 1970s the liberal opposition Progressive Federal Party was more concerned about political prisoners than the conditions under which ordinary criminals were imprisoned. Similarly, in the post-1976 period the bulk of critical academic literature was less concerned with 'conventional' youth criminality than on youth and politics, with the focus on children in detention.

Discursive Shifts

From the mid-1970s the state adopted a range of reform initiatives in an attempt to maintain a faltering hegemony in the face of growing unemployment, strikes, the national liberation struggles in Angola and Mozambique and the ideological revival of the Black Consciousness movement (Marais 2001, 2011, Posel 1984, Tikly 2003). Following on the 1979 Riekert Commission proposal, that control and revenue generation in townships be decentralized, local black township councils were elected and assigned the duties that had previously been performed by white civil servants (Marais 2011).

The effects of this rollback neoliberalism were substantial rent increases and increased competition for jobs between black workers and their migrant counterparts. This resulted in increasing politicization and resistance (Marais 2011: 43). These reforms took place in the context of a global recession and in the first three months of 1976 the South African economy lost one quarter of its foreign exchange reserves, resulting in the government taking an emergency loan from the IMF (Marais 2011). In the face of political resistance, apartheid ideology started to falter and even Afrikaner capital began to question the utility of racial segregation, pressing the ruling Nationalist Party to face the reality of a growing, permanent, urbanized black population.

Concomitant with political and economic reforms, with the political ideology of separate development replacing that of segregation, there was a shift in the dominant explanations for crime. The original theories underpinning racial segregation based on 'scientific racism' started to lose their hegemonic status (Van Zyl Smit 1989, Dubow 1995). By the 1970s, Willemse and Rademeyer's (1933) first South African textbook on criminology, *Kriminologie*, which had expounded a hereditary theory of criminal behaviour, was no longer the only textbook.

Even arch conservatives such as Cronje were no longer explicitly linking race and crime. Cronje's thesis of 'bio-psycho-sociocriminological' causality incorporated a multi-causal framework for explaining criminal behaviour. An individual's 'criminopredisposition' was located within the individual but fostered by background factors. According to Naude (1988a: 16), whereas previously psychological and social treatment techniques were brought to bear on behavioral problems, now the 'biopsychosocial viewpoint' prevailed. The standard line, in terms of a 'biopsychosocial' approach, was that crime was a 'complex phenomenon' and 'the result of multiple causes' (1988a: 16). This complemented the new state ideology that South Africa comprised 'plural' communities with different, and indeed conflicting, value systems and necessitated a 'multifactorial approach … in its treatment and prevention' (Naude 1988a: 16). Given this diversity, there could be no overall one-size-fits-all theory of criminology, of why people committed crimes, especially one which was based on race alone.

This shift in criminological theories should be seen in the context of a governmental project that sought to responsibilize a select group, by creating a black middle class whose members had the rights to reside in urban areas, whilst shunting the rest into the homelands. In their drive to obtain a 'stable source of African semi-skilled and skilled labour' (Marais 2001: 43) the 'verligte (enlightened) Nats' sought only a limited form of inclusiveness for blacks that did not entail the conferral of full citizenship (Charney 1983: 151). Durkheim's theory of anomie was given an apartheid spin and, in terms of an overall political ideology, which presented South Africa as being composed of a variety of ethnic communities, whites, blacks and coloureds were regarded as being differentially affected by urbanization. Official criminology justified the homelands on the basis of black people's apparent inability to cope with city living.

Socio-Economic Conditions

From the 1970s on, left, liberal and right political discourse increasingly blamed socio-economic conditions for causing crime and official criminology embraced the position that crime experts could no longer solve the problem of crime. The 1976 Viljoen Report marked an epistemological shift in this regard. It found that for the majority of South Africa's population, crime was an 'almost inevitable sequel to deprivation and miserable socio-economic conditions' and that 'among the white community' it was 'affluence and the selfish and materialistic outlook' (*Cape Times*, 1 February 1977). The Annual Reports of the South African Police referred to 'normal' worldwide increases in crime and ascribed the increased crime statistics in South Africa to population growth, work shortages, socio-economic conditions and 'recent unrest' (Department of Justice, Police and Prisons 1978a).

Linking unemployment with crime in the 'old' South Africa was used to justify repressive policies, such as influx control and the homelands. Thus in 1980 Adrian Vlok, a Nationalist Party MP who subsequently became the Minister of Law and Order, in reply to a question by a Progressive Federal party MP, stated that:

> the hon member is constantly telling us in this House that the unemployed people are the people who commit crime, and that is true. The police are engaged in preventing them from streaming into our towns and cities where unemployed people create the potential of a higher incidence of crime. (*Hansard* 1980a, col: 5997)

Blaming unemployment for crime was also used as a means of disclaiming responsibility, particularly on the part of the police. Thus in 1981, when the police gave evidence to the Bloomberg Commission on Crime and Law Enforcement, they reiterated that the cause of the townships' crime problem was socio-economic, and that the responsibility did not lie with the South African Police (*Cape Times*, 29 July 1981).

At the same time the discourse of some Nationalist Party MPs sounded almost left in their call for socio-economic upliftment of black people. Thus, for example, in the debate on the 1981 Prisons Appropriation Vote an NP MP stated that:

> if we wish to see how we could reduce the prison population in South Africa in the long term … it could not be achieved by way of the single measure of rehabilitation within the prison, but that a total socio-economic upliftment effort and a total programme of action by the Government is necessary to get the communities and the individual within the communities stabilized. If we are unable to re-establish the anchors of proper family control and family discipline among our Black people…, we are heading for an ever-increasing prison population (*Hansard* 1980b: cols: 6103–4).

In the 1986 debate on the Abolition of Influx Control Bill the Minister of Constitutional Development and Planning, in what was perhaps the final death knell for the theory that crime could be stopped by keeping black people out of urban areas, stated that:

> Social problems cannot be solved by merely applying coercive measures … crime in an urbanization context is not merely the result of people being in cities. It could rather be ascribed to inadequate housing, poverty, broken homes. (*Hansard* 1986a cols: 7045–9368)

Subculture

The Viljoen Report referred to a 'subculture of violence', citing American criminologists Wolfgang and Ferracuti, who in their book *The Subculture of Violence* (1967, 1982), argued that violent values were uniquely widespread among African-Americans because of a 'subculture of violence' (1982: 149) In 1976 Schurink and Strijdom (1976: 9–10) ascribed the fact that crime in Soweto was 'generally committed by two or more persons' as supporting Shaw's subcultural theories of deviance and juvenile delinquency.

According to Cloete (1979: 235), Professor of Criminology at UNISA, the visibility of 'conventional goals, values and norms … to the community of the sub-culture' caused 'a common problem [of conflict] in the group', resulting in 'crime and delinquency in certain sectors and strata of the community'. Cronje (1982: 115) argued that 'incompetent and irresponsible parenthood' was a 'criminogenic factor', 'especially at low socio-economic levels'. He referred to 'growing permissiveness' as being a breeding ground of crime. Thus, a 'morally undesirable family with a bad value concept' would transmit a 'bad value concept productive of low moral norms' which would expose offspring 'to, or precipitate, antisocial behavior' (Cronje 1982: 544). He explained the high rate amongst blacks of crimes against property, murder and assault as being related to a 'low standard of living' (Cronje 1982: 265). Although he conceded that 'adverse sociocultural factors' coupled with 'poor norms' could be 'criminogenic' it was divergent 'attitudes to and quality of life' (Cronje 1982: 523) that explained the higher crime rates among 'non whites'. His research into the 'marital states' of convicted people revealed that a high percentage of coloured and black delinquents had never married and that 'a low social, material and occupational level' led to an 'unstable lifestyle, delinquency and possible stigmatisation'(Cronje 1982: 420). This high rate of 'illegitimacy amongst blacks' was apparently 'unthinkable in a tribal context' (Cronje 1982: 421).

Haysom's 1981 ground-breaking study, which analysed gang formation in South African prisons, exemplifies how a more critical perspective also deployed subcultural theory. He identified the 'structural causes of crime' (1981: 23) as being due to the fact that Africans had been pushed out of the rural areas into the cities in order to supplement their income to pay hut taxes. Once in the urban areas they had become part of a 'reserve army of labour'. According to him (1981: 21), the fact that the black townships suffered from a 'lack of adequate housing, lighting, transport, educational and, recreational facilities' coupled with the 'dominance of the all male institutions of the compound and the prison' made them conducive to criminal operations. Influx control legislation contributed to further criminalization by causing pass law offenders to come into contact with prison gangs. Being confronted with 'vast wealth on the one hand and on the other with structural constraints' which prevented the majority from 'acquiring such wealth legitimately', gangs emerged as an 'ideological response to an unequal society' and from a society with an 'abnormally high' crime rate (Haysom 1981: 33).

1990–94 (Transitioning into the 'New' South Africa)

During this period there was a lot more concern about crime, especially political crime, and departmental annual reports increasingly included sections on crime causation. The argument that crime was to a large extent a normal outcome of adverse socio-economic conditions was increasingly put forward by the police and politicians during this period. It constituted an admission that the state, especially the police, could not stop crime on its or their own. As such, its use as an explanatory device also doubled up as an excuse and it was often combined with a lamenting of the ills associated with 'uncontrolled urbanization'. As a House of Delegates representative put it:

> uncontrolled urbanization is coupled with squatter problems. It is in this situation that socio-economic deterioration, as a result of unemployment, poor infrastructure and overpopulation, takes place. For this and other reasons crime is increasing at an alarming rate (*Hansard* 1991b, col: 7625).

It was also presented as being normal in the sense of being an 'international phenomenon' (Department of Law and Order 1993: 51).

The 1992 SAP Annual Report stated that more than 65 per cent of crime was 'aimed at obtaining property and the basic necessities of life'; hence South Africa's 'economic problems' – the Report referred to a 45 per cent increase in the registered unemployment rate – were considered to be the 'greatest single variable ... particularly [in respect of] those crimes related to the economy' (Department of Law and Order 1993: 55). In 1993 the increase in theft was attributed to the high unemployment rate, 'accompanied by the deteriorating economy' (Department of Law and Order 1994: 101). Although it was acknowledged that the political situation also impacted on crime the official position was that it had an indirect rather than a direct influence and that 'socio-economic factors such as unemployment, poor housing and a lack of the basic necessities of life should rather be seen as influencing factors' (Department of Law and Order 1993: 54). In this way, then, the discourse about the increasing crime rate as symptom of socio-economic and social decline became mantra-like, so much so that exactly the same phrase appeared in consecutive police annual reports.

Even 'crimes of violence' which had both a 'political and criminal dimension' were also 'fundamentally rooted in the same socio-political and economical circumstances' (Department of Law and Order 1994: 104). This was of course ammunition in the ideological battle against the ANC and its blaming of the political situation for causing crime. Official criminology's emphasis on socio-economic conditions and unrest as causing crime had a conservative subtext which totally omitted to look at the role of the state and the impact of apartheid policies in causing crime and the very socio-economic conditions which were now considered to be so problematic. On the other hand the position taken by the ANC and left-wing activists was almost the complete antithesis – the argument being that lawlessness was encouraged by an illegitimate and corrupt government that did not set an example.

'Unrest and the 'Culture of Violence'

The perception, circulated by the state, was that the increase in violence during the transition was due to inter-group conflict amongst blacks.[3] Thus the 1991 Annual Report of the Commissioner of the South African Police stated that:

> Whereas crime related to inter-group conflict previously occurred principally in Natal it has, especially since July 1990, spread to other areas. This has given rise to large-scale manslaughter and devastation in the ranks of especially black people. (Department of Law and Order 1992: 1)

'Unrest', discussed under the 'Internal Security' part of the South African Police Annual Reports, was regarded as originating in

> *inter alia*, the occurrence of conflict between various ethnic, ideological and social groupings, as well as from a spirit of anarchy stimulated by hooliganism and a high degree of criminality. (Department of Law and Order 1991: 51)

3 See Chapter 2.

Similarly, de Minnaar and Esterhuysen (1990: 70), writing in a 1990 HSRC publication, attributed the fact that one community was more 'homogenous … being made up almost entirely of Zulus' as the reason that 'it … enjoyed more stability and [was] prone to less unrest than others'. This discourse echoed the cultural diversity and plurality framework, which had at one stage been used to justify apartheid. Mainstream criminologists depoliticized the violence, in which state agents were often complicit with Inkatha 'impis',[4] by referring to it as 'faction fighting'. Ndabandaba (1990a: 429) presented it as a species of 'organized crime'. He also referred to right-wing American criminologist Banfield and his theory of a high propensity for crime in the 'underclass'. Of course he made no mention of the role of the state in this violence. One of his explanations for this 'violent collective behaviour' was that the 'possibilities of conflict' attributable to the 'ideology of vengeance' (1990a: 437), which had always been present in black societies, had increased with urbanization, contributed to the malaise and reinforced the violence.

The 'culture of violence' which the 1992 Police Annual Report referred to as having arisen in 1976, in the context of the Soweto uprising, was attributed to the 'apparent inability of black political groupings to control the radical elements within their own ranks' (Department of Law and Order 1993: 57). Thus murder was to be

> judged [not] only in the light of the struggle for political power and because of intolerance, but should also [be judged] … in the light of a collapse of society, economic decline (with the concomitant unemployment) and the ill discipline of a sector of the community which has grown up in a culture of violence and criminality in general. (Department of Law and Order 1993: 59–60)

In 1993 a Nationalist Party MP referred to 'a new and truly alarming pattern of interracial violence'. He blamed both the 'fiery' words of Dullah Omar[5] and the 'angry, uneducated youth' – the so-called 'lost generation', stating that:

> What at first seemed to be classic terrorism is now claiming victims in city and country areas alike … the use of the words 'Kill a Boer'[6] aroused great anger across the country. This anger was justified, because boers were killed … then we have Dullah Omar who tried to wiggle himself out of his fiery speech by invoking metaphor. He asked people to turn their guns on the real enemy. Of course he did not mean guns in their literal sense, and the enemy he spoke of was apartheid, as if that were some disembodied entity [but the disaffected

4 The Inkatha Freedom Party (IFP) was a political party that was dominant in Natal. It consisted mainly of Zulus and the word 'impis' refers to groups of armed IFP sympathizers.

5 An ANC member who became the first Minister of Justice after the 1994 elections.

6 *Boer* is an Afrikaans word for farmer.

youth] – are not going to bother with such niceties (*Hansard* 1993–94a, col: 9082–83).[7]

The 'culture of violence' explanation also embraced the argument that bad parenting produced delinquent children who were conditioned in a social milieu that encouraged negative values. This theory was very popular with mainstream criminologists Glanz, Lotter and Ndabandaba. They all agreed that crime was more rampant among lower class youth (Glanz 1990: 295) because 'delinquent behavior [was] learned through social interaction with significant others who support pro-delinquent values'. Lotter and Ndabandaba (1990) referred to the proponents of labeling theory as being 'usually humanistic and often neo-Marxist in outlook' and proposed that there was considerable evidence that supported control theory, as did Glanz. Similarly, Chinkanda and Maphatane (1990: 309), citing Afrikaner Nationalist criminologist Venter (1972), blamed criminal parents for delinquent children and parental 'neglect' was regarded as constituting an important cause of delinquency.

Because increasing 'lawlessness' was perceived as an indication of a state that was losing control and could only regain it by being tough on crime, there was also a call for stricter bail and sentencing regimes and more effective policing. This discourse presupposed that slackness in keeping order was a cause of crime, along the lines of zero tolerance and order maintenance theories that assumed prominence in the USA in the late 1990s.[8] In 1991 the Deputy Head of the Criminal Investigation Department identified 'ineffective punishment' and the moratorium on the death penalty as one of the contributing factors to crime (Kneen 1991).[9] The South African Security Federation, Security Association of South Africa, police and banks called for a review of the conditions for the granting of bail in cases involving 'serious crimes of violence' (Kneen 1991). The Academy of the South African Police at Graaf Reinet, in a report on the causes of crime, stated that (apart from socio-economic factors and social decay) people who committed crimes while out on bail also influenced the high crime rates (Department of Law and Order 1992: 6). This was grist for the mill of harsher bail laws, discussed in Chapter 6.

---

7 It is ironic that some 18 years later Julius Malema, now expelled as leader of the African National Congress Youth League, caused great consternation by his singing of the 'Kill the Boer' song while he was still an ANC member and head of the Youth League.

8 Proponents of the 'broken window thesis' (which is the informal name for the zero tolerance and order maintenance theories) (Wilson and Kelling 1982, Kelling and Coles 1996) propose that communities will only be able to use informal social control mechanisms if they are propped up with zero tolerance policing of incivilities.

9 See Chapter 6 where I refer to the 1991 moratorium on the death penalty.

ANC Explanations for Crime

The ANC also deployed the socio-economic argument to explain crime. In 1991 its Western Cape spokesperson referred to a 'socio-economic disease of epidemic proportions' that was afflicting South African society and blamed the 'low quality of life and no recreational facilities' for causing crime (*Cape Times*, 23 March 1991). In its 1992 'Ready to Govern' policy document the ANC (1992a) emphasized that 'a just criminal justice system [would] enhance respect for the courts and obedience to the law'. The implication was that crime was caused because people did not respect the illegitimate apartheid justice system. It blamed the 'militarized' nature of South African society for high levels of violence and crime and stressed the need to create 'legitimate security institutions' while promising a 'new approach to security' which incorporated 'political, economic, social and environmental dimensions' (ANC 1992a). It also referred to 'crimes of the poor such as street crime' and linked these to 'the structural violence of the apartheid era' (ANC 1992b: 7).

The ANC referred to a 'lost generation' which had come into being during the 'political struggle of the last 6 years' (ANC 1992b: 3) and which had experienced 'substantially weakened' attachment to the socializing structures of 'family, school, peer pressure, the older generation, political and civic organizations'. These losses put this generation at risk of adopting 'criminal lifestyles' and 'militant political views'. It was also 'the sloganeering around redistribution of wealth' that had created a tolerance for crime and a huge market in illegal goods (ANC 1992b: 3).

Another reason adduced for the escalation of 'conventional crime' was because there had been a vacuum in 'crime-policing' during the 1980s which, coupled with the 'suppression of political organizations' that militated against the 'informal policing and ordering role' (ANC 1992b: 3) that these organizations played, resulted in crime increasing. This notion that political organizations played an important social ordering role is one which underpinned the communitarian ideas that became dominant in critical criminology during this time. It was very much linked to the call for 'people's power', grassroots democracy and community-based governance initiatives.

Although communitarianism embraced a range of positions and theories, all with a somewhat different nuance and focus, the point of departure was recognition of the need to involve the community in creating its own security and to govern through empowering local communities. Its leading proponents were the child justice advocates Julia Sloth-Nielson and Anne Skelton and academic Clifford Shearing. It was to resurface in a different form in the post-1996 call of the Moral Regeneration Movement for a return to the 'revolutionary morality' of the struggle. It also resonated with the turn to community-based crime prevention that had become popular in the West. Shearing's (1991, 1992) work on security, as entailing a broad rather than narrow conception of policing, influenced the way in which the ANC framed 'underdevelopment, poverty, lack of democratic participation and the abuse of human rights' as 'security threats' (ANC 1992a).

The fact that both the government and the ANC referred to lawlessness and adverse socio-economic conditions as causing crime highlights the political nature of these explanations. Blaming crime on socio-economic conditions is a flexible discourse that can be and is used in various ways depending on the politics of the speaker. The policy implications of using the socio-economic argument are by no means a foregone conclusion. In the 1990s the NP blamed crime on unemployment but the causes of unemployment were ascribed to boycotts and sanctions, as opposed to government policies such as racial capitalism. The blame was firmly placed on externalities over which the government professed to have no control. In the 'new' South Africa the fact that illegal aliens are blamed for exacerbating the problem of unemployment and hence of crime is used as a justification for keeping foreigners out. Thus the socio-economic explanation is very much linked to the political context in which it is deployed and brings to mind Garland's notion of a 'discursive maneuver'. It is not just a tool of liberal discourse for explaining, and in a sense excusing, crime.

1994–2004 (Consolidating the 'New' South Africa)

The Field

The 'new' South Africa has seen a massive growth of non-state expertise, with experts no longer legitimated just by being situated in state institutions. They are now to be found in think tanks such as the Council for Scientific and Industrial Research (CSIR), the Human Sciences Research Council (HSRC), the Institute for Security Studies (ISS), the Centre for the Study of Violence and Reconciliation (CSVR), the MTN Crime Prevention Centre at Rhodes University and the Institute for Human Rights and Criminal Justice Studies at Technikon South Africa (Dixon 2004c). The largely privatized HSRC has expanded and a National Research Foundation has come into being. Both institutions conduct mostly policy-based research. Consultants also play a central role in the production of criminological knowledge.

In the initial euphoria of the first democratic elections many formerly critical criminologists worked with the new government in developing new policies on crime and punishment.[10] One of the key developments was the creation of a civilian secretariat, a type of policy-making think tank, in the department of Safety and Security. This enabled non-governmental and community-based organizations to be involved in policy decisions about the direction of policing in the new South Africa.

---

10 Janine Rauch, Clifford Shearing, Bill Dixon, Elrena van Der Spuy, Dirk van Zyl Smit, Etienne Marais, Martin Schonteich, Julia Sloth Nielson, Anne Skelton, Peter Gastrow, Mark Shaw, Irvin Kinnes, Lukas Muntingh and Antoinette Louw are a few names that are worth mentioning in this regard.

For the sake of simplicity I have identified four 'ideal type' *official* explanations about crime causation in the 'new' South Africa: they are 'transition theory', 'blame it on apartheid', 'socio-economic' and 'pragmatic criminology'. None of these models focuses on the unequal nature of South African society or the fact that poverty and inequality actually increased as constitutional democracy was institutionalized (Zuern 2006). They all incorporate elements of the 'old' theories. I start with 'transition theory'.

Transition and the Lack of Legitimate Authority

The theory that crime increases with transitions to democracy was popular not only amongst mainstream think tanks such as the Institute for Security Studies, left-of-centre criminologists/consultants (such as Kinnes 2000, Shaw 1995, 1996, 1997) and opposition politicians, but also with the state. It goes something along these lines:

> Crime tends to increase during periods of political transition coupled with instability and violence. During periods of instability, routine policing activities are diverted towards controlling violence, and crime consequently increases. (Schonteich and Louw 2001: 5)

Transition theory is rooted in the Durkheimian hypothesis that rapid social change leads to societal deregulation and anomie which in turn leads to higher anomic homicide rates.[11] The latter occur as a result of 'social conditions accompanying increased egoism or individuation *in the absence of* well-defined norms and values' (Pridemore and Kim 2006: 82–5). Thus, in 1995 the Minister for Safety and Security stated that:

> it is historically well-established that whenever an authoritarian regime is replaced by a democratic regime, an increase in the crime rate is immediately observable, arising out of the economic conditions which have been left as a legacy. (*Hansard* 1995a, col: 231)

The 1996 National Crime Prevention Strategy (NCPS) makes explicit reference to transition theory in the part on 'factors giving rise to crime in South Africa'. It was when the 'undemocratic, unaccountable and largely repressive methods of social control which resulted in a substantially over-regulated society' (Department of Safety and Security 1996a: 4.2.3: 14) were withdrawn after 1990 that crime rose. This occurred because

11 Durkheim also stated that *altruistic* homicides are 'associated with strong sentiments about the collective and its protection' (cited in Pridemore and Kim 2006: 84).

> the negotiated transition to democracy and the accompanying unshackling of democratic political processes, also had the unintended consequence of breaking down the existing (often illegitimate) mechanisms of social control – without immediately replacing them with legitimate, credible, consensus based alternatives. (Department of Safety and Security 1996a: 4.2.1: 14)

The NCPS (Department of Safety and Security 1996a: 4.2.7: 15) blamed 'the extensive destruction of the family, the school and even the workplace as vehicles of social cohesion during the preceding era' for 'a society of 'lawlessness'. Similarly the 1998 White Paper on Safety and Security refers to 'opportunities for organised crime and sophisticated criminal operations due to weakened state and social controls' (Department of Safety and Security 1998: 9).

Blame it on Apartheid and the Need for Moral Regeneration

Mandela used the term 'moral regeneration' in 1998, in his speech at the closing of Parliament. The first 'Moral Summit', arranged by the ANC's Commission of Religious Affairs (Rauch 2005), resulted in the 1998 'Moral Renewal of the Nation' pamphlet. The notion of a need for 'moral regeneration' also linked in with Mbeki's African Renaissance initiative (Rauch 2005: 19) that was centred around a drive to revive Africa's former glory, which it had enjoyed prior to the advent of colonialism, and which was cemented by the values of *ubuntu*.[12] As Marais (2011: 380–81) points out, corporate South Africa was very amenable to the African Renaissance Project because the discourse of having Africa regain its 'rightful place on the world stage' included a neoliberal angle centred around bringing the South African economy onto a global footing.

The point of departure was that apartheid had resulted in a breakdown of the 'moral infrastructure' of South African society due to its failure to set 'moral standards' and its embracing of 'an unethical position' that stained everyone with corruption (ANC, 1998). In 2001 then Deputy President Zuma made a speech to Parliament where he blamed apartheid for having 'brutalized all' and causing the 'breakdown of the moral fibre' of all sectors of society (*Hansard* 2001, col: 7827).

In blaming apartheid for the moral degeneration of society the ANC counterposed an ANC 'revolutionary morality' with apartheid immorality:

> Those who were involved in the struggle against apartheid, in the field, in prison, or in exile, experienced a comradeship of very high order. It inspired a high moral tone, and enacted an equality which embraced all South Africans irrespective of race, age, sex, colour or creed. People committed themselves and everything they had to the struggle for a new just and moral community. Self-sacrifice of personal enjoyment, time and money was real: they shared resources

12 This is a Xhosa term. Marais (2001) refers to it as denoting an ethos of reciprocity and mutual aid. See Chapter 6 where I discuss its usage in more detail.

> and dangers, hopes and fears. Far from being helpless victims of terror, they had an integrity and sense of commitment which brought out the best of humanity within them. They built a self-questioning corporate approach to decision making which gave them a "hands on" experience of the principles and policies they professed. (ANC 1998)

In a rather neoliberalesque manoeuvre South Africa's moral renewal was individualized and the 'people shall govern' clause of the Freedom Charter was interpreted in a responsibilizing way:

> The dictatorial apartheid regime was driven by the idea that 'The State will do it'. Many spent years opposing oppression by saying: 'The State must not do it.' Now some have carried the same notion into the quest for transformation by saying: 'The State must do it.' Our tradition is that the people shall govern. The responsibility – including the responsibility for the State – is ours. The transition is from a dictatorial command society, to a responsible society which empowers people to make their own choices. (ANC 1998)

It was thus the individual citizen who would be the 'crucial driving force of transition to a new era' in exercising 'personal choice and responsibility' (ANC 1998). Moral regeneration was needed to rebuild 'the positive social values' that had been eroded by 'decades of oppression, state violence, poverty and social dislocation' (ANC 2001) and to undo the effects of South Africa's 'culture of violence' (Mbeki, cited in Rauch 2005: 20).

This 'culture of violence ... and the low state of morality' (*Hansard* 1998a col: 8067–8) was a way of explaining why the police couldn't solve the problem of crime, of shifting blame from the police, to the 'communities' who 'actively participate in the perpetration of crime' (Hansard 2001b, question 160, col: 2472). The implication was that criminals not only needed to be inculcated with the ANC's 'revolutionary values' but that they were also conceived of as rational actors who could choose to change their behaviour.

The ANC thus embraced a form of 'neoliberal penality' inasmuch as it stressed cracking down on crime and punishing offenders and, at the same time, responsibilizing South African citizens for preventing crime in their personal capacities. Yet, contrary to O'Malley's (1994: 15) definition of 'neoliberal penality', which stresses the amoral nature of accepting responsibility for one's actions,[13] in South Africa the construction of responsible citizens is very much premised on the acceptance of a specific form of morality. This morality is central to the concept of the African Renaissance and to the revolutionary morality that was touted as being the antithesis to apartheid's immorality.

---

13 In the sense that it 'does not imply accepting or obeying any specific set of morals', but taking responsibility for 'the consequence of one's actions' (O'Malley 1994: 15).

Socio-economic Causes of Crime

Mertonian[14] and left realist[15] theories of 'relative deprivation'[16] were also melded together with transition theory to explain South Africa's high crime rates by both state and think tank discourse. In 1994 the Reconstruction and Development Programme (RDP) was regarded as critical to combat crime because crime was viewed as being predominantly caused by poverty. The underlying premise was that legitimation of the police would go a long way to solving crime along with reconstruction and development (Dixon 2006). Since the RDP was geared towards uplifting the lives of poor South Africans, it was thought that it would have a major effect on crime (*Hansard* 1994, col: 2413, ANC 1994). Thus, for example in 1995 the Minister of Safety and Security identified root causes of crime as being 'poverty, disempowerment and social alienation' (*Hansard* 1995b col: 2939). He stated that for crime prevention to be 'lasting' it had to address these root causes and that the RDP would substantially contribute towards addressing this.

Another angle to the poverty argument is that 'relative deprivation' coupled with urbanization is a major crime risk factor. The official explanation is that the lifting of influx control resulted in 'compacted urbanization' (Department of Safety and Security 2003: 24): what 'should have occurred naturally over a period of at least fifty years, has now occurred in 17 years'. These 'higher levels of urban unemployment' coupled with the mushrooming of 'squatter/informal settlements', where policing is 'extremely difficult', have resulted in an increase in crime (Department of Safety and Security 2003: 24–5). Yet the NP government had said similar things about crime in the 1970s, 1980s and early 1990s and the socio-economic explanation is not new to the 'new' South Africa. Of course the

14 Merton's 'strain theory' posits that, in an anomic state, social goals and the means to achieve them do not correspond and that because of this, individuals will sometimes use illegitimate means to attain institutionalized goals.

15 In the 1980s, as a response to early critical criminology, which had ignored the very real problem of crime, especially insofar as poor crime victims were concerned, the 'left' and 'new' realists emerged in British criminology. The 'new realists' focused predominantly on the 'control' of crime – hence producing 'administrative criminology' whereas the left realists focused on causes. The new realists referred to notions of innate wickedness, moral degeneration and greed whereas the left realists acknowledged that individual differences were always mediated by social and economic conditions and that class played an important role (Young 1999).

16 Relative deprivation, as opposed to absolute deprivation, refers to the condition where individuals subjectively perceive themselves as being worse off than others, with whom they compare themselves and whom they think are undeserving of their perceived privileges. It is in contrast with absolute deprivation. As Jock Young (1999) explains, relative deprivation is felt not only by people looking towards those in better economic positions but also by those in higher class structures looking downwards, seeing undeserved rewards accruing to those who do not deserve it because they lack a work ethic/moral restraint. This engenders feelings of punitiveness.

political context is entirely different and whereas the ANC government blamed the NP for the adverse socio-economic conditions the NP blamed the communists, unrest, sanctions and a general worldwide recession.

As Marais (2001) points out, the RDP was not exactly a radical document. However, from 1996, with the adoption of GEAR and the emphasis on economic growth as opposed to poverty alleviation, the demand by the public for the ANC government to take the crime issue more seriously and the ANC drive to be seen to be providing a quick fix for crime, the left realist approach of former struggle activists and the socio-economic explanation became somewhat sidelined. High density policing was now justified as 'stabilizing' crime in 'crime combating zones'/'geographical hotspots' so that there could be 'normal crime management and ... a climate conducive to socio-economic development' (Department of Safety and Security 1999: 3). In this way, then, socio-economic causes, although still part of state discourse, were now joined by more immediate pragmatic solutions – the short term, quick fixes of 'reactive' as opposed to 'proactive' policing, the integrated justice system, the production of facts and figures about crime. It was now crime which was presented as causing the RDP to fail as opposed to the RDP being deployed to solve crime – as such there was a subtle shift in preconditions.[17] This is exemplified by the following quotation from Shubane (2001: 200):

> while factors such as poverty and unemployment are often cited as "root causes" of crime, there is little prospect, under current conditions, of addressing problems by, for example, public works programmes or other job creation schemes. Where the risk of arrest, prosecution and incarceration is low, the incentive to abandon fairly lucrative criminal activity in favour of relatively low-paying work is small. Only if the cost of crime is increased and its benefits reduced will a decision to abandon it to take up employment become rational.

Indeed, the NCPS specifically stated that South Africa should 'attract the confidence of investors and the interest of tourists' (quoted in Dixon 2006: 178) and that safety was 'an essential precondition for the protection of individual rights and the development of a successful society' (par 1.3.1.4. quoted in Dixon 2006: 178). The private sector NEDCOR Project on Crime Violence and Investment, published in June 1996, shortly after the NCPS, was critical of the government's 'lack of urgency' (Dixon 2006: 179) and pushed for 'successful short term programmes' as a route out of the 'culture of crime' that South Africa was in the grip of.

The fact that poverty alleviation is always mentioned together with more reactive and short term crime prevention strategies results in it being distinctly sidelined. Its use in official discourse is therefore somewhat disingenuous. Whilst recognizing and acknowledging the fact that it is one of the precipitating causes of crime, poverty is simultaneously decentred because it is a long term issue, and

---

17 See for example the Department of Safety and Security 1996b: 2, Department of Safety and Security 2001 and the National Crime Combating Strategy.

there is a need for more immediate policy solutions. These politically expedient short term interventions very often, through harsh punitive policies that emphasize the importance of arrest and imprisonment – in the drive to be tough on crime – militate against the long term solution itself. Thus the deeper, underlying causes of crime are glossed over at the same time as further immiseration is produced through policies that target the poor and pathologize neighbourhoods.

Despite the fact that the 1999 ANC Election Manifesto stated that 'We must be Tough on the underlying causes of crime such as poverty and inequality **and** Tough on crime and corruption themselves' (emphasis in manifesto), this understanding was not carried through in its five-year programme, where nothing was mentioned about how to go about alleviating the socio-economic conditions linked to crime (Gould 2009). Instead the programme mentioned:

- reducing 'the number of guns in circulation'
- 'tougher gun controls'
- 'harsher sentences for serious crimes'
- 'alternative sentences for petty crimes, including electronic monitoring systems'
- improving 'conditions within the police service'
- improving 'co-operation between all elements of the criminal-justice system
- taking 'decisive action against organised gangs'
- strengthening the Directorate of Public Prosecutions (with 'special integrated units to deal with serious crimes')
- paying 'special attention to serious and violent crimes, including abuse of women and children' (ANC 1999).

The 2004 ANC Election Manifesto jettisoned any reference to poverty and inequality as causing crime and focused instead on partnership and responsibilization. It was billed as 'A People's Contract to Create Work and Fight Poverty' where 'we need community participation, as citizens to co-operate with the police, provide information and refuse to buy stolen goods' (ANC 2004). To combat crime and corruption the ANC promised to deploy better trained, managed and visible police, strengthen the prosecution system, improve co-ordination, set up additional special courts, improve border protection to stem illegal migration and cross-border crime and implement anti-corruption measures.

Pragmatic Criminology

Police Annual Reports have from 1996 on reflected a shift from identifying the causes of crime in the context of social crime prevention initiatives to a more pragmatic 'problem-solving approach' where the causes of crime – at community level – translated into a greater focus on situational crime prevention and sector policing. In 1996 the Minister of Justice referred to the need for adequate deterrent mechanisms since 'as long as a potential offender thinks that he will be able to escape justice, there will be no deterrence' (*Hansard* 1996a, col: 4974). Although the 1996 National Crime Prevention Strategy identified poverty and underdevelopment, the historic marginalization of youth and gender inequality as being some of the 'historical factors' which contributed to South Africa's high crime rate, it also contained an overtly managerialist discourse[18] which prioritized the need to establish an efficient and effective criminal justice system as a means to deter crime.

The 2002–3 Annual Report of the South African Police Service (SAPS) refers to an 'integrated intelligence driven approach', 'the Movement Control System' and 'other new technology such as mobile luggage scanners, x-ray scanners, body scanners, a traffic flow system and the Automated Fingerprint Identification System (AFIS)' (Department of Safety and Security 2003: 21). The foreword identifies the 'crime risk factors' of economic strain and deprivation, low education levels, high rates of urbanization, high levels of gun ownership, high levels of substance abuse, an outgoing lifestyle, socio-economic and political transition and the risk of repeat victimization. These risk factors emanate from statistical equations, wherein a truth is established so that the experts can predict who should be targeted, such as the youth in marginalized areas and drug users (Department of Safety and Security 1996a: 20). Indeed drugs are conceived of as being a major cause of crime, as is inadequate law enforcement and the lack of prison capacity. HIV/AIDS is also regarded as a crime risk factor since orphaned children are at a greater than average risk of engaging in delinquent and/or 'anti-social' behaviour, due to inadequate parenting and support (Department of Safety and Security 2003: 25, Schonteich 1999b). The failure to imprison sufficiently large numbers is another crime risk factor which is addressed by calling for more imprisonment (Altbekker 2007).

The problem with the risk factor discourse is, as pointed out by Martel et al. (2011: 240), that structural hardships often translate into risk factors (or being intrinsically criminogenic). Where social status is taken as a risk marker a 'permanently marginal' segment of the population emerges as 'irredeemably high risk' (Martel et al. 2011: 240). Risk factors, such as socio-economic disadvantage and HIV/AIDS, are difficult to change and the steps taken to reduce the risk do not actually address the risk factor (i.e. they don't decrease poverty, or supply anti-retrovirals).[19] In addition the crime risk factor discourse does not aim to explain individual involvement in criminal behavior but to identify characteristics (of neighbourhoods, individuals, communities, cities, etc.) that lead to high rates of criminality (Sampson 1995: 193). Thus, when the neighbourhood becomes a crime risk order maintenance policing is the easiest 'zero tolerance solution'. This identification of risk factors often underpins targeted policing, or what Valverde

---

18 See Chapter 5, where I discuss these contradictory points of departure.

19 This point is taken from O'Malley 2004a: 152.

(2003: 439) refers to as 'targeted governance'[20] and results in saturation policing and immigration profiling. Thus, for example, in 1999 President Mbeki referred to urban renewal in a parliamentary speech, stating that 'multi-disciplinary interventions' would be made to ensure that the NCPS was implemented in areas where crime was high, in areas that were poor and black (Rauch, cited in Dixon 2006). The National Crime Combating Strategy similarly targeted those police stations that were responsible for more than half of serious crime and included the urban 'nodes' (Dixon 2006: 183) identified for implementation of urban renewal projects based on their risk. Yet a risk-based approach to explaining crime is not 'neutral' and the discourse of risk both constitutes and is constituted by 'moral and political strategies of governing' (O'Malley 2004a: 27). As O'Malley (2004a: 27) points out, a seemingly neutral risk-based discourse can in fact contain a strikingly normative and conservative subtext precisely because risk is 'a fluid, inclusive, heterogeneous array of practices with diverse effects and implications' which can be assembled into 'complex configurations with other technologies'.

Conclusion

Criminological theories play an important role in shoring up state policies and do not arise in a vacuum: they are both shaped by and shape shifts in overarching political programmes and rationalities. Explanations for crime are also produced by policing practices and, since 'crime' is itself a political construct that changes over time and consists of 'very different and, historically speaking, varying activities' (Schinkel 2002: 137), the explanations for crime will also change as does the political context. Yet the new theories build on old theories and on past policing practices to explain the forms and targets of criminality that came into being by virtue of these earlier policies, laws and practices. The results of past criminalization can thus not be undone overnight and discursive shifts are not always rigid breaks.

The Nationalist Party government came to power in 1948 on the platform that it could solve the problem of crime by enforcing strict apartheid rules, but by the mid-1970s, as the racist criminology of Afrikaner Nationalists lost its dominance, and mainstream/hegemonic criminologists substituted the term 'socio-economic circumstances' for race, so did the government have to acknowledge that it could not solve the problem of crime on its own and certainly not via the imposition of apartheid. Given the ANC's history as a socialist left-leaning liberation movement and the general tone of its (albeit scarce) pre-1994 pronouncements on crime, one might have expected that as a government it would have prioritized solving crime through situating it, and hence explaining it, in a context that drew on something

20 Since the entire city cannot be policed, targeted governance uses indicators to make a 'rational' selection of locations to be policed and is site- and risk-specific (Valverde 2003: 439).

more than the bland and mainstream administrative criminology which has become dominant in post-apartheid South Africa. Back in the 1980s one would have thought that the ANC would have made more of the constitutive nature of criminal law and orthodox criminology, yet it has in fact used the same epistemological constructs as official criminology in the old South Africa. Explaining crime as a result of development/urbanization/transition and criminal law as the natural counterpoint to such social problems fails to see how the criminal law itself constituted those problems through, for example, the pass laws and how policing techniques created likely targets of criminalization, discussed in the next chapter. This omission is common to both the 'old' and 'new' official criminology.

I have argued that official criminology in the late apartheid period adopted a racialized version of the modernist theory that high crime rates in the 'Third World' were due to rapid social change that was not accompanied by adequate social regulation. The similarities between this and 'transition theory' are remarkable and indeed even in 2006 then President Mbeki (2006: 13) argued that the 'impact of abrupt social change without adequate provision for acquiring of non delinquent social values' leads to high crime rates, especially property crimes. It would thus seem that 'structural functionalist' criminology in the form of 'transition theory' remains dominant in South Africa.

Both the NP and the ANC referred to a 'culture of violence' and 'criminality' and both branded the youth as being out of control. In the case of the ANC this strand is apparent in the discourse of the Moral Regeneration Movement. Through blaming apartheid the ANC infused the struggle against apartheid with morality – as an organization it would be in the forefront of reinserting morals into South African society. Alongside this there has also been an emergence of what I have referred to as 'pragmatic criminology', which decentres deep-rooted explanations for crime in favour of a managerialist exposition that focuses on risk factors, such as illegal immigration, and utilizes the science of numbers. These arguments may seem rather innocuous and politically hard to fault, yet it is not so much what they say about the causes of crime as what is left unsaid: there is a dearth of official theories on crime that seriously engage in and with the structural conditions that are conducive to crime and the legacies that were wrought by apartheid policies. Whereas Cavadino and Dignan (2006: 98) note that managerial techniques have not had an impact on the 'multiple' problems of 'penality' in South Africa, the discourse is still important insofar as it produces a certain way of looking at the world, of constructing and identifying problems.

Perhaps we should not be too surprised at the continuities between apartheid and post-apartheid discourses on crime, especially not if we situate them in the context of the transition to a neoliberal economy that started in the late 1970s – in other words the apartheid state, and the political rationality underpinning the economic system, was changing *well before* the official 'transition' began in 1990. If we situate the ANC discourse on crime causation in the context of its adoption of an overarching political rationality that stresses individual responsibility, in the context of a South Africa that underwent a dual transition to a liberal democracy *and* a stronger embracing of neoliberal economics (Zuern 2006, Bond 2000, Marais 2001, 2011, McCord 2007, McDonald 2002, Terreblanche 2012) and where the act of governing has come to be measured in terms of how it (i.e. the ANC) deals with crime, then the surprise factor is lessened. It is then not so difficult to see why in post-apartheid South Africa attention has shifted to dealing with the effects of crime, rather than its causes (Garland 1996: 447) and why there has been no concerted attempt to explain and deal with crime in a more in-depth and progressive fashion.

Chapter 4
Constructions of Criminality

> For a long time ordinary individuality – the everyday individuality of everybody – remained below the threshold of description. To be looked at, observed, described in detail, followed from day to day by an uninterrupted writing was a privilege ... The disciplines reversed this relation, lowered the threshold of describable individuality and made of this description a means of control and a method of domination ... This turning of real lives into writing is no longer a procedure of heroization; it functions as a procedure of objectification and subjectification. (Foucault 1977, 1995: 191)

Introduction

Although one might have expected the official understanding of the 'dangerous criminal classes' to undergo a major shift with the advent of the 'new' South Africa, in this chapter I argue that many of the same tropes and targets are still being used by the post-apartheid government. Policing practices and the targets of crime policies continue to criminalize the poor (the vast majority of whom are black), illegal immigrants (the 'new' pass law offender) and, the coloured *skollie*.[1]

The pass, anti-squatting and trespassing laws are of enormous significance because they licensed the police to treat black people as if they were always under suspicion, always open to search, always open for interrogation and inspection (Kynoch 2011, Gillespie 2011, Super 2010, Edwards and Hecht 2010). These laws made black people police property and hence subject to criminalization. I argue that this police power never ended with the repeal of apartheid laws: the new target population are foreign blacks from other countries and race and the concept of foreignness still play a major role in defining the techniques that get deployed and the resultant subjectification and objectification. Likewise, insofar as private non-state security initiatives are concerned, it is poor blacks who are still excluded from largely white middle class neighbourhoods (Steinberg 2008, Benit-Gbaffou 2008, Samara 2011).

The purpose of this chapter is not to simply point out that the ANC government uses the same strong-arm tactics, in the crime control arena, as did the apartheid government, but to link the official explanations for crime, discussed in the previous chapter, with policing practices and the resultant emergence of criminal categories. Viewing apartheid as both productive and repressive enables us to

1 An Afrikaans word meaning hooligan or thug.

better explain the continuities between two seemingly opposed regimes and to see how certain strategies of rule have remained, even though the governmental programmes which utilized them have disappeared.

1976–89 Reform of Verwoerdian Apartheid

Infringements and Criminality

The deep linkages between crime and race were both constitutive of and constituted by the post-1948 Nationalist Party (NP) project of promoting Afrikaners and developing an Afrikaner capitalist class. The fact that 'poor whites' were constructed as committing crimes because of their poverty, whereas Africans did so because of genetic inferiority, tied in perfectly with the socio-economic project of 'racial Fordism' (Marais 2001: 11). Black people, who were regarded as non-citizens, were institutionally excluded from the South African style welfare state and, restricted as they were from movement into cities, provided a concentrated source of cheap labour, as indeed they had done since colonial times (Marais 2001).

Apartheid involved contradictory drives towards both exclusion and inclusion. On the one hand there was, as Savage (cited in Budlender and Davis 1984: 159) states, an 'exclusionary need' to 'obtain political security by controlling and policing the number of blacks in "white" areas' and, on the other hand, 'an "inclusionary" need to ensure a supply of cheap labour in these areas'. The migrant labour system, in terms of which blacks were kept in the rural homelands but allowed into urban areas only if they had permits ('passes'), was crucial to obtaining this supply of cheap labour.

The gaze of the state was directed at black people, who were arrested and prosecuted for 'infringements' of the law. These petty offences, which only applied to blacks, included:

- violation of curfew regulations
- foreign 'Bantu' entering urban areas
- violation of regulations in respect of registration and production of documents
- violation of the Bantu Urban Areas Consolidation Act (the act which regulated the movement of blacks in urban areas)
- unlawful trespass or intrusion
- 'Bantu' taxation
- illegal possession of 'Bantu' liquor and drunkenness
- arrest for not being in possession of identity documents.

In 1978 the state asserted that a racialized personal identity document coupled with fingerprinting was the way to protect against foreign black invaders (Edwards and Hecht 2010: 625). Yet, as Edwards and Hecht (2010) point out, the plan never worked: passbooks were forged and the system never brought about the effective control of black movement. As such, 'the passbook was useful mainly as a pretext for random policing (inspections on the streets) and violent harassment' (Edwards and Hecht 2010: 626). What the police described as 'routine crime prevention' often received bad press due to people being arrested for 'technical contraventions' rather than for 'genuine crimes such as murder, rape, assault, armed robbery, house-breaking, theft, drug peddling, receiving stolen goods' (*Cape Times*, 18 September 1978).

Between 1976 and 1977 more than 150,000 people were prosecuted for failing to produce documents, 160,000 for violation of the Bantu Urban Areas Consolidation Act and almost 200,000 for illegal possession of alcohol and drunkenness (Department of Justice, Police and Prisons 1977). Between 1975 and 1985 more than 600,000 black people (and no whites) were arrested for failing to produce identity documents (*Hansard* 1985b). Raids on hostels (the almost 'total' institutions which housed male migrant workers for the mines) constituted a type of targeted policing of so-called 'squatters' and resulted in the criminalization of those who did not have the necessary documentation to live in the hostels. Thus, for example, in January 1982 766 black men were arrested after a raid on a single men's hostel in Soweto and charged with contravening the regulations governing 'the control and supervision of an urban black residential area' (*Hansard* 1982a, question 6, col: 213). More than 15,000 people were prosecuted for violating curfew regulations between July 1979 and June 1980 (*Hansard* 1981b). Police raids on shebeens[2] were justified as 'preventative action', taken because 'police realise that although shebeens are of cultural value to their patrons they are often gathering places for criminal elements' (Calitz 1988: 141). Although 7,777 people were detained, in terms of the State of Emergency, between July 1985 and February 1986, 8,065 people were arrested for trespass offences in just one month in 1986 (Department of Law and Order 1987). The fact that statistics were kept on violations of the Immorality Act (the Act that prohibited sexual relations between whites and 'non-whites') but not on assaults by farmers of farmworkers (*Hansard* 1982a, question 13, col: 939), was evidence of how politics and the construction of particular forms of criminality were intimately connected.

This pattern of exclusion and segregation, based on apartheid principles of separating likely victims (whites) from likely offenders (poor blacks) was perceived to be effective, insofar as whites were concerned. Thus, although the 1976 Report of Commission of Inquiry into the Penal System of the Republic of South Africa (the 'Viljoen Report') criticized the pass laws it also voiced concern that their removal from the statute book would deprive the police of ready access to a pool of potentially serious offenders (para 4.2.2.4).

The Viljoen Report had a chapter on the 'criminality of the non-white population' where it approvingly quoted Advocate Labuschagne (Para 1.16), who stated that not only did the

2 Illegal liquor outlets in the townships.

> Bantu and the Coloured figure largely in all forms of non-serious crime [but … the non-whites also have a proportionately greater share in serious crimes than whites.

Citing establishment criminologists, such as Retief, the Commission (Para: 1.24: 10) concluded that although there were 'no grounds' on which to base a 'theory of congenital criminal tendency', the fact

> that a person belongs to a certain race is not entirely without significance in providing some key to his criminal behaviour [but because of] … differences in the general level of development and civilization between Blacks and Whites in their respective personal, social, economic, cultural and other settings … it [is] impossible to place Blacks on an equal footing with Whites for the purposes of comparing their respective criminal tendencies.

The standard conventional argument was that a violent 'black subculture' existed. This explained why 'they' burnt 'their schools' and 'violence' was regarded as 'South African as *boerewors*', meaning that it, and that peculiar sausage invented by white Afrikaners, were both characteristic of the 'South African way of life' (Nash 1976).

There was a distinctive link between unemployment, criminality and race. It was the 'black unemployed loiterer', the '*rondloper*' (a derogatory Afrikaans name for a person with no fixed abode) who 'robbed and stole' (*Hansard* 1979, col: 722) because of a lack of income, who represented a stereotypical danger and was regarded as a type of vermin that had to be dealt with. Similarly, 'mopping up operations in residential and business areas [were] aimed at all idlers and unemployed persons' (Viljoen Report 1976: para 147). The fact that 'no European prisoner [was] hired out or placed to work on public roads where he would be constantly seen by the public' (Viljoen Report 1976: para 885) but that this was legitimate in the case of 'Black' prisoners contributed to their criminalization in the sense that the public gaze was on them, as if they had no dignity which could be lost. The sight of public works being carried out by black offenders (but never by whites) would of course reinforce the public perception that criminals were always black. This image also fed into the ideology of reform through labour because imprisonment was justified on the basis that it was tailored to 'fit'/'reform' the coloured/black lumpen proletariat.[3]

And so the iatrogenic feedback[4] mechanisms went: black people were policed via crime blitzes, raids and swoops on alleged 'crime hotspots' (*Cape Times*, 29 April 1978). This led to greater rates of imprisonment, in turn producing the

---

3 See Chapter 6, where I discuss rehabilitation in prison.

4 Stanley Cohen (1985) uses this term. It comes from Illich and refers to doctor-induced illness. I use it in the context of emphasizing how the policing of black people resulted in their criminalization, imprisonment and marking them for further criminalization.

criminal class which vindicated the policing in the first place. Even after arrests for influx control violations were suspended in April 1986 and trespass was no longer reported on in the Police Annual Reports, because it was not 'justified economically' (*Hansard* 1986b, col: 546), with prosecutions for contravening the Group Areas Act having petered out (*Hansard* 1988a, Brogden and Shearing 1993), the damage had been done and a certain type of criminal had been produced. Indeed, 15 million fingerprints were held in terms of the pass laws and draconian anti-squatting legislation filled some of the gaps left by the pass laws (Sher 1985). Thus, poor blacks from the township remained the subjects of state criminalization policies (Brogden and Shearing 1993: 64) and establishment criminologists explained black criminality on the basis of a black subculture, a culture of poverty and urbanization. As Foucault so eloquently wrote in *Discipline and Punish*:

> In short, the carceral archipelago assures, in the depths of the social body, the formation of delinquency on the basis of subtle illegalities, the overlapping of the latter by the former and the establishment of a specified criminality (1995: 301).

Racialized Criminology and the Production of Delinquency

As discussed in the previous chapters, from the mid-1970s the state embarked on a series of reforms. Coercion alone was not working to maintain control in South Africa and the South African state sought to create a buffer black and coloured middle class in order to govern more effectively. This strategy played out in the area of alcohol regulation with the 1977 Liquor Amendment bill purporting to 'normalize' alcohol usage and teach the lower class how to drink responsibly:

> liquor is being made more accessible to the other race groups … with the necessary protection and control of course ... So we find that Asiatics and Coloureds may sell liquor under a defined authority and that the Minister may authorize any person to sell drink to any Bantu. (*Hansard* 1977c, col: 2003)

This liberalizing of the laws regulating alcohol usage was evidence of the embracing of a more governmental type of power which entailed a governing through the techniques of the self. As a Nationalist Party MP stated:

> a great responsibility rests on each one of us, as members of a family, as members of a community, to contribute to responsible usage; to educate people so that we will be able to combat evils in our own society as well (*Hansard* 1977b, col: 4627).

See also Foucault (1979, 1995), who also wrote about the effects of subjectification and disciplinary power.

From 1977 onwards the South African Institute for Sociological, Demographic and Criminological Research (SAISDCR) started to supplement its hitherto mainly quantitative methodology with qualitative studies of 'deviant behavior' (Schurink 1982: 48). As a Human Science Research Council (HSRC) researcher put it: 'studies of deviant behavior are at present turned *increasingly* to deviant subcultures in the community for the composition of their samples' (Schurink 1982: 48). Thus for example, Schurink and Ndabandaba refer to an increasing tendency among South African researchers to study 'sex for sale' and in 1977 the HSRC introduced prostitution in the studies of deviant behaviour. The titles of some of the studies give an indication of how criminological problems were constructed along racial lines:

- The use of alcohol and tobacco among Blacks (Schmidt 1976)
- The attitude of urban Black ethnic units towards the law, crime and aspects of the criminal justice system (Van den Burgh and De Beer 1977)
- The inner reality of the Black man and his criminal responsibility (Buhrmann 1980)
- Child Abuse among the Zulus: A People in Cultural Transition" (Loening 1981)
- *Die Meting van Alkohol inname in die Kleurling Woonbeurt Eersterus – 'n Toepassing van die Khavafri Alkohol Toets* (The measuring of alcohol intake in the coloured township of Eersterus – the application of the Khavafri alcohol test) (Rocha 1983)
- A study of juvenile delinquency among Zulus in Natal, with particular reference to accounts and views of the delinquency (Brown 1984)
- Crimes of violence in black townships (Ndabandaba 1987).

By the late 1980s this heightened concern with studying the black subject manifested in a new emphasis on juvenile delinquency, gangs and prison studies. Research directives given by the government to the HSRC resulted in studies on:

- Gang activities in Reform Schools and other Institutions falling under the Children's Act
- Investigation into the Structure, Functions and Organisations of Black and Coloured Street Gangs in the Open Community
- The Processing and Treatment of Juvenile Offenders: South African Policy and Practice
- A Study of Overseas Models for the Processing and Treatment of Juvenile Violent Offenders
- A Psycho-sociological Investigation of Juveniles who have been sent to Prison as a Result of Committing Violent and other types of crime
- An evaluation of Services Provided by Aftercare Centres in the RSA
- Aftercare Systems for Ex-offenders: A Literature Survey with the Purpose of Developing a Model for Aftercare

- The Perceptions of Families Receiving Reconstruction Services of the Welfare Service
- The provision of services by social and assistant workers to Black male board prisoners: an exploratory study
- Juvenile delinquency: (a) the appearance and extent of juvenile delinquency in the RSA according to official crime statistics and (b) the etiology of juvenile delinquency and the processing and treatment of juvenile offenders
- The value of training received by prisoners as perceived by prisoners and training personnel, the implementation of a treatment programme in South African prisons
- The nature, extent and pattern of violence in South African prisons
- An investigation into the preparation for release of violent offenders
- Supervision of violent offenders after release
- A study of gang activities amongst Black prisoners in South African prisons
- Prison gangs: An investigation with special reference to number gangs amongst Coloured prisoners (Department of Justice 1986, Department of Justice 1987a, *Hansard* 1987c, col: 205).

Thus, as apartheid began to reform, 'non-whites' became the objects of criminological studies and new categories of criminality were created, which served to further cement the recognition of a 'non-white' criminal class. In a Foucaultian sense, then, social scientists created their own objects of study that they mapped onto real events in the world. The more knowledge that was generated about these subjects, the more they were both subjectified and subjected (Foucault 1995: 27–8). The information that was generated by these studies helped to cement the categories of criminality that both informed, and resulted from, these criminological investigations. None of these studies made any mention of power, inequality, policing techniques or state violence. On the other hand, as I argued in the previous chapter, critical criminologists studied state crime and did not really engage with these categories of criminality on their own terms.

The Drug Offender

Rehabilitation centres for 'non-whites' were virtually non-existent and when one looks at the numbers convicted it is clear that a policy of imprisonment was followed in respect of the 'non-white' drug offender.[5] The pass raids resulted in mass arrests for offences such as possession of cannabis. The 1977 Police Annual Report reflected that whilst only 1,755 whites were arrested for drug offences, 4,189 'Coloureds', 898 'Asians' and 15,067 'Bantu' were (Department of Justice, Police and Prisons 1977).[6] Given that Coloureds constituted only 10 per cent

5 See statistics in *Hansard* 1977d, 1977e, 1978a and 1978d.

6 Interestingly, in subsequent reports cannabis offences were not divided on a racial basis.

of the population these figures represent extraordinarily high rates of arrest for coloured men.

Between 1972 and 1978 there were 80,000 convictions for use and possession of *dagga* (the colloquial term for cannabis), the vast majority of which affected black people (*Hansard* 1978a, col: 6328). Out of 14,000 convictions in 1976, 9,000 were black and most of the remainder were 'Coloureds' and 'Indians'. The 1971 Abuse of Dependence Producing Substances and Rehabilitation Centres Act provided for minimum sentences and a presumption of dealing when caught with more than a certain amount of cannabis. As opposition Progressive Federal Party MP Helen Suzman (*Hansard* 1978a: col: 6328) stated:

> We have cluttered up our gaols with thousands and thousands of these people. If one adds to this number the 10,000 people who were sentenced over the years to serve at least five years in prison for dealing in drugs, one can see that our gaols were very full indeed as a result of these laws … In 1976 only 18 people were sent to rehabilitation centres although over 20,000 people were convicted for all drug offences relating to dagga and other drugs.

In the 1980s as more white youth started to be seen to be using cannabis, concern with the minimum sentence drug legislation found its way into official discourse. This was reflected in studies such as: 'Criteria for sentencing for dealing in dagga' (Raath 1982) and 'The Drug-Using behavior and View on Illicit Drug Use of Post-School White Male South Africans' (Van der Burgh 1984). In 1983 the first South African conference on the 'dagga problem' (Department of Health and Welfare 1984: 1) was held under the auspices of the Department of Health and Welfare. In the discussion around the 1986 Substance Abuse Amendment Act, which did away with mandatory minimum sentences for possession of cannabis, the fact that blacks had used *dagga* for centuries was ascribed to their culture whereas in the case of whites it was regarded as a new thing, thus more of a threat, and more discretion was needed by the courts to deal with this new problem (*Hansard* 1986c, col: 11281). In 1988, for the first time, the Annual Report of the Commissioner of the South African Police contained more in-depth statistics on the activities of the South African Narcotic Bureau.

The Coloured Criminal

As a racial group coloureds occupied a unique place in South Africa's repressive welfare state and were treated differently from blacks and whites. They did not enjoy the same privileges as whites yet in the Cape they enjoyed preferential labour treatment over blacks and from 1983 onwards they were included in the Tricameral Parliamentary System, along with Indians and whites. Blacks were excluded. Despite the fact that they constituted a buffer between black and white they were not accorded full citizenship rights (Jensen 2008: 2) and even though they were not affected by the pass laws coloured men were much more likely to go to prison than black men (Pinnock 1984: 74, cited in Jensen 2008). In 1979 and 1980, 729 out of 100,000 coloureds went to prison, 425 blacks, 86 whites and 57 Indians. Coloured men also stayed in prison for longer than other groups and were imprisoned for mainly alcohol-, drug- and violence-related offences (Jensen 2008: 36, Gould 2012, Badroodien 2000). This overrepresentation of coloureds in prison was blamed on more 'deep-seated problems – cultural conflict and urbanization' (*Hansard* 1980b, col: 6099).

The Viljoen Report (para 1.25.1) ascribed coloured criminality to largely the same reasons as black criminality (urbanization, detribalization and westernization) with the added factors of the 'lack of a cultural background' and 'exceptionally high liquor consumption' combined with 'poverty and apathy' (para 1.21.2). It was, according to an NP MP (*Hansard* 1977e, col: 6351: 3), the

> work-shy coloured ... the *sonsitters* (sun worshippers) who were now coming to Cape Town and making their living ... by making their home in the bushes and running around at night like jackals, seeing where they can steal and rob

who were the problem. It was the coloured *skollie* – the unemployed coloured gangster – who epitomized all that was wrong with the coloured 'race'. As discussed in Chapter 3, this link between unemployment and criminality was one of the foundations of the construction of 'non-white' criminality.

As a stereotype the *skollie* was the subject of numerous studies and commissions of inquiry with the 1976 'Theron Commission of Inquiry into Matters Relating to the Coloured Group' being central. It was based on the need to save coloureds and cement white Afrikaans middle class values (Jensen 2008: 35, Gould 2012, Badroodien 2008). In the 1970s, in a somewhat similar development to that of the child-saving movement in progressive-era America (Platt 1969, Feld 1999) there was a thrust towards sending coloured children to reformatories and industrial schools in order to 'save' them from the 'culture of poverty' and to 'save coloured women and children from their drunken husbands and fathers' (quoted in Gould 2012). The sending of young coloured boys 'en masse' (Gould 2012) to reformatories resulted in their consequent institutionalization (Jensen 2008, Badroodien 2008). Efforts to deal with the alcohol problems amongst the coloured community via a policy of restricted trading hours, backfired with the establishment of illegal alcohol outlets, resulting in further criminalization when people were arrested for breaking these laws (Gould 2012).

This South African version of the American child-saving movement took place together with a governmental attempt to bolster the 'self-respecting middle class [that had] arisen among the coloureds' (*Hansard* 1977c, col: 53). Thus, the 1977 Liquor Amendment Bill was justified because

> the Coloured peoples in this country, have become more sophisticated under the policy of the NP and have developed specific tastes which they, as citizens, and inhabitants also have the right to satisfy (*Hansard* 1977c, col: 2003).

In 1984, a Nationalist Party MP explained that coloured people no longer drank cheap wine by virtue of their having 'become educated and [achieving] a higher standard of living … [as such] their wine consumption also become normalized' (*Hansard* 1984s, col: 4038). The Department of Coloured Affairs gave financial assistance to coloured women via maintenance grants, the number of which increased from 25,000 in 1976 to 42,000 in 1982 (Jensen 2008: 38). Because coloured criminality was different from black criminality, in 1977 'depth classification', a form of classification that took place according to the 'particular characteristics of each person' (*Hansard* 1977f, col: 9359), was extended to imprisoned coloureds in the Western Cape – it had previously been only for white males who were sentenced to more than two years.

1990–94 (Negotiation and Contestation)

In *The Policing of Families* Donzelot argues that at the end of the nineteenth century, in France, the more comfortably off families experienced an increase in their autonomy *vis a vis* the state whereas poor families were policed in the repressive sense of the word. The coming to the fore of a more governmental, as opposed to sovereign, type of power, entailed that the marginal were dispossessed of their private rights whereas the bourgeois family was encouraged to pursue happiness through private means and positive integration (Donzelot 1979). A similar process took place in South Africa during the transition to a new dispensation. The turn to ruling through the community as a mode of legitimization that started in the 1970s became deepened and entrenched and this occurred throughout the government departments, not only in the police. Yet those who were not fit to be empowered (such as illegal immigrants and drug offenders), or who did not make the cut of self-sufficiency, experienced the 'might' of the criminal law.

In this section I discuss how there was a dual shift to 'freedom' and also to further criminalization and targeting of the usual suspects: the illegal immigrant and the out-of-control militant black youth entered the discourse, yet the figure of the threatening black outsider was still there, as was the coloured *skollie*. Although the concept of welfare promotion was very strongly present in the discourse, the interventions that were aimed at high risk areas also resulted in the further criminalization of the residents of these areas.

Despite the concern with political violence and 'unrest' during this period, official criminology continued to be concerned with drugs and 'illegal aliens'. In 1992 more than 17,000 people were arrested for drug offences, the vast majority being for cannabis, a mostly 'black' crime, and the SAPS established an Illegal Immigrants Investigation Unit (Department of Law and Order 1994: 105–6). The coloured male continued to be over-represented in prison statistics (Department of Correctional Services 1993) and the 'black squatter' continued to be pilloried as someone who 'takes your work away from you' (*Hansard* 1990b, col: 8000).

The 'Lost Generation'

Despite the fact that apartheid was being dismantled at a rapid pace, black people continued to be criminalized, particularly via drug legislation and the notions of a 'culture of poverty', 'lost generation' and 'marginalization.'

A community liaison intra-departmental committee was established to implement the 'Population Development Programme', which focused on enhancing the quality of life and the living standards of specific communities. 'Community work' was prioritized in

> overpopulated and subeconomic residential areas characterized by low living standards and a high risk of developing social problems; border areas and areas where factors where such as depopulation, disasters or any other disruptive events threaten stability. (Department of Health Services and Welfare Administration 1990: 38)

These areas would later be referred to as 'zones of disorder' – areas which needed development, in the form of services, but where the levels of crime were simultaneously regarded as threats to development (Jensen 2005, 2008, Dixon 2006).[7]

Thus, even when used in a sympathetic way the very delineation of an 'underclass' runs the risk of 'reifying some notion of "Otherness"' (King 1999: 290). There is easy slippage between this and the moral judgement that conservative commentators bring to bear when they refer to a 'culture of poverty' or a 'culture of violence' as causing poverty and criminality and thus the uncivilized and undeserving poor are somehow to blame, somehow responsible, for the abject conditions in which they find themselves (King 1999: 235). The misrepresentation of the correlation between poverty and criminality can result in an automatic assumption that inequality and poverty lead people into crime (Caldeira 2000: 137) and when crime is associated with poverty and marginality the stereotypes that link criminality to poverty are strengthened (Foucault 1979, Caldeira 2000).

In the second half of 1990 the government commissioned the Human Sciences Research Council (HSRC) to research the possibility that the 'black youth [would] be able to wreck the negotiation and reconciliation process' and 'whether it would be possible to 'integrate the black youth into the new South Africa' (De Cock and Schutte 1991, cited in Seekings 1995: 107). The government's Constitutional Development Service also formally requested the HSRC to research the position of black youth in Soweto and whether they posed a threat to orderly constitutional

---

7 See, for example, the report by KPMG and TRL (2009), commissioned by the Western Cape Department of Community Safety. It refers to 15 'priority areas', based on the 'number of serious violent crimes recorded in these areas' and identifies these communities as 'zones of poverty and unemployment' where there was a high rate of 'contact crime, gangsterism and substance abuse' (para 1.1:20).

change (Seekings 1995: 30). It was the conservative editor of the *Sunday Times* newspaper, Ken Owen, who coined the term 'lost generation'. He used it to describe black South African youth in light of their behaviour which was, according to him, symbolic of the ANC's 'insatiable passion' for 'unfettered power' (quoted in Seekings 1995: 31).

The more sympathetic left-wing view presented the youth as being marginalized as a result of the 'political struggle of the last 6 years'. This had weakened their 'attachment to socializing structures (family, school, peer pressure, the older generation, political and civic organizations)' (Seekings 1995: 31). The non-government Joint Enrichment Project, set up in 1986 by the South African Council of Churches and the Southern African Bishops Conference[8] (Seekings 1995: 113) and the Community Agency for Social Inquiry, a research consultancy which focused on research for the democratic movement, were concerned with 'marginalized youth' (Seekings 1995: 113–14). Although they did not refer to the 'lost generation', they gave credence to the notion of the existence of a problem in respect of South Africa's black youth and their penchant for violence.

1994–2004 (Consolidating the 'New' South Africa)

The vast majority of South Africa's prison population are still poor and 'non-white'. On 31 May 2003, blacks constituted 69.7 per cent of the female prison population, coloureds 21.2 per cent, Asians just under 1 per cent and whites 8.3 per cent. Black men made up 76.6 per cent of the male prison population, coloureds 20.7 per cent, whites 2.2 per cent and Asians 0.5 per cent. According to the 2001 census, blacks constituted 79 per cent of the population, coloureds 8.9 per cent, Asians 2.5 per cent and whites 9.6 per cent. Thus, coloured men and women were the most overrepresented in the prison population. White men had the lowest rates of imprisonment in proportion to their presence in the population (Vetten and Bhana 2005: 259).

Whereas previously all blacks were denied citizenship, and criminalized on this basis, in post-apartheid South Africa it is the undocumented migrant from other African countries who is criminalized, often via techniques of racial profiling and racist stereotyping. The coloured male is still the object of governmental interventions that are based on essentializing and reductionist stereotypes and is still disproportionately imprisoned.

There have also been definite shifts in categories of criminality and new subjects, which are distinctive to the 'new' era, have emerged: the category of the 'organized' criminal, the 'sophisticated' criminal and the drug dealer with international ties. This has taken place alongside some distinctively neoliberal processes such as the installation of prepaid water and electricity meters in townships (as devices

8 Both sympathetic to the struggle for democracy and staunch supporters of human rights.

for self-administering service cut-offs) and the implementation of public works projects, which Marais (2011: 139) considers a way to 'productivise what are essentially forms of indigent support' in a context where social grants are not universally obtainable and 'handouts' are stigmatized (Marais 2011, Bond 2000, McCord 2007, Terreblanche 2012).

Stranger Danger

It is commonplace to associate black foreigners in South Africa with crime, HIV/AIDS and unemployment and xenophobic incidents are regular occurrences (Landau 2005, 2011, Legget 2003, Crush and McDonald 2001, Crush and Williams 2003, Jensen and Buur 2007). Arbitrary arrests and detentions of asylum seekers are common occurrences and based on appearances in the sense that language (accent and pronunciation of words), being unable to speak one of South Africa's official 'African' languages and physical appearance (looking foreign by virtue of hairstyle, clothing, vaccination marks and other physical characteristics) are all definitive (Human Rights Watch 1997, South African Human Rights Commission 1999, Crush and McDonald 2001, Landau 2005, Jensen and Buur 2007, Klaaren and Ramji 2001).

In 1994 the Minister of Justice stated that 'the influence of a large number of illegal aliens in South Africa – as many as an estimated two million people – had a significant impact on the incidence of criminality' (*Hansard* 1994, col: 2074). Illegal immigrants stand accused of being involved in organized crime, and special operations such as Operation Aliens, aim to arrest and deport 'illegal immigrants, involved in organized and serious and violent crimes' (Department of Safety and Security 2002: 6). Official statistics also distinguish between citizens and non-citizens in the context of arrests for commercial crimes, thus contributing to the alienation and criminalization of foreigners.[9]

On 13 March 2000, at the start of Operation Crackdown, part of a three year crime combating strategy, more than 1,000 police went to the Johannesburg suburbs of Hillbrow, Berea and Yeoville and embarked on a 'high density, cordon, search and seizure operation' (Pelser 2000). 14 people were arrested for alleged involvement in serious offences (such as murder, rape, drug dealing and robbery), 512 for less serious offences such as prostitution and urinating in public and a whopping 7,068 on suspicion of being illegal immigrants. In 2000 the Minister of Safety and Security referred to 'havens of criminality' (*Hansard* 2000b question 49, col: 892) as being the places where many illegal aliens were netted in clean-up operations and between March and August 2000 43,000 illegal aliens were arrested in the greater Johannesburg metropolitan area alone (*Hansard* 2000a, question 4220, col: 1276). In 2003 the City of Johannesburg and the Department of Home Affairs launched a joint operation which deployed helicopters and almost

9 See for example Table 23 – Commercial Crime Cases, Annual Report of the National Commissioner of the South African Police Service, 1 April 2002–31 March 2003: 63.

1,000 private security officers in the name of crime prevention and urban renewal. After sealing an apartment block, officials confiscated four illegal firearms and arrested 198 illegal immigrants, leading to the conclusion that in fact the entire exercise had been aimed at ridding the city of unwanted foreigners (Landau 2005: 10). Similarly Operation Clean Sweep in Pretoria resulted in 32 arrests for serious offences, 513 for less serious offences and 740 for being illegal immigrants. This mode of policing is reminiscent of the pass law raids of the apartheid era where the liberal press accused the police of arresting pass law offenders under the pretext of cracking down on serious crime. It is also an example of what Landau (2005: 9) refers to as 'targeting non-nationals' to 'help police meet arrest targets'. As Steinberg (2012: 355) puts it, the visibility of the deportation

> produces state power on a terrain where the state is seen to be failing in its duties, and it creates a bond between state and citizenry where the bond is troublingly frail.

The South African media shows a propensity towards negative reporting on black foreigners from other parts of Africa, and it is Zimbabweans, Mozambicans and Nigerians upon whom the most opprobrium is heaped (Media Tenor 2008). In other words the greatest negativity attaches to those foreigners who hail from countries with a high number of refugees, asylum seekers and/or migrant workers living in South Africa (Media Tenor 2008). Similarly, newspaper reports use ethnicity as a means of reporting; for example a '*Zimbabwean* national' (*Cape Times*, 6 April 2009) was arrested for the mugging of a tourist on Lions Head (my emphasis).

In South Africa, the bureaucratic/administrative face of immigration law fits very snugly with the more punitive technology of criminal law. As is the case in Europe and the USA, suspicion of drug dealing increases when it is 'linked with immigration and the presence of resented minorities' (Woodiwiss and Hobbs 2009: 118). Not only does official discourse on immigration feed into a 'general anxiety about difference' (Bosworth and Guild 2008: 712) but when the activities of drug dealing and illegal immigration converge, in the context of high rates of unemployment, the moral panic escalates and in the process legitimate refugees are criminalized.

The Emergence of the 'Sophisticated' Criminal and 'Organized' Crime

Standing (2006) refers to an 'alien conspiracy' or 'parasitic' model as being hegemonic in official discourse on organized crime in South Africa today. In terms of this theory the transition from apartheid to democracy has ushered in a dramatic shift in the level of sophistication of, and heightened threat from, criminal groups. As he points out, this discourse is in keeping with international mainstream discourse which views states in transition as particularly susceptible to crime due to changes in policing, the opening up of borders and a more open movement of people and goods both within and into the newly democratizing country.

As such, the post-apartheid criminal is constructed as a very intelligent human being, as a

> super-criminal – the criminal who has...modern technology, ample resources and everything else to enable him and his syndicate to menace our society. (*Hansard* 1996a, col: 4991)

The National Crime Prevention Strategy devotes a section to the problem of 'organized crime', describing a 'crime syndicate'

> as a collection of organised criminals with a national, and even international scope, controlling any vice, business or criminal operation. (Department of Safety and Security 1996a: para 5.7.2.0.2)

It refers to:

> structured hierarchies of control, clearly designated rank structures, sophisticated payment and promotion systems, and a veil of secrecy which all operate to ensure that the detection and prosecution of organised crime is a difficult and costly venture. (para 5.7.2.0.4: 33)

Similarly the White Paper on Safety and Security states that:

> The work of fighting crime is becoming more complex and, therefore, more challenging. Criminals are becoming more organized and more sophisticated, operating with little regard to national boundaries. Foreign criminal groups are extending their operations as organized crime becomes increasingly globalised. (Department of Safety and Security 1998: ii)

The *organized* part of organized crime connotes rationality, efficiency and complexity. Since it cannot be tackled through standard crime control techniques the whole organization needs to be destroyed, through an 'organized crime approach' (*Hansard* 2000b, question 39, cols: 418–19), which utilizes draconian tactics. Because, according to an ANC MP, 'even home made criminals have become more and more sophisticated and operate their vile trade with military precision' (*Hansard* 1999, col: 1651) the 'organized crime strategy' of the SAPS is targeted at identifying syndicates and dealing with the sophisticated criminal. Responding to this threat includes 'prevention (regular roadblocks and patrols); response (rapid response capability); and investigation (specialized investigation)' (Department of Safety and Security 1997: 10).

The first organized crime unit in the South African Police Service, established in 1995, entailed the reorganization of more than 500 SAPS Specialised

Investigation Units and the creation of the Directorate of Special Operations (known as the Scorpions) (Department of Safety and Security 1999).[10] Their principal objective was, according to the Minister of Justice and Constitutional Development (*Hansard* 2000c, col: 7166), to

> inject into these criminals the venom of criminal law to attack and paralyse the nervous system of organised crime and terrorism as effectively and efficiently as possible.

The Gang Problem and the Coloured Skollie

The ANC government continues to subjectify and objectify the coloured male, making him the subject of its penal gaze, even although it packages the gaze in a different discourse and utilizes different forms of governance. As such the *skollie* continues to be a problem that animates government policy and the *skollie* identity is still very much regarded as a problem to be solved, to be governed through a penal framework, even though the political programmes which produced the initial (criminalizing) interventions and the subjects themselves, have been jettisoned. Operation Lancer, Tsipam, Crackdown, Akantus II, Slasher – the latter particularly against the 'gang threat' – were launched in Mitchellsplein, Phillipi, Hannover Park, Manenberg, Bishop Lavis, Elsies River and surrounding police stations between 2001 and 2002 – all predominantly poor coloured areas in Cape Town (Department of Safety and Security 2002: 49).

As discussed previously, a disproportionate amount of coloured men still land up in prison. In addition, the high rates of imprisonment from gang hotspots – at one point in 1999 five out of 48 households in Heideveld magistrate's court area had someone in prison (Jensen 2008: 82) – contribute to further criminalization of young working class males from coloured areas (Leggett 2004). Coloured communities are strongly prisonized in the sense that everyone knows someone who has been or is in prison. Ironically, in July 2012, the Premier of the Western Cape, and leader of the official opposition party, called for the deployment of the South African Army to quell gang violence in coloured neighbourhoods on the Cape Flats (Butana and Hartley 2012).

The 1998 Prevention of Organised Crime Act (POCA) was passed to combat 'organized crime' and 'criminal gang' activities. In the debate on the bill the ANC Minister of Justice referred to a 'culture of violence in our country and the low state of morality' (*Hansard* 1998a, col: 8067–8), using similar language to apartheid ideologues in regards to the 'culture of violence'. Thus, on the one hand the government blames society's damaged moral fabric on apartheid, but on the other it demonizes criminals – the *unethical* citizens who have a low state of morality.

---

10 The Scorpions were controversially dissolved in 2009 and replaced by The Hawks.

It is not at all clear as to who or what constitutes an organized criminal or what 'organized crime' is since the concepts are slippery, broadly defined and fuzzy. Based on the US RICO Act (Racketeer Influenced and Corrupt Organizations) POCA does not contain a definition of 'organized crime' but prescribes a punitive approach to 'criminal gangs'. This is surprising given the 1992 ANC discussion document on 'Crime and Crime Control', which ascribed gang formation to 'structural and political reasons' and presented gang members as having 'legitimate economic needs' (ANC 1992b: 8–9). Although by no means a radical or Marxist document it explicitly recognized that 'crimes of the poor such as street crime and other crimes had some link to the structural violence of the apartheid era' and that

> consequently the strategies for combating such crimes have to demonstrate an understanding and compassion for the structural predicament of the perpetrator, who is at the same time a victim, however much one condemns those deeds. (ANC 1992b: 2–3)

The ANC called for

> a creative process, such as the one NICRO is using in Cape Town … a multi-faceted approach which draws on all the social forces in the affected area and binds them into an alliance that does not have a gang busting ethos, but engages with gangs in such a way as to diminish the negative impact of the gang … Significantly absent in the process are the police, who have special, cowboy-style gang-busting units in Cape Town. (ANC 1992b: 8–9)

Despite these lofty ideals the hodge-podge foundation through which gang membership is proved, in terms of section 11 of POCA, feeds into the stereotype of the poor young coloured male as being a potential gangster (Standing 2005, Jensen 2008, Gould 2012). Section 11 provides for the following criteria:

- whether the person is identified as such by a parent/guardian
- resides in or frequents a particular gangs area and adopts their style of dress, their use of hand signs, language or their tattoos
- associates with 'known members' of a criminal gang
- has been arrested more than once in the company of identified members of a criminal gang for offences which are consistent with usual criminal gang activities.

Yet studies show that gang membership is indistinct, contested, ephemeral and shortlived (Jensen 2008, Standing, 2006, Glaser 1998) and is part of a 'continuum of possible masculine identities' (Glaser 1998: 309) which are often blurred, even from the perspective of the 'gangsters' themselves.

Making up the Numbers

By utilizing similar 'crime prevention operations' to that of the police in the 'old' South Africa the result is that the usual targets and the usual suspects are still the objects of the state's police power. Official crime statistics point to the existence of crime 'hotspots' – concentrations of criminal conduct in a single location (Department of Safety and Security 2003: 41). These are therefore the 'crackdown stations' where crime prevention programmes (of the crackdown type) are targeted and result in further criminalization of the poor, the foreign, the black and the coloured male.

The 2003–4 police statistics reflected an increase in 'victimless crimes': illegal possession of firearms increased by 4 per cent, drug-related crime increased by 14 per cent and driving under the influence of drugs or alcohol increased by 10 per cent. Between April 2002 and March 2003 there were 17,676 arrests for commercial crimes as compared to 647,951 for drugs and other 'victimless' crimes and 444,738 for 'priority crimes' (serious and violent crime) (Department of Safety and Security 2003: 63). Because victimless crimes are linked to 'various other forms of criminality' (Du Plessis and Louw 2005) the police were congratulated on the crackdown but it is often the petty and poor criminals, South Africa's 'underclass', who get imprisoned as a result of these high profile blitz operations. The results of a December 2001 survey revealed that only 28 per cent of probationers and parolees in urban areas, and 16 per cent in rural areas, had access to both telephones and electricity (*Hansard* 2002b, question 198: col: 3327–8). In 2004, 8,859 awaiting trial prisoners never paid bail set at R500.00[11] (*Hansard* 2004d, col: 1307). This is evidence of the way that poverty, race and incarceration are still intimately associated with each other in South Africa.

Although the Reconstruction and Development Programme was an important strategy for bringing development to the 'ungovernable' townships, the areas zoned for development intervention were defined and identified through criteria that were based on development *and* security (Reconstruction and Development Programme 1994: 1, cited in Jensen 2005: 557). Thus the need to combat criminality featured alongside the need to provide for basic services (such as health, housing and electricity). It is indeed ironic that the townships, the sites of people's power during the 1980s, have become an impediment to transformation (Jensen 2008: 197) in the 'post' apartheid era. Perhaps this is not so surprising given that apartheid produced these 'lawless' zones, through both its penal gaze and policing techniques (creating a pool of likely offenders), and also through ignoring the very real violence and crime that played out in these 'non-white' spaces. The widespread service delivery protests that have become almost endemic to present day South Africa have also resulted in criminalization of the poor, due to the hard hitting and repressive techniques used to quell protests.

11 About 50$.

Conclusion

As the forms of power exercised by the South African state moved from a predominantly exclusionary (sovereign) form to a more inclusive form of repressive/disciplinary welfarism to liberal governmentality so too were various forms of criminality produced, subjected to different forms of governance, and rendered thinkable in new ways. Thus we have the pass law offender, the black loiterer, the coloured *skollie*, the gangster, the organized criminal and the illegal immigrant. Yet all of these are based on notions of danger that are founded on stereotypes that have survived regime change – in this sense they are centuries old. As such the continuities between the 'old' and the 'new' South Africa are particularly apparent in the realm of who gets excluded from citizenship on the basis of their criminality and how this criminality is constructed.

By emphasizing state repression, assuming that the problem of crime, of disorder, would be solved through legitimation – a legitimate government, a legitimate police force – the ANC ignored the problem of criminality and its deep-rooted causes. Once faced with the problem of crime, it constructed policies on the edifice of the stereotypes that had been created by previous regimes, constituted in the face of rampant inequalities. In South Africa just after the transition – the ruling elites growing fear of criminality, coupled with heightened economic inequality, the uncertainty of the transition, unemployment and the influx of foreigners brought substantial pressure to bear on law-makers. Whereas before 1994 the ANC had emphasized legitimating the police and the law as a means to get people to buy into the new democracy, once in power, once faced with the enormity of the crime problem that it had ignored prior to coming into power, it flipped and blamed criminality for impeding development, without delving into the complex history of exactly how this criminality had been produced. Given this, it is not surprising that race and class are still huge determinants of who goes to prison and who gets surveilled.

Official discourse on crime not only involves repressive measures but also constitutes an official way of knowing, constructing and organizing the various categories of offender. Policy-makers construct target populations (such as the pass law offender, the supercriminal, the illegal immigrant, the gangster, the organized criminal) and based on these constructions policy solutions are created and implemented and further categorization and/or criminalization occurs. But the knowledge that prevails as 'truth' is linked to power and networks and 'the better [one] is networked, the more likely it is [one's] beliefs will catch on and persist' (Hacking 1999: 203). Thus the existence of the 'criminal' is not just a matter of discovering an essential and unchanging entity called a 'criminal' since 'truth is not outside power or lacking in power' (Foucault, 2000: 131). Exactly where the gaze of the state, and increasingly non-state actors, is focused, is crucially important in the construction of criminality in the 'new' South Africa.

Chapter 5
Crime Prevention and the Turn to the Community

> Although crime prevention is a complex concept, it can in general be defined as an attempt to stop a crime before or while it is being committed to prevent further criminal activities.
>
> Crime prevention can also be regarded as a strategy to control crime in the sense that, if you do not prevent the occurrence of crime, you cannot eliminate the possibility that criminal activities will be carried out. Crime prevention, the detection and punishment of offenders, the protection of life and property and the preservation of public peace and order is not the responsibility only of the SAPS, but also of the public. The police and the public should therefore follow a joint partnership approach. Police agencies over the world have realized that because of the complex and diverse nature of crime and because of their limited resources, they alone are not capable of implementing crime prevention strategies. The international trend in policing is for communities and other government agencies to become increasingly involved in crime prevention, representing a more holistic and effective approach. (Department of Safety and Security 2003: 16–17)

Introduction

In this chapter I track the rise of the term 'community' from the mid-1970s in state discourse about crime and situate it within the turn towards neoliberalism and the embracing of the 'criminologies of everyday life' (Garland 1996: 450), such as situational crime prevention. I show how the liberal politics of the 'new' South Africa have ushered in new forms of positive and productive, as opposed to repressive, power. These include the technologies for preventing (and governing) crime through the family, the social and the individual. This has involved the emergence of new ways to understand and manage crime (Singh 1999, 2005a, 2005b, 2008). I argue that the concept of crime prevention is transforming the notion of what it means to be an ethical citizen in South Africa and that the technologies of restorative justice, social crime prevention, familialization and actuarialism are important tools in this neoliberal shift to governing at a distance.

A large part of my analysis is focused on the 1996 National Crime Prevention Strategy (NCPS) because it represents an attempt to both transform crime prevention *and* to achieve transformation via crime prevention within the context of a governmentalizing state. The NCPS is an interesting example of a political programme – to prevent crime in democratic South Africa – which expresses the tension between the developmental and neoliberal aspects of the South African political economy. It also exemplifies the tension which the ANC, a former liberation movement, displayed as it battled to reassert its struggle credentials, once it assumed the reigns of government, in the face of a crime problem which it had, as a liberation movement, largely ignored. As such the NCPS embraces a range of seemingly contradictory technologies for preventing crime, developed not only in relation to their role in implementing the programme but also in relation to the broader governmental strategies of the Growth, Employment and Redistribution (GEAR) strategy and 'transformation'. It is because of this that the NCPS is a markedly apolitical document which, despite its paradigmatic embracing of social crime prevention, exhibits an overall bias towards the creation of a leaner, meaner and more efficient criminal justice system – an 'integrated criminal justice system'.

The fact that the ANC and the Nationalist Party both supported crime prevention via the ubiquitous 'community' is not only indicative of the polyvalence and flexibility of this term – it can and has been appropriated by both left and right – but its usage also complements the neoliberal call for more empowered citizens and less state intervention, an ideology that both the ANC and the NP came to embrace, at different periods in time.

1976–89 (Reform of Verwoerdian Apartheid)

From Control to Development

In the face of the political and economic crises of the 1970s the state embarked on a series of reforms, discussed in Chapter 1. The 'private enterprise system' was presented as 'the way to wipe out discrimination' (*Hansard* 1977a col: 809) and the State President's 1979 speech to the opening of parliament specifically called for a 'profit orientated free market economy [as] the most effective system to achieve the highest rate of economic development' (*Hansard*, 1979a, col: 6). Through these reforms the NP government hoped to

> involve the masses of South Africa in the free market system ... to make capitalists of the underdeveloped people in South Africa ... the Black man in particular. (*Hansard* 1982b: col: 2758)

In the 1988 debate on the Transport Deregulation Bill the Deputy Minister of Transport Affairs stated that

> the approach to regulation must mainly emphasise the promotion of economic activities and be less directed towards their control, while greater dependence

> is placed on natural market mechanisms and self-regulation. (*Hansard* 1988b col: 14506)

This had implications for the criminal justice system.

The Liberalization of the Criminal Justice System

The 1977 Riekert Commission of Inquiry pointed out that the night permit/curfew system, which prescribed hours for which black people needed permits to be in white areas, and was justified as a crime prevention device, did not work effectively because permits were quite easily forged. Not only did the curfew laws net 'innocent people' but those blacks with 'ulterior motives' were not prevented from committing crimes (Riekert Commission of Inquiry, para: 178). Apart from serving as a crime prevention mechanism the curfew system was also meant to 'realize the ideal of separate development' by keeping 'White and Black population groups in separate residential areas at least at night' (Riekert Commission of Inquiry, para 4.269: 178).

Riekert's recommendations called for the more effective 'utilisation of manpower' and a 'shift of emphasis from control to development' (para 6.13: 248) so that black communities in urban black residential and rural areas could develop. The new Department of Plural Relations and Development was 'a speciality and development department ... faced with the ... challenge of creating stable, contented and happy Black communities in the White areas' (para 6.13: 254). This would of course also contribute to crime prevention. There was thus a shift from a policy of keeping blacks out of white areas, as a blanket mode of crime prevention, to one which sought to allow greater numbers access to the cities.

On 29 May 1980 the Minister of Justice announced that black people could now apply for permits to sell alcohol in townships and that the practice of the Administration Boards selling liquor was to be phased out. As of June 1980 the Liquor Board was no longer under the Ministry of Justice but under the Minister of Industries, Commerce and Consumer Affairs. In his speech on the 1981 Liquor Amendment Bill the Minister of Trade and Industries referred to 'Black' people as being brought into the traditional criminal law/penal system and as no longer just being excluded or controlled by influx control (*Hansard* 1981c). Instead it was 'orderly and controlled contact' which would now ensure the preservation of separate communities. Regulation was justified as being in the interests of commerce rather than morals and certain black people were to be responsibilized rather than demonized. Since the Immorality Act could no longer be scripturally justified, reliance was instead placed on the concept of the 'continued orderly structuring of communities' and its repeal in 1985 was justified on the basis that legislation was no longer necessary to enforce the policy of separate development because people would police themselves.

As a result of this 'defining deviance down' (Garland 1996: 455), policing practices changed. Whereas in 1971–72 offence statistics were almost at same level as infringements,[1] in 1982–83 infringements had declined by 60 per cent, indicating that fewer people were being arrested for these technical offences. In 1989 a departmental investigation into decriminalization and depenalization was held. It was precipitated by the steep increase in the number of criminal cases in the magistrates' courts. It found, unsurprisingly, that due to too many statutory by-laws, enforced by criminal sanction, there was a situation of over-criminalization (Department of Justice 1991a: 4).

The Verwoerdian era call by 'Afrikaner Nationalist' criminologists for racial segregation on the basis of biological differences did not resonate with the new governmental project to create a 'sweetheart', compliant African petty bourgeoisie class and a 'multi-racial' South Africa. As such the ideological fit between a racist criminology – which had portrayed 'Africans' as being immoral and genetically inferior to whites and hence undeserving of citizenship in white South Africa – and the state reform project started to loosen. The justifications for and modes of punishment began to shift and the state embraced the concept of community-based crime prevention. The 'community' was firmly rooted in the notion of creating a 'strong stable urban middle class' (*Hansard* 1982c col: 2742). Distinctions were now drawn between the 'developed' and the 'under/non-developed' peoples of South Africa, based on class rather than race.

The Turn to Crime Prevention and Responsibilization in the Community

With the 'marketization' that occurred in South Africa in the 1970s the state's role shifted to responsibilizing rather than providing – to help people to help themselves (Hay 1996: 18). This impacted on crime prevention in the sense that the government no longer accepted full responsibility for preventing crime. Crime became a problem to be managed, as opposed to being solved, in terms of an overall governmentalization of the state. This saw the government adopt technologies of rule which no longer relied solely on sovereign, exclusionary and overtly repressive forms of power. Instead, via 'action at a distance', it sought to govern through the 'conduct of conduct'. In terms of a 'responsibilization strategy', which Garland (1996: 451) defines as

> central government seeking to act upon crime not in a direct fashion through state agencies (police, courts, prisons, social work etc) but instead by acting indirectly, seeking to activate action on the part of non state agencies and organizations

the state began to call on the 'community' and the individual to take responsibility for preventing and protecting against crime and managing the crime risk. What

1 Infringements were statutory offences that were aimed at certain races, mainly black people. They included curfew violations, 'foreign blacks entering urban areas' and 'registration and production of documents'.

was previously called 'Rehabilitation Week' became 'Crime Prevention Week' (*Cape Times*, 29 July 1977), with the state acknowledging that it could not solve the problem of crime on its own. This took place within the context of a state strategy that was based on the divide-and-rule tactics of creating a small, relatively privileged class of urban blacks, while keeping the majority in the Bantustans.[2]

In its drive to responsiblize, the NP relied extensively on the notion of 'community'. For example, the 1977 Community Councils Bill was justified as offering

> Black communities the opportunity to channel their activities in a way that imparts a life, a pulse, a character … a Black community is now being given the opportunity … to control itself, to discipline itself and to maintain law and order by means of a civil guard for its community. It is a basic right of every civilization. (*Hansard* 1977g col: 11235)

One of the responsibilities of the newly established community councils, established in terms of the 1977 Community Councils Act, was 'slum clearance' and the *makgotla* (traditional court) system was reactivated on the grounds that 'Black people prefer to settle their differences according to their own legal system' (*Hansard* 1977g col: 11250).

The 1985 'Report on Investigation into the Present Welfare Policy in the RSA' called for 'privatisation to the highest possible degree' via 'community involvement'. 'Community services were proposed to replace 'residential care' with the stress being on 'prevention and development' rather than 'care and remedy' (Department of Health and Welfare 1985: paras 3(f); 3(b) 3(c): 2 –3)).

Although the police continued to engage in cordon and search operations as modes of crime prevention, targeted mainly at arresting illegal sojourners (influx control violaters) and squatters, by 1980 there was a distinctive discursive embracing of individualized responsibility for crime prevention. The 1980 South African Police (SAP) Annual Report stated that

> The most effective manner in which to prevent crime is to make the broader public more aware of crime. There are attempts at making the public realize that the fight against crime is the responsibility of each individual in the community. (Department of Police 1981: 7)

---

2 As Budlender and Davis (1984: 174) describe these reforms, influx control was to be shifted from:

> control of mere presence in the area to tight control of employment and accommodation in the area. For urban insiders life would become much easier but for outsiders it would become much more difficult to gain access to cities because it would be tied to accommodation (which was extremely scarce) and lawful employment.

In terms of this new approach a crime prevention officer was to be appointed for every police division (Department of Police 1981: 7).

As petty apartheid was being dismantled in the 1980s, in the face of increasing resistance from the ANC and other banned organizations, the SAP separated out the combating of crime and the maintaining of 'law and order', assuming responsibility for the latter but not the former. In 1981 the Minister of Justice and Law and Order claimed that the state was dealing with the crime problem but could not do so on its own. The 'community' had a vital role to play and communities had to start taking responsibility for crime prevention. Black municipal authorities were permitted to appoint their own municipal police in terms of the 1984 Black Local Authorities Act and municipal police, known as 'community guards', were responsible for day-to-day policing in the townships with powers of order maintenance and enforcing municipal by-laws (Brogden and Shearing 1993: 81). The infamous *kitskonstabels* ('instant constables'), known as such because they were only given three weeks' training, were appointed and let loose on the townships in September 1986, further entrenching this turn to self-policing by allowing the SAP and South African Defence Force (SADF) to withdraw from the townships (Brogden and Shearing 1993: 83). This was all part of the counter-insurgency strategy of low intensity warfare that the state had adopted to fight against its enemies in terms of which it sought to obscure the connections between state agents and violence (Haysom undated).

Despite the fact that the dramatic increase in the official crime rate in 1986 was attributed to 'unrest' – the argument being that 'unrest' caused crime – the 86-page 1988–90 SAP Annual Report included, for the first time, a section on crime prevention and the importance of partnership with citizens.[3] The 1989–90 report stated that it was

> a principle recognized throughout the world that a police institution cannot, on its own, prevent crime. Effective crime prevention can take place only when there is an active partnership of the Police and the law-abiding members of the public against crime. (Department of Law and Order 1990: 40)

The decrease in the offence of house-breaking was ascribed to the neighbourhood watch systems of which there were more than 1600 in 1987 (Department of Law and Order 1990: 41). It is interesting to note that the first neighbourhood watch, which started in 1985 in Randburg, was very much linked to the fear of terrorism and was perceived as necessary to avoid the killing of innocent civilians (Department of Law and Order 1988).

Mainstream academic criminologists such as Stevens (1988: 164) stressed the fact that because an increase in crime 'against the person' was a worldwide trend,

3 The previous year's Annual Report had been only 43 pages and the 1982–83 Annual Report had been critiqued by the Opposition because it was only nine pages long (*Hansard* 1983).

'it is every individual's duty to take his own precautionary measures in order to protect his person'. This discourse set the stage for the turn to community policing, as a mode of attaining legitimacy for the police and as a form of crime prevention, during the deeply contested transition period.

1989–94 (Transitioning into the 'New' South Africa)

Community Policing as a Legitimation Technique

Together with a shift towards constitutionalism and human rights, the idea of 'community' was utilized extensively in government policy documents during the negotiations about how to transition towards democracy. The turn to community was justified as a cost-cutting measure and as a cure for a deficient criminal justice system. This cohered with an overarching neoliberalized political discourse that eulogized the idea of 'self-sufficient', (Department of Health and Welfare 1992: 3) empowered communities. 'Community development' was linked with:

> the empowerment of people to enable them to become co-creators of a better future ... to enter as facilitators, enablers and catalysts of self-help ... to promote growth (economic, physical, physiological and social), equal opportunities [and] general welfare (Department of Health and Welfare 1992: 3).

The text of the September 1991 *National Peace Accord* – an agreement in which the signatories (political leaders, trade unions, security forces, business, industry and the church) committed themselves to peaceful negotiations in the period leading up to the 1994 elections – linked the notion of community policing to the quest for partnership and legitimacy. Through accountable, 'friendly, effective and prompt service' the police would try to 'obtain the co-operation of the public whose partnership in the task of crime control and prevention [was] essential' (National Peace Accord 1991: para 3.1.3).[4] The civilian Police Board, established in terms of the Accord, was responsible for advising the Minister of Law and Order on the training and use of the SAP 'in order to reconcile the interests of the community with that of the Force' (Department of Law and Order 1993: 11–12). It was explicitly recognized that the 'service' aspect of the police had been underdeveloped and that more time needed to be devoted to 'community-orientated service' (Department of Law and Order 1993: 1). This was in keeping with the then State President De Klerk's January 1990 address to top police officers where he expressly divorced politics from policing, stating that 'we do not want to use you any more as instruments to reach certain goals. We as politicians must take responsibility for politics' (ANC 1992c: 1).

4 Cited in Department of Law and Order 1993.

The word 'community' was repeatedly used throughout the introduction to the 1991 SAP Annual Report and the Community Relations division, established in December 1992, was responsible for facilitating and implementing this 'new policing approach' (Department of Law and Order 1994: 82). Police-community liaison forums were established at station level, the aim being to draw up plans to combat crime, in co-operation with 'the community' within the structure of these forums (Department of Law and Order 1993: 1). In terms of 'corporate image development' the division on Community Policing was 'commissioned to educate and inform the community about the new policing approach'. Community Police Officers were appointed at station level and 'community-directed projects' such as 'adopt a cop' youth projects and youth camps were launched (Department of Law and Order 1994: 83). The fact that academics at the University of South Africa were calling for 'police to play a proactive and preventive role in enforcing law and preventing crime' is indicative of the hegemony of this discourse in the early 1990s.[5]

Because the term 'community' is polyvalent and flexible enough to bear different meanings, depending on the context, it functions in multiple ways and appeals to diverse parts of the political spectrum. The enhanced use of the term 'community' in state discourse during this period was a form of 'corporatism' (Lacey and Zedner 1995: 311) insofar as it functioned in a way that sought to obscure the conflict which South African communities were in fact experiencing during this time of heightened political violence and rising vigilantism. It did so by incorporating 'non-state groups ... within structures of governance in the quest for consensual implementation of policy' (Lacey and Zedner 1995: 311). As such, it was a mode of papering over the class and racial divides that might otherwise have been damaging to political legitimacy and policy implementation and it represented an attempt by the government to create a new unifying moment. The 'community' was both a technique of responsibilization in the realm of crime prevention and also a body on which (and location in which) crime prevention was to be implemented and initiated. It was also used as a site/space for a new form of policing, even though the very communities which were most in need of the 'new' policing were those that had been most eviscerated and fragmented by the old, authoritarian approach.

A Foregrounding of Crime Prevention

There was a distinct emphasis on violence and crime in the 1990 Police Appropriation vote and, for the first time, specific mention was made of 'crime prevention and corrective services' in the 1991 Health and Welfare Annual Report (Department of Health and Welfare 1991: 40). The 1991–92 Annual Report of the Department of Justice also contained more on crime than past reports. In

5 See for example Du Preez, Director of the Institute for Criminology at UNISA (1992), Police and Policing in the New South Africa.

1991 the Security Branch of the SAP was replaced by the Crime Combating and Investigation Division (CCID), encapsulating a discursive shift from threat to state security, emanating from terrorists, to threat to 'everyman', emanating from criminals. The SAP launched a campaign to convince residents that they (i.e. the police) were 'community servants' (*Argus*, 12 April 1991, quoted in Steytler 1992: 160) and pamphlets were distributed among township residents calling for residents to 'take the liberty in trusting us with your crime problems' at a time when 'criminals are walking among our people like wolves in sheep's clothing' (ibid.). In terms of an overall civilianization, of what had previously been a militarized service image, the police sought to portray themselves as sympathizers for those who lived in the crime-ridden townships. The camouflaged *Casspirs* (colloquial name for the military vehicles that patrolled the townships) were repainted in blue and yellow and called *Inyala* (meaning antelope) and there were high publicity crime prevention swoops (Steytler 1992).

The SAP established more internal divisions that highlighted the problem of crime and the role of the community in crime prevention. Thus the Division: 'Visible Policing' was divided into Crime Prevention Operations, Neighbourhood Watch Systems, Senior Citizens, Business Watch and a Tourist Assistance Unit. The 'Visible Policing Division' was established after a merger between the former Uniformed Branch ('pro-active service') and the Operational Branch ('Reactive Service') (Department of Law and Order 1992). In fact, because of this emphasis on crime prevention the 1991 Annual Report of the SAP had a different format to previous reports. This represented 'for the first time in the history of the SAP, the realization of the ideal to make provision for the execution of crime prevention as a primary task'. Crime was referred to as 'the cruelest destroyer of our rapidly urbanizing society' (Department of Law and Order 1992: 1) and, somewhat ambitiously perhaps, 'successful crime prevention' was presented as 'the absence of, or the decrease in crime', rather than being based on 'statistics for arrest' (Department of Law and Order 1992: 83). At the same time it was explicitly recognized that crime was an 'international phenomenon', which the SAP could not remedy.

In March 1992 at a meeting on the 'question of crime in the country' it was decided to establish an inter-departmental secretariat comprising the departments of Justice, the SAP and Correctional Services. The secretariat would, amongst other things,

> with the aid of criminologists, sociologists, penologists and other experts investigate the establishment of a national research centre to conduct a co-ordinated study of all aspects of crime and the combating of crime in the unique circumstances that prevail in South Africa and to make recommendations … on how to promote a sense of community responsibility for the combating of crime. (Department of Justice 1992: 8)

A National Campaign for the Protection of Senior Citizens, sponsored by a local supermarket, was launched in 1993 and a '10 point plan to combat crime and violence' was drawn up. Cabinet also subsidised radios for farmers. Through its Chaplains' Services, the SAP presented seminars on 'Crime and sin' so as to 'sharpen the Christian conscience with regard to its co-responsibility in the prevention of crime' (Department of Law and Order 1993: 26). The 'lethargy of members of the public to take certain simple basic preventive measures against theft' (Department of Law and Order 1994: 3) was blamed for adversely affecting crime prevention and, in terms of 'Operation M', arrangements were made for possessions, such as video machines, to be marked free of charge so as to prevent house-breakings. There was also an emphasis on 'strategic planning', devising 'three year objectives' (Department of Law and Order 1994: 1), the 'monitoring [of] quality service', 'performance auditing', 'cost effective management', 'the principles of liability, accountability, affordability, but also effectiveness' (Department of Law and Order 1994: 6).

It should not be forgotten that these developments were taking place against the backdrop of an increasingly fraught political landscape. The focus was on political violence, the problem of illegal firearms and keeping the peace during the negotiations about democracy. Many whites feared that the country was going to degenerate into an anarchic bloodbath. At the same time left-wing reformers outside the government promoted solutions that enhanced autonomy at the local level, attempting to build on the 'people's power' initiatives which urban black South African communities had started to develop during the 1980s (Van Zyl Smit 1989).

The ANC and People's Power

The idea of community as crime-combating mechanism was utilized not only by government but also by the ANC. This was rooted in the notions of 'people's power' and grassroots democracy which peppered the discourse of left-wing activists in the 1980s. 'People's power' was presented as the 'collective strength of the community' as opposed to 'coercion', which was 'the use of force *against* the community' (Sisulu 1986). The key distinction between people's power and coercion was whether a 'democratic mandate from the community' existed or not. Thus when

> bands of youth set up so called 'kangaroo courts' and gave out punishments, under the control of no-one with no democratic mandate from the community, this is <u>not</u> people's power ... [but] a 'crime'. (Sisulu 1986, emphasis in original)

On the other hand, when

> disciplined organised youth, together with other older people participate in the exercise of people's justice and the setting up of people's courts; when

> these structures are acting on a mandate from the community and are under the democratic control of the community, this is an example of people's power. (Sisulu 1986: 17)

People's power was regarded as a particularly good form of 'crime control' since it 'was disciplined, democratic and an expression of the will of the people [and] … in the areas where people are taking control, crime [was] being wiped out' (Sisulu 1986: 17–18). In 1990 Raymond Suttner, one of the movement's ideologues, stated frankly that one of the weaknesses of the South African democratic movement was that it had, at times, only been able to 'deliver boycotts' when 'for many people one of the most pressing problems is crime'. The golden age of the United Democratic Front was proffered as a yardstick when street committees had been

> able to reduce crime significantly … [thus making] a significant impact on communities and [had] given people a sense of their own power, their own capacity, to deal with problems. (Suttner 1990: 44)

In 1992, at a conference on 'Policing in the New South Africa', the ANC stated that it supported community policing because it was 'in line with international thinking' and it was 'the community who are largely responsible for criminal prosecutions [and] … not the police alone who combat and prevent crime' (ANC 1993: 9). The ANC focused on securing the legitimacy of the police in terms of the processes of civilianization, affirmative action, changing investigation techniques and projecting a politically non-partisan image of policing (ANC 1993: 11–12). As such, the major preoccupation on the part of the ANC immediately before 1994 was how to legitimate the criminal justice system, particularly the police. This was not that surprising, considering that the police had hitherto been a symbol of the apartheid state, yet they were now called on to play a neutral role in order maintenance during the transition period.

This bent towards communitarianism and grassroots democracy was rooted in the 'people shall govern' clause of the Freedom Charter and it echoed a global shift towards informal justice (Abel 1982). But it also resonated with the more neoliberal turn to community that had started under the Nationalist Party in the 1970s and that I referred to in the first part of this chapter. In this way then there was a shift towards governing the self through crime – not only a shift towards democratic political processes but also a democratization through crime.

As crime became the subject and object of plans and strategies to combat it, so too was the 'community' increasingly drawn into the ambit of crime prevention by both the state and the ANC. Although the turn to community started in the 1970s, this sense of having to devise strategies to combat the problem of crime, of being confronted by it, was a new development, one which became increasingly apparent in post-apartheid South Africa. As the democratic South African government started to 'govern through crime' (Simon 1997: 174) it became the lens through which social policies were implemented and national discourse became securitized.

1994–2004 (Consolidating the 'New' South Africa)

Crime Prevention and Transformation and the Transformation of Crime Prevention

The 'new constitutional dispensation', ushered in on 27 April 1994, entailed an immediate focus on incorporating the former homeland departments of justice, welfare, prisons and police into united departments in terms of a complicated 'rationalization' process. The logistics of amalgamating 11 separate police forces into one was extremely challenging (Laufer 2001, Schonteich 2001, Shaw 1996, 2002). It also had to take place within the framework of 'human rights and a [racially] representative civil service' as well as 'recognition of the need to address violence and serious crime' (Department of Justice 1995: 1). Community policing was presented as the midwife of the 'rebirth' of policing in South Africa and it was twinned with 'transformation' – based on 'partnerships and ... sharing responsibility' (Department of Safety and Security 1996b: 1, Nathan and Colin 1993). Thus the partnership discourse which had arisen in the 1970s was strongly intertwined with the way in which the new government approached the problem of crime. Whereas Steinberg (2001) argues that the police discourse changed abruptly as the language of community policing replaced the language of law and order, I have argued that we can trace this back to the 1970s.

The dominant thinking was that legitimizing the SAP would lead to crime reduction and that a 'fundamental reassessment of and transformation of the nature and style of policing' was crucial in order to effect a 'complete and decisive break with the past' (Department of Safety and Security 1996b: 2). The police had to be 'rehabilitated' and people had to be 'mobilized' to 'participate in the provision of safety and security' (Department of Safety and Security 1998: i). There also needed to be a shift from 'bandit catching' to 'problem solving' (Department of Safety and Security 1996b: 12). These ideas were exemplified in the 1996 National Crime Prevention Strategy (NCPS), which presented crime prevention as being distinct from 'crime control' and as being part and parcel of transformation (Department of Safety and Security, 1996a). Indeed, the very fact of democracy was, to a certain extent, in and of itself thought to be a crime prevention device. As one person, on a somewhat cynical note, stated: the ANC thought that, with the advent of democracy, crime would fade away, 'just like the state under socialism'.[6]

6 Personal communication from Willie Hofmeyer, former struggle activist and Head of the Special Investigating Unit (Scorpions) at time of the interview.

The Construction of a 'New Common Sense'[7]

Ethics and morals have become central to South African state discourse on crime prevention. Just as in the past they were central to the ANC's discursive accompaniment to its armed struggle against apartheid, they were now called upon in the struggle against crime. Yet this was not just an inversion; instead, the state sought to construct a new morality, one which 'structured and transformed how crime was thought about' (Singh 2008: 14). Crime was now problematized as a violation of human rights, a threat to democracy and a major constraint on development (Department of Safety and Security 1996a: 43).[8] Because of this the preamble to the 1996–97 SAPS Annual Plan referred to a need for transformation:

> transformation of how our society approaches criminality and victimisation. This transformation must be successful both because reconstruction and development is dependant on a basic level of stability, and because it is the fundamental right of all people to live without fear in a safe and secure environment. (Department of Safety and Security 1996b: 1)

In November 1994, six months after the first democratic elections, the Interdepartmental Crime Combating Secretariat was replaced by the Interdepartmental Committee on a National Crime Prevention Strategy. It was tasked by Cabinet to draft a National Crime Prevention Strategy (NCPS) to be put into operation in 1996. Although the NCPS was not implemented in its entirety, it is important because it was representative of a new discourse in the governance of crime, one which relied on techniques of the self, the self situated within the social, within the community.

The 'new paradigm' (Department of Safety and Security 1996a: 6) proffered in the NCPS was premised on a shift from an exclusive emphasis on 'crime control' to 'crime prevention', from crime as a '*security* issue' to crime as a '*social* issue' (emphasis in the original). Whereas in the past there had been a 'state centred' system the NCPS proposed that this should be replaced by a greater emphasis on a 'victim centred, restorative justice system' (Department of Safety and Security 1996a: 6). It was aimed at supporting 'the creation of crime resistant communities' and contributing towards a 'reduction of the culture of violence' (Department of Safety and Security 1996a: 66) through the creation of a new 'common sense' with regard to crime' (Department of Safety and Security 1996a: para 23.1.1: 73). The critical factors for 'reducing tolerance towards crime, and hence reducing crime-levels' were the 'prevailing moral climate within communities, attitudes towards

7 This term is used in the National Crime Prevention Strategy (Department of Safety and Security, 1996a: 23.1.1: 73).

8 Singh's (2008: 14) observation that crime was constituted as a threat to the very ties that bound citizens together in the 'new' South Africa is apt.

crime and the willingness of citizens and communities to take responsibility for crime' (Department of Safety and Security 1996a: para 23.1.1: 73).

The consultants who developed the NCPS were ex-left-wing activists and as they themselves later admitted, extremely idealistic at the time.[9] They were clearly influenced by left realism, as theorized by Jock Young. In the words of Janine Rauch they were 'clueless'[10] but, having been tasked to develop a strategy on crime prevention at the behest of the President himself – one which was to be distinguished from law enforcement (this would continue under the ambit of the police) – they set about drafting. When they presented the first draft to the Cabinet Subcommittee on Security, chaired by then Deputy President Mbeki, it was rejected on the basis that they needed to include short-term solutions to the crime problem. The NCPS was eventually launched in February 1996. Given the extreme compromise position that it represented, coupled with the Business Against Crime's influence, it resulted in an eclectic, apolitical and managerialist document (Dixon 2004c).

Intersectoralism and the Moral Citizen of the 'Newoliberal' South Africa

The NCPS was published a few months after the government adopted the neoliberal 'Growth, Employment and Redistribution' (GEAR) strategy. The latter reemphasized and formally enunciated neoliberal economic policies and in particular promoted 'private corporate profitability' as the main way through which 'social delivery' would occur (South African Comrades for the Encounter 1997: 3, Marais 2001, 2011, Bond 2000, Gillespie 2008, Peet, 2002, Terreblanche 2012). As Gillespie (2008: 76) states:

> at the time that Mandela was launching the "RDP of the soul", the ANC had shifted its economic policy further to the right by *abandoning* the RDP economic framework and replacing it, after considerable discussion with the IMF and the World Bank, with the neoliberal policy framework known as GEAR.

In keeping with the managerialist principles which were fast attaining hegemony in South Africa, the NCPS sought to create an integrated criminal justice system where criminal justice officials – governed through victim complaints and customer satisfaction audits – would be made responsive to the needs of customers and clients, particularly victims and multi-agency structures (Department of Safety and Security 1996a: 67). But the NCPS drafters had presumed a degree of co-operation and co-ordination in government practice that was in fact non-existent. According to Graeme Simpson, in ignoring the narrow approach that typified government departments, the drafters produced a document that

9 Personal communication from Janine Rauch 2011.

10 Personal communication from Janine Rauch 2011.

represented all the 'gravest dangers of vision based policy making'.[11] Yet even if the NCPS had been properly implemented, with marginalization being redressed by a 'process of human development, one which created a sense of belonging and stake in society'[12] the vision was still remarkably silent about how to redress the inequality that defines social relations and, indeed, the relations of production, in the 'new' South Africa.

The NCPS emphasized the importance of a 'coordinated approach' through the creation of an 'Integrated Criminal Justice System (Department of Safety and Security 1996a 6: 6.1). The point of departure was that a focus on managing the separate departments involved in the criminal justice process 'as an integrated whole' would result in an 'increase in the ratio of convictions to reported crimes and reduce time lags in the justice process' (Department of Safety and Security 1996a: 53). According to Rauch the NCPS was a bureaucratic document and not a criminological study and because there was very little data on victims or perpetrators at the time, it contained 'broad brush descriptive stuff'[13] rather than hard data on which to base policy. It focused more on how to achieve an integrated criminal justice system because the criminal justice system was a known entity and perceived to be easier to change than complex social problems.

The new ANC government did not trust the bureaucracy inherited from the old regime: it was distrustful of the SAPS and criminal justice functionaries. Thus when the private sector Business Against Crime (BAC) initiative offered its assistance ANC politicians were inclined to take it. The BAC's point of departure was that the investigation and response skills of the police needed to be strengthened so that more people could be arrested for committing crimes. As such the BAC gave extensive funds towards the implementing of the 'integrated justice system' at the expense of that of social crime prevention (Dixon 2004a). This is probably why the first project that the NCPS funded was the building of prison fences – because preventing prison escapes was regarded as a form of crime prevention. The next was a project on computers – a somewhat far cry from spending on the deep-rooted social problems that characterized South African society. As Giffard (unpublished: 48) points out, the NCPS paid scant attention to prisons:

> paradoxically if the NCPS is effective, it will diminish the possibilities for reform and transformation in prisons, as it will increase the ability of the police to detect and apprehend offenders, and the ability of the courts to process cases quickly ... what is obvious is the 'black box syndrome' in which the prison system is merely seen as a dumping ground for a criminal justice system that has its priorities elsewhere.

11 Personal communication from Graeme Simpson 2010.

12 Personal communication from Graeme Simpson 2010

13 Personal communication to the author 2011.

Empowerment and Neoliberalism

Just as crime prevention was democratized in the sense that it was now to benefit not only whites, but *everyone*, and it was also now *everyone's* responsibility to prevent crime, so too did the White Paper for Social Welfare envisage a

> departure from the old, expensive model of service delivery (which benefited a few) to a new model that seeks to empower individuals and communities so as to reach previously underserviced areas. (Department of Welfare 1996a: 19)

'Intersectoral collaboration' was the 'most important element' (Department of Welfare 1996a: 27) for the new 'community development' approach with its principles of 'community participation and control … and empowerment' (Department of Welfare 1996a: 26). This meant that 'if money [was] allocated for poverty alleviation programmes … the programme [had] to ultimately enable economic and social independence of beneficiaries' (Department of Welfare 1996a: 27). To this end the development of Small, Medium and Micro Enterprises (SMMEs) was encouraged, as was a 'policy of volunteerism' since, as was the case for crime, the 'government [could] never deliver on its own' (Department of Welfare 1996a: 27). This 'transition from welfare to social development' (Department of Welfare 2001: 6) was reflected in the name change that the department underwent in 2001, from the Department of Welfare to the Department of Social Development.

Because the South African state embraced elements of neoliberalism together with developmentalism and/or because neoliberalism is a pathway to developmentalism – the latter being a panacea for the rollback neoliberal policies of an earlier era – there was (and still is) a tension between an emphasis on growth, productivity and competitiveness and the need to effect social inclusion. This tension is characteristic of 'third way' governments which seek to legitimate their rule via the discourse of inclusion whilst at the same time adopting economic policies which result in exclusion (Marais 2001, 2011, Stenson 2001, Muehlebach 2007, Gillespie 2008, Terreblanche 2012). The post-apartheid state could not be seen to be supporting a blatant law-and-order approach but at the same time it was not prepared to over-promote long term social interventions, specifically those needed to address inequality, because this was politically unfeasible. The fact that restorative justice and 'morality' figure strongly in the NCPS is linked to this 'thirdwayism' because restorative justice is attractive to all parts of the political spectrum. It also resonates with the call to grassroots justice by left-wing activist organizations in South Africa in the 1980s and has definite links with the notion of people's power. Thus, the discursive links between development theory and neoliberalism centre around the notion of empowerment and draw on the radical participatory development theories of the 1960s and early 1970s with their stress on self-reliance and local empowerment (Marais 2011: 222).

Blaming apartheid for the 'serious breakdown of the moral infrastructure of our society' meant that South Africa needed 'reconstruction and development of the Soul' (Department of Safety and Security 1999: 9)[14] and the forging of a new morality, as part of nation building. This morality did not need to be constructed from scratch; instead it entailed a 'renewal process', a call to the past, to *ubuntu*, a recreating/reinvigorating of something that had once existed in 'traditional African cultures'. This entailed a continuation of the liberation struggle rhetoric since 'the movement' was based on a 'culture of high social and personal values, rooted in *ubuntu*, which were articulated repeatedly through the years of its growth' (ANC 1998, Rauch 2005). It also entailed a return to people's power in terms of a discourse that conveniently ignored the Stalinesque aberrations when people's power went wrong. As such it constituted an ideological legitimating device.

In South Africa *ubuntu* is also fused with neoliberalism because it is compatible with the neoliberal doctrine of absolving the state from the basic responsibilities of social provision (Marais 2011). As Ferguson (quoted in Marais 2011: 224) states: 'neoliberal motifs of 'empowerment' restyle the unemployed as 'micro-entrepreneurs'. Whereas in the past, employment was linked to legal residence, in the 'new' South Africa it is the moral citizen's duty to be active and to work, even if it is only in the part-time poorly paid sector or as an unpaid volunteer.

Rose's 'ethico-politics' of advanced liberalism and Muehlebach's 'ethical citizen' are useful concepts with which to frame this 'socialised actuarialism'[15] (O'Malley, 2004a: 268). Rose distinguishes between discipline, which 'individualizes and normalizes', bio-power, which 'collectivizes and socializes' and 'ethico-politics', which

> concerns itself with self-techniques necessary for responsible self-government and the relations between obligations to oneself and one's obligations to others. (Rose 1999: 188)

Muehlebach argues that 'ethical citizenship' is a configuration of citizenship that is shaped under neoliberal conditions. It is a means for the

> so-called 'social inclusion' of those citizens who linger at the margins of the 'active,' that is employed, population. With ethical citizenship, these populations are presented with a possibility of partaking in the collective good through new modes of participatory 'activity'. (Muehlebach 2007: 85)

14 Quoting from Mandela's opening address to Parliament in 1995.

15 A term that O'Malley uses to indicate the *sharing* of risk, as opposed to it being borne by individuals who exercise rational choice.

Brave New Past – Restorative Justice, Familialization and Social Crime Prevention

The NCPS specifically mentions restorative justice as a form of crime prevention, stating that

> A restorative justice system is one which seeks to encourage full rehabilitation, participation for juvenile offenders and where treatment is aimed at enabling the minor offender to avoid a life of crime. (Department of Safety and Security 1996a: 6–7)

It states that a justice system which provides a 'real role for victims' will function as a crime prevention device in the sense of imposing a more meaningful moral burden on offenders' (Department of Safety and Security 1996a: 66).

The South African Law Commission Discussion Paper on 'Community Dispute Resolution' referred to restorative justice as having:

> elements which echo indigenous African procedures. They echo the practice of *makgotla, inkundla, ibunga* and *imbizos* where members of the community directly participate in questions and decisions. These popular justice systems have evolved and their practices have been adapted to urban circumstances (South African Law Commission 1997).

In this way then restorative justice was Africanized and given credibility by being aligned with the notion of *ubuntu* and legitimated through its alleged links to past indigenous practices. It has also been incorporated into an overall neoliberal political rationality, which promotes state withdrawal from the provision of certain services.

Because of its flexible nature the notion of restorative justice has been appropriated by a range of political parties and can in fact legitimate a harsh/punitive outcome, especially when linked to victim satisfaction (Auckerman 2002: 77). Martel et al. (2011: 247) critique restorative justice for playing into the 'myth of the community being a zone of healing', yet in the early stages of risk assessment, the community is often considered to be a dangerous space. Even the conservative African Christian Democratic Party, which was against gay marriages and abortion and in favour of the death penalty, asked questions about whether the government was applying restorative justice principles in the criminal justice cluster (*Hansard* 2004c col: 418). Of course these questions always seemed to be asked in the context of child justice[16] and, to a large extent, politicians (including ANC MPs) conflated restorative justice with victims' rights. The NCPS also states that

16 See for example *Hansard* 2001c, cols: 4209–5840.

> Empowerment of victims is aimed at creating a greater role for victims in the criminal justice process … offenders are required to take responsibility for their actions and the victims satisfaction with the outcome becomes a benchmark for meaningful justice. (Department of Safety and Security, 1996a: 66, 1.9.2.3)

The family has been similarly romanticized in the new South Africa. 'Family-centred and community based services and programmes' (Department of Welfare 1995) are represented as being 'more appropriate, more integrative and potentially more cost effective' (Department of Welfare 1995: 5). A National Family Policy was developed (Department of Social Development 2002) and the family was central to the Moral Regeneration Movement (MRM). In fact during the 2002 parliamentary debate on Moral Regeneration, 'A call on South Africans to work together to restore the social fabric', the focus was on the family and its role in upholding the moral fabric of society (*Hansard* 2002a). As then Deputy President Zuma (*Hansard* 2001, col: 7826) stated:

> We cannot expect the police to be social workers, parents and everything. Their task is to help apprehend lawbreakers (that is, to act upon immoral behaviour) whereas ours is to ensure that there are less, or no, lawbreakers (that is, helping people to make ethical decisions from the start).

Since failure to discipline children within the family was a form of 'moral degeneration' (Gillespie 2008: 74) it was crucial that 'children, youth, women, families and older persons' contributed to the creation of 'an enabling and caring society' (Department of Welfare 1999: 22). Thus, the new paradigm of developmental, as opposed to dependent, social welfare services was based on the principles of 'empowerment, continuum of care, restorative justice and family preservation' (Department of Welfare 1999: 22). The state has thus, according to Gillespie (2008: 74), positioned the family 'as a central category of interpretation', thereby deploying the 'reified tropes of family values' in its construction of criminality as 'remediable through familial and moral intervention'.

Yet, the idea of the family being an inherently good alternative to the state is in and of itself a social construct with a particular history. Donzelot (1979: 58) wrote about how the 'liberalization and valorization' of the family that occurred at the end of the nineteenth century was not a 'triumph of modernity', not a 'profound mutation of sensibilities' (in Elias's civilizing sense) but a strategy of liberal government. In a similar way the familialization strategy in the new South Africa is both a site and technique of government. Although Donzelot was looking at nineteenth century France, his ideas are relevant to the 'newoliberal' South Africa where state strategies sought to govern welfare (and crime) through families. Thus existing State Maintenance Grants were 'revamped' and in order to qualify for grants 'care-givers' now had to register children with the Department of Home Affairs with immunization and 'health care monitoring' being done through the Department of Health programmes (Department of Welfare 1996a: 18).

Social crime prevention, 'aimed at reducing the socio-economic and environmental factors conducive to criminality through the targeting of particular causal factors conducive to crime' (Department of Safety and Security 1998: 44), was probably the most left of the NCPS crime prevention technologies and based on the 'socio-economic explanation' for crime. Yet it has hardly been implemented. The 2004 Annual Report of the SAPS referred to social crime prevention as being implemented through a focus on victims, and implementation of Programmes on Youth Crime Prevention Capacity Building, Prevention of Violence, and Local Crime Prevention Development. The last mentioned programme was based on the philosophy that the community had to 'take ownership of their situation' and it recognized 'the indigenous knowledge of communities during the conceptual phase of projects that address the root causes of crime and anti-social behaviour' (Department of Safety and Security 2004a: 14–15). This construction of social crime prevention was based on the premise that 'all levels of government and civil society must work together to combat crime', that 'law enforcement on its own' was not enough and that crime prevention also had to focus on victims and 'deal with people's fear of crime' (Department of Safety and Security 2004a: 14–15). As Janine Rauch has subsequently stated, one of the most serious problems of interpretation and implementation of the NCPS was that social crime prevention became misunderstood as *prevention of social crimes*: this focus on victims was a 'weird twist'[17] which had not been anticipated by the drafters.

Conclusion

The NCPS embraced an eclectic range of approaches to deal with crime in South Africa, including situational crime prevention (the management of opportunity structures through manipulations of the physical environment), social crime prevention, restorative justice and corporatism (a multi-agency approach). In doing so it amalgamated the amoral rational choice individual of situational crime prevention, who weighs up the costs and benefits and commits a crime only when the benefits outweigh the costs, with the construction of a moral post-apartheid quintessential South African. According to Rauch there are pragmatic reasons for the eclectic nature of the NCPS, particularly because it was the outcome of an inter-departmental process of writing. This is indeed the case but it is also important to note that interdepartmentalism is symptomatic of a neoliberal approach and eclecticism is always the result of unevenness, itself a feature of the variegated neoliberalization processes discussed in Chapter 1. Although Rauch notes that the NCPS was a blank slate insofar as there was no pre-existing crime prevention policy, in this chapter I have argued that there were clear contexts, rationalities and ways of thinking that framed the writing, the thinking, the final product and its implementation.

17 Personal communication 2011.

This chapter has tracked the concept of communitization and the rise of the term 'community' back to the 1970s and 1980s when it started to be used more frequently in official discourse. I have argued that community policing has precursors in both the democratic movement, in overseas consultants, international trends and also in the apartheid government's neoliberal turn. As the South African state started to neoliberalize in the late 1970s, so too did the term 'community' start to be appear more frequently in state discourse and there was a distinctive embracing of community-based crime prevention in official criminology. This turn to community, or 'co-operative governance', continued and became entrenched after the first democratic elections and is one of the hallmarks of governance in democratizing South Africa. It is precisely because 'community', the 'social', the 'family', *ubuntu* and restorative justice are flexible and seemingly unproblematic, neutral, wholesome-sounding concepts that they are attractive to and appropriated by people on different ends of the political spectrum. Because of this they can be used in diverse ways to underpin varying political rationalities.

Although the NCPS does identify poverty and underdevelopment, the historic marginalization of youth and gender inequality as being some of the 'historical factors' which contributed to South Africa's high crime rate and social crime prevention is, to some extent, aimed at making interventions beyond the narrow ambit of the criminal justice system – in the socio-economic sphere – it is still a markedly apolitical and managerial document. There is no in-depth examination of criminalization, of the power relations that constitute criminality and the construction of crime, no attempt to understand the history and status of South African criminology in political terms, no attempt to see how the construction of the problem of crime impacts on the policies adopted to deal with it, or to locate criminological theory in the broader political economy of the South African state. Instead, crime itself is a taken for granted construct, social control institutions such as prisons are not subjected to historical scrutiny and the salience of class, race and gender as political determinants of enforcement are largely ignored.

The fact that political programmes are influenced by broader governmental strategies, such as developmentalism and neoliberalism, and are always uneven, negotiated and hence incompletely implemented, results in the partial 'installation of the appropriate techniques' (O'Malley 1992: 259). This explains the eclecticism of the NCPS and indeed, as I argue in this book, the eclecticism that characterizes penality in South Africa.

Chapter 6
Punishment and the Body[1]

> As soon as power gave itself the function of administering life, its reason for being and the logic of its exercise and not the awakening of humanitarian feelings made it more and more difficult to apply the death penalty. How could power exercise its prerogatives by putting people to death when its main role was to ensure, sustain and multiply life, to put this life in order? (Foucault 1980: 74)

Introduction

In 1992 the ANC stated that 'our crime problems are *NOT* being solved by large-scale imprisonment' and that 'however much one condemns those deeds' the state response should show compassion for the perpetrator (ANC 1992b: 7, emphasis in the original). Yet despite its support of people's justice, its pro-poor stance, explicit pronouncements on the degrading nature of imprisonment (Sachs 1982: 14) and the latter's inability to solve South Africa's crime problems (ANC 1992b: 14),[2] once it became the ruling party the ANC did not adopt a programme of progressive penal reform. Instead, and notwithstanding the prison's strong associations with the punitive apartheid regime, long-term imprisonment has actually increased under an ANC government. Thus, between 1996 and 2003 the incarceration rate in South Africa rose from 280 to 402 per 100,000. Between 2001 and 2003, the number of people serving sentences of 10 years or more grew by almost 35 per cent (Gordon 2006: 259). By 2000, sentences of 7 to 10 years, 10 to 15 years, 15 to 20 years and 20 years to life had increased by 50 per cent, 67 per cent, 70 per cent and 124 per cent respectively. The longest sentences were, in other words, increasing the most (South African Law Commission 2000).

In Chapter 4 I argued that despite the fact that the different political programmes adopted by the apartheid and post-apartheid governments were grounded in, and

1 This chapter is an amalgamated version of two articles (Super 2011 and Super 2011b) which were published in the *British Journal of Criminology* and *Theoretical Criminology* respectively.

2 It is significant that the Freedom Charter, despite the fact that it dates back to the 1950s, was still regarded as a central document in the 1990s (ANC 1990b: 29). It promised a situation where imprisonment would only be for 'serious crimes against the people', aimed at 'at re-education, not vengeance' in terms of an overall framework which was represented as being 'completely in harmony with the wider goals of a socialist South Africa' (Suttner and Cronin 1986: 250).

drew on, distinctive ideologies, social contexts, 'discursive resources' (Garland 1985: 152), goals and technologies they targeted the same categories – poor black and coloured males, black foreigners and drug users. This chapter traces the ways in which the transition to democracy has ushered in a shift from punishing these categories via the infliction of physical punishment (hangings and whippings) to an increase in the use of long-term imprisonment and the reinvention of rehabilitation. I track the shift from physically violating an offender's body to deprivation of liberty and the discursive justifications for this.

Penality under apartheid was a complex entity, which embraced at least some of the tenets of liberalism. Even though there is no doubt that the apartheid regime deployed repressive punishment practices, particularly against black people, the death penalty being a prime example, this 'evil beast' was not a static monolithic entity. One of the liberal features of apartheid penality was the fact that, for the most part, the judicial process was employed. In this chapter I argue that the punishment regime under the Nationalist Party (NP) government also reformed, liberalized if you will, from the 1970s on. Thus, for example, the 1982 Internal Security Bill, although draconian, abolished mandatory minimum sentence provisions. In addition the courts were given more sentencing discretion, the death penalty was limited to acts of violence and juveniles were afforded greater protection from ordinary adult punishment. This liberalization, limited as it was, was accompanied by an increase in imprisonment and a lengthening of prison sentences, a trend that has continued under the post-apartheid state. One might therefore ask whether there is some intimate relationship between democracy and imprisonment and whether, like Foucault, we could view the ascendancy of the prison in the 'new' South Africa as part of a subtle (or not so subtle) repressive social control apparatus of the modernizing South African state.

1976–89 (Reform of Verwoerdian Apartheid)

The 'uniqueness' of South Africa, harnessed to arguments of racial superiority, was used to justify racially differentiated punishments, including the death penalty. The official line was that South Africa was a 'heterogenous' society which consisted of different races which were at different stages of development. 'Whipping' was 'something that Africans ... understand' (*Hansard* 1977b cols: 3275) and hanging was also deemed to be an appropriate punishment given the 'unsophisticated' nature of the majority of the population (*Hansard* 1977b: col: 4392). This differentiation also played out in the prisons, where prisoners were divided into 'whites', 'Bantu', 'Asians' and 'coloureds' and distinctions started at the very basic level of the types of bedding that were made available.[3]

3 Even in 1988 at Pollsmoor prison, 538 whites had 'beds with mattresses and bedding' and only 23 had felt mats with bedding. 787 coloureds had 'beds with mattresses and bedding' whereas 3,394 had the inferior combined sisal and felt mats with bedding.

Corporal Punishment

The Viljoen Commission of Inquiry heralded a definite liberalization of the criminal justice system, strongly criticizing mandatory minimum sentences and calling for pre-sentence reports, assistance by psychologists, social welfare workers and other experts prior to the court passing sentence. It also recommended that urgent attention be paid to the investigation of community-based alternatives to imprisonment and that there should be diversion, as opposed to imprisonment, for pass law infringements. The Commission recommended that corporal punishment should be curtailed to a maximum number of five strokes administered no more than twice and only for violent offences or in defiance of 'lawful' authority. It supported its retention, on the grounds that African witnesses were unanimous in their support for it (Midgley 1982: 401).

The government did not implement all of the Commission's recommendations in respect of corporal punishment because of the 'great faith' that many black South Africans had in it (Minister of Justice quoted in Midgley 1982: 402). It did, however, in the 1977 Criminal Procedure Act, reduce the maximum age at which corporal punishment could be imposed, from 50 to 30 years, reduce the number of strokes that could be imposed, from ten to seven, and provide that adults could only be whipped on two occasions. The latter provision did not apply to juveniles. There was thus a decline in the use of whipping as a mode of punishment for adult offenders (D'Olieveira and D'Olieveira 1983). In an attempt to 'humanize' this punishment the Criminal Procedure Act also stated that juveniles had to be whipped over their clothing, as opposed to their bare buttocks. Between 1985 and 86, 164 whites were sentenced to corporal punishment coupled with imprisonment, 648 coloureds, 8 Indians and 1,553 blacks. Whites who were sentenced to only corporal punishment numbered 1,730, coloureds 13,875, Indians 468 and blacks 22,389 (*Hansard* 1990a: question 32: cols 129–30). The fact that far more offenders were sentenced to corporal punishment alone, than to corporal punishment coupled with imprisonment, was indicative of the court's attempt to use it as a means to avoid a sentence of imprisonment.

The NP government supported the imposition of corporal punishment by informal courts set up by 'tribal' or 'homeland' representatives in the townships. Known as *makgotla*, these courts settled disputes based on purported 'indigenous law'. Presented as voluntary and progressive, as part of the 'black man's' heritage, *makgotla* bolstered the neoliberal state reform project of providing limited self-government to blacks. Another reason for encouraging the punishment and control of 'young hooligans and criminals' by traditional authorities was because, in the

Only 128 blacks had 'beds with mattresses and bedding' and 933 slept on sisal and felt mats. At Modderbee prison where there were no whites at all only 119 blacks had the 'luxury' style bedding (i.e. mattresses) whereas 4,000 had sisal and felt mats (*Hansard* 1988a, question 870, col: 1300).

post-Soweto era, these two groups posed great challenges to the apartheid regime. As one NP MP stated:

> It really is necessary for young hooligans like those in our Black residential areas to be dealt with in a traditional way ... parents prefer to take the children to the makgotla, instead of to the police, because ... the punishment is much more effective. The makgotla gives the uncontrollable boy or tsotsi a thorough thrashing – as they put it: 25 strokes without counting. (*Hansard* 1977g, col: 11251)

Since probation services were used on a token basis for the black offender (Brown 1985: 53), corporal punishment served as a form of diversion from prison sentences. As such the body was a major site of punishment in respect of the young black juvenile offender and by the early 1990s the state was carrying out more than 32,000 whippings per year on young people (Harcourt-Baldwin 1981, Skelton 2005). In a country where whites were a distinct minority it was telling that in 1978 there were only 618 'Non-White social workers' – 83 Indian, 233 coloured and 302 black – as opposed to 3,000 white social workers (*Hansard* 1978b, col: 6897). Given the policy of 'canalization' in terms of which social workers had to be of the same race as their clients, this explains the total lack of probation services for blacks and the disparity in treatment between the different races. Because white probation officers lacked the knowledge of the 'black man', it was 'unscientific' to think that white volunteers or probation officers could work in coloured or black communities. These communities had to take responsibility for themselves. This was the justification for the 1986 Probation Services Amendment Act being made applicable to whites only, the rationale being that probation services could only succeed in a 'developed' community (*Hansard* 1986–7, col: 1138).

In 1986 the Criminal Procedure Act was amended to provide for community service. The Act also stipulated that an adult could not be sentenced to a whipping in addition to imprisonment unless the whole or part of the imprisonment was suspended. This package of alternatives to imprisonment was presented as a means of decreasing the population of the prison, about which the state was becoming increasingly concerned. However, the introduction of community-based sentences was coupled with a widening of the offences for which corporal punishment could be imposed, to include arson, public violence, sedition and malicious damage to property. At the same time bestiality and homosexual acts were removed from the list of offences for which an adult could be whipped. Quite clearly this new list of corporally punishable offences was intended to deal with offences against public order in a climate of intensified political unrest (Corpun 2005). A similar thing had occurred in 1976 and 1977 when many black schoolchildren were whipped for participating in the widespread political resistance of the time, including the Soweto uprising (Institute of Race Relations, cited in Midgley 1982: 402).

Rehabilitation and the Prison

Contrary to official representations of it rehabilitation is not a scientific formula or a concept set in stone, but instead, a moving resultant in a field of relational practices. As such the different treatment regimes and justifications for imprisonment of blacks, whites, coloureds and Asians, were both constituted by and constitutive of broader ideological discursive shifts that were taking place in South Africa from the late 1970s.

Work and rehabilitation The ideological justification for imprisonment in the case of black men was the connection between work and rehabilitation and in fact the definition of rehabilitation contained in the 1959 Prisons Act was:

> as far as practical to apply such treatment and training to convicted prisoners as may lead to their reform and rehabilitation and to train them in habits of industry and labour. (1959 Prisons Act, s. 2, author's emphasis)

During the era of Verwoerdian apartheid, when there was a need for cheap unskilled labour, the ideology that pass law offenders could be rehabilitated through work could fit, because of the need for unskilled labourers. Once in prison, pass law offenders were recycled into a constantly replenishing trove of 'usable delinquents' (Bright 1996: 295). The problem that they constituted drew attention to the category of crimes engendered by the pass laws and established a high watermark against the 'deviant other' – the layabout lazy black person who had to be taught the benefits of labour and how to become a good worker. As such the prison aimed to support other institutions, such as the farm colonies established in terms of the 1945 Blacks Urban Areas Consolidation Act. These colonies served as repositories for those declared to be 'idle and undesirable' in terms of s. 29 of the Act, where they could 'learn habits of diligence and industry' (Department of Justice, Police and Prisons 1980: 14). Thus, the category of 'idle and undesirable' that was pinned onto a black person who needed 'rehabilitation' translated into a drive to produce a steady supply of cheap labour. Once in prison black people were, for the most part, not 'treated' at all. In 1979, there were 71 white social workers to service 5,649 white prisoners; four coloured social workers for 36,577 coloured prisoners; and 23 black social workers for 194,735 black prisoners.

Release on parole was not confined to long-term prisoners, but was also used in the large-scale release of short-term prisoners (the majority of whom were pass law offenders) and was conditional on short-term contracts of employment being entered into (Sloth-Nielson 1986: 31). In 1979, the Minister of Prisons stated that although 90,000 people were sentenced to terms of imprisonment of one to four months, the reality was that they never all landed up in prison: where there were employers who were looking for short-term workers, these prisoners were immediately placed on parole. It was only 'recidivists' who served their full sentences (*Hansard* 1979b). This type of release took place within 48 hours of being sentenced and was called 'parole' because on an ideological level, the government had to justify the imprisonment and release of pass law offenders, the notion being that work would rehabilitate them (Sloth-Nielson 1986: 31). Thus, the discourse on parole 'forged conceptual links' (Bright 1996) between what was done (or not done) to prisoners inside the prison and the perception of who the criminals were on the outside (i.e. pass law offenders), what should be done to them (what punishment they deserved, i.e. work) and how the 'criminal' problem could be contained. As the Minister of Justice, Police and Prisons stated in 1978:

> I do not believe there is any better form of rehabilitation than to have a man work with his hands in the soil … As soon as a Black prisoner is released after having learnt to work on a prison farm, he is snatched up and appointed as foreman on a farm. The reason is that he has been properly trained in that type of work. Thus we have various projects in progress to train people … Some of the prisoners are trained in kitchen work, and as waiters, etc. As soon as they are released, those prisoners are snatched up by the hotels. We are almost unable to keep up with the work of rehabilitation. (*Hansard* 1978c. col: 7158–9)

In this way, then, criminalization and imprisonment were inextricably linked to apartheid's labour policies and needs.

Shifts In the 1980s there was a distinctive embracing of a rehabilitative approach at the same time as political discourse was deracializing. There was a purported shift in the treatment regime, to a more specialized 'team approach', with the replacement of Prison Boards by Release Boards and the establishment of Institutional Committees. Custodial staff would now be involved in the treatment of prisoners, the justification being to bring in 'a new dimension' of 'greater sympathy and involvement' (Department of Justice 1981: 48). The fact that the 1982–83 Annual Report had a much more in depth section on medical treatment available in prison covering optometric, dental, infants and confinements is indicative of a shift in the treatment regime to one which purported to be more caring and inclusive. In 1983 more privileges were extended to prisoners: they were allowed more visits and for longer and increased amounts of money were permitted for purchases. The 1986–87 Annual Report followed a different format from previous reports and, for the first time, there were statistics on the age groups of prisoners in custody as well as tables: on the number of social workers, auxiliary workers, social work services, educational services and classification of prisoners. These new figures were generated by the centralization of statistical updating and indicated a greater level of analysis than before. They also produced new categories and subjects of knowledge.

In the 1982 debate on the Prisons Amendment Bill, an NP MP stated that 'we have moved away from penal measures as retaliatory measures or deterrents' (*Hansard* 1982e, col: 3610) and that, as such, prisons were becoming more rehabilitational. In an attempt to depoliticize the status of those who were incarcerated because of having threatened the political order, the Minister of Justice and Prisons conceded that 'security' prisoners could earn remission. He stated that since security prisoners enjoyed no status above that of other criminals, they would now be treated 'in a way which takes factors such as security and treatment into consideration' and would be able to earn 'mitigation of punishment on an individual basis' (*Hansard* 1982f, col: 1001). They were no longer to be detained on a centralized, but on a decentralized basis, and only those with a 'good prognosis' who could show that they had 'turned their backs on crime' would be considered for remission. Yet in June 1987, at the height of the State of Emergency, the Minister of Justice announced that those who were guilty of acts of violence were not entitled to parole (*Hansard* 1987b, col: 2863). At the same time, renunciation of violence was regarded as an indication of rehabilitation and this applied especially to political prisoners. When Mandela was released in 1990, the state tried to present what was obviously a political decision as a rehabilitational/advisory release board issue. This flip-flopping vacillating construction of the multiple meanings of rehabilitation is indicative of the linkages between the carceral and the political realms (Simon 2000).

By 1988, the concept of 'behavior modification', rather than treatment, became the dominant theory governing prisons, with the discourse of rehabilitation being incorporated into that of 'reintegration', the new buzzword. On admission, prisoners were no longer observed in an observation centre. Instead, they were given a 'standardized and weighted questionnaire' (Department of Justice 1987: 62) and then classified as maximum or medium. This was presented as being consistent, cost-effective, objective and conducive to scientific research. Thus, science and safe custody were interwoven with each other. The offender was no longer seen as emotionally ill, but as responsible (Naude 1988b: 108). Privileges were decoupled from security classification and made conditional on 'behaviour, adaptation, discipline and co-operation' (Department of Justice 1987: 63) so that prisoners could be 'motivated to ensure co-operation and good behaviour' (Department of Justice 1987: 64).

Hanging by the Neck until Dead

The report of the 1947 Lansdown Commission on Penal and Prison Reform stated that the death penalty was necessary because the 'majority of South Africa's population had not yet emerged from a state of barbarism' (cited in Turrel 2004: 87). It was mandatory for certain offences, unless the court found extenuating circumstances.

According to a 1982 study on the exercise of discretion by judges in deciding on extenuating circumstances, between 1971 and 1979 only 8 per cent of 'tipplers' received the death sentence whereas 28 per cent of cannabis users did (Olmesdahl 1982). Where the victim was white the 'risk of death verdict' was 68 per cent, with an Asian victim it was 50 per cent and in respect of black victims it was only 13 per cent (Olmesdahl 1982: 209). This was evidence that black lives did not have quite the same value as whites and that black violence was largely ignored by the state, unless it threatened the public order – then it was classified as 'unrest' and took on a whole new meaning and significance.[4] The chances of the death sentence, where the victim was a casual acquaintance or co-employee, were 16 per cent, but this rose to 34 per cent where the victim was a stranger, thus reinforcing the stereotypical image of black stranger danger (Turrel 2004, Olmesdahl 1982). Half of the death sentences were imposed where the motive of the accused was theft (Olmesdahl 1982: 212) – a crime that was committed more by poor blacks than middle class 'tippling' whites.

Capital punishment in South Africa was also used as a tool to control and punish opponents of apartheid, particularly in respect of accused members of banned liberation movements (Holt 1989: 298). Thus, for example in 1983, the execution of three convicted ANC combatants was timed to coincide with the seventh anniversary of the Soweto uprising. 1,219 people were executed during the ten-year period between 1980 and 1989 and 1,842 death sentences were handed down (Davis and le Roux 2009: 127). In 1987, a new category of death row prisoners was created: those prisoners who were sentenced to death for 'political unrest' between 1984 and 1986, and 164 people were executed – a substantial increase from 115 in 1984. These penalties were imposed at a time when political resistance was at its peak and the country was subject to a State of Emergency.

Despite the fact that in 1987 the death sentence was at an all-time high, 42 per cent of those convicted were reprieved by the State President (*Hansard* 1990c, col: 111612) and, although the first politically related crimes went to the gallows in September 1987, the decrease started thereafter: in 1988 117 were executed and this dropped to 53 in 1989. A close reading of the 1988 *Hansard* (1988a) reveals that many questions were asked in Parliament about the manner in which hangings were carried out and reprieves rose from 18 in 1987 to 49 in 1988 and 63 in 1989. This represented the first time that the number of reprieves exceeded the number of executions (Devenish 1992: 13). The last execution took place on 14 November 1989.

The ANC and Bodily Punishment

The ANC is generally presented as being opposed to the death penalty (Shubane 2001), yet, just as the apartheid government used the death penalty as a tool for controlling political threats from the liberation movement, so too did the ANC use execution as a tool to control those who committed treason against the movement (ANC 1985, Sachs 1986).

4 See Ayers (1984: 231) who, writing about the nineteenth century American South, refers to a police officer referring to three classes of homicide: 'If a nigger kills a white man, that's murder. If a white man kills a nigger, that's justifiable homicide. If a nigger kills another nigger, that's one less nigger.'

The harshness of ANC rule in exile, particularly in the camps, has traditionally been underplayed as a function of keeping discipline and dealing with the threat posed by the apartheid forces (Alexander and Kynoch 2011). This perspective obscures the fact that the ANC engaged in some distinctively punitive practices against deviants (Alexander and Kynoch 2011, Machava 2011). The way that necklacing by young militant activists in black South African townships was tacitly condoned is also indicative of a punitive strand running through the ANC, and those who acted in its name, during the liberation struggle (Kynoch 2011).

The 1981 campaign against *dagga* smoking is one such example. In 1981, Moses Mabhida, head of the Revolutionary Council in Angola, blamed *dagga* smoking in the camps on the apartheid regime, stating that 'the chief aim of the apartheid government was to corrupt our people and introduce bad morals' (quoted in Ngculu 2009: 161). Because of this he declared war against those found 'sneaking out of the camps in search of dagga, or those found to be smoking dagga' (Ngculu 2009: 161) and camp security was given orders to shoot people caught leaving the camp without permission. Offenders were tied to a tree as part of their punishment or they were locked in a windowless container. A number of offenders were severely beaten by the Angolan Regional Command, resulting in some of them dying (Ngculu 2009, Skweyiya et al. 1992).

There were communal and isolation cells at Quatro Camp in Angola, also known as Camp 32 and the Morris Seabelo Rehabilitation Centre. The name 'Quatro' itself comes from the Johannesburg Fort Prison known as Number 4 (Kynoch 2011: 407). The communal cells were overcrowded and inadequately ventilated and there was a lack of adequate health care, with a doctor visiting the camp only rarely. Blankets could be washed only once every six months and detainees bathed in the left-over water. Toilets consisted of plastic buckets cut in half and emptied once per day. Food deprivation was frequently used as form of punishment. Those punished performed hard labour which consisted mainly of felling trees, chopping wood, breaking stones, digging trenches and hauling water in a cart. The latter was regarded as extremely unfair by detainees, given that the camp had no running water and they were required to fetch water and run with the cart uphill (Skweyiya et al. 1992). Ngculu (2009: 160) refers to instances where 'comrades' had to don a heavy overcoat and stand in the centre of the camp in the burning sun for the whole day and how severe punishment was imposed on those found drinking or drunk or who had slipped out of camp to find alcohol.

The foregoing exposition is not intended to be an exhaustive or in-depth catalogue of human rights abuses in the camps, merely to show that by constructing certain behaviours as counter-revolutionary, and hence deviant, the ANC excommunicated wrongdoers and imposed punitive punishments. Thus, in constructing cannabis smokers as 'counter-revolutionary' they were subjected to cruel punishments, justified in the name of the struggle against apartheid. This was contrary to the wholesome words of the Freedom Charter and the inclusive notion of people's power and the ANC morality that struggle idealists believed in. It also contained the seeds of the punitive forms of penality that the ANC would come to adopt in the 'new' South Africa. The division between politics and criminality that became apparent after 1994 did in fact have some precursors in liberation struggle constructions of the 'counter-revolutionary'. As Alexander and Kynoch (2011: 410) point out, just as liberatory projects lauded as reformist could become instruments of repression so too could projects intended to be liberatory become tyrannical.

1989–94 (Transitioning into the 'New' South Africa)

Human Rights and the Crime Crackdown

On 2 February 1990 FW De Klerk, then State President, announced that mandatory capital punishment was to be removed from the statute book. The list of offences for which the death penalty could be imposed was restricted and it could no longer be imposed for 'housebreaking with aggravating circumstances'. Death row prisoners were now also afforded an automatic right of appeal (Davis and Le Roux 2009: 128). This scaling down, an attempt to humanize and civilize through the killing of fewer people, was presented by the Nationalist Party (NP) as part of an evolutionary 'civilizing process' (*Hansard* 1990c, col: 11185). It resulted in 105 people being sentenced to death between July 1990 and March 1992 as opposed to 406 in the corresponding period in the previous two years. The 'constitutional state objective' (Department of Justice 1992: 25) was later extended to include a moratorium on executions. The recommendation made by South African Law Commission in the 'Interim Report on Group and Human Rights' was that the death penalty be 'depoliticized' and dealt with by the future Constitutional Court. This resulted in a suspension of executions as of 27 March 1991 (Department of Justice 1992: 10). The University of South Africa's department of Criminal and Procedural Law referred to the reform as being 'motivated by a genuine concern for the interests of criminal justice and of South Africa as a whole' (*Hansard* 1990c, col: 11595).

There was much discussion in parliamentary debates about how to legitimate the justice system via the appointment of assessors and lay people to courts. The consistent statement was that although 'people's courts were being rejected there was a need for "small claims" courts and alternative structures for meting out justice' (MP Koornhof *Hansard* 1991b, col: 8054). The state, in other words, was seeking an alternative to the ANC's version of informal justice, referred to in the previous chapter. In the debate on the 1991 Decriminalization bill the Deputy Minister of Justice stated that

> the imposition of punishment by the courts is a serious matter that ought to be reserved solely for those offences which pose a danger to the community or are morally blameworthy. Whenever punishment is imposed by the courts too

> readily in other instances, this can not only undermine the authority of the court, but also cheapen the criminal sanction. (*Hansard* 1991c, col: 9023)

He stated that 'it's accepted worldwide that a prison sentence alone, as a method of curbing crime, has failed' (*Hansard* 1991c, col: 8123) and the argument was that a 'state of over-criminalization' would have an adverse effect on the efficacy of the criminal justice system (*Hansard* 1991c, col: 9023). Yet in practice decriminalization was reserved mainly for traffic offences.

In contrast to this liberalization there was also a concurrent shift towards making bail more stringent, a lengthening of prison sentences and greater restriction of parole. In 1992 the Minister of Justice referred to 'new and fresh ideas on the abuse of bail and the fact that it is granted too readily … coming from all over' (*Hansard* 1992a, col: 5719). Even the liberal opposition Democratic Party (DP) complained about the ease with which bail was granted, and one MP suggested looking at the USA where high bail was set for serious offences (*Hansard* 1992a, col: 5682). Tony Leon, a Democratic Party MP, who later became the leader of the Democratic Alliance, referred to a 'scourge of violent crimes' and recommended a minimum sentence for offences committed with firearms. In May 1992 the penal jurisdiction of the Magistrates Court was increased from R4,000 to R20,000 and the Regional Court from R40,000 to R200,000. The 1992 Criminal Procedure Second Amendment Act introduced strict measures to deal with 'unrest related' and other forms of violent crime. The Attorney General could now issue a certificate to restrict bail and minimum penalties were introduced for the use of automatic weapons. The 1982 Intimidation Act was also broadened such that there was no longer a need to prove actual intimidation in order to find someone guilty of the offence of intimidation.

The 1992 Drugs and Drug Trafficking Act introduced a 25 year maximum sentence for dealing in drugs as well as search and seizure provisions and evidential presumptions which were loaded against the accused (*Hansard* 1992f). This followed on the 1990 Abuse of Dependence Producing Substances Act, which provided for heavier penalties in order to 'combat the drug menace, and heed the public's call for firmer action against drug offenders' (*Hansard* 1990d, col: 10736). Yet the 1992 Prevention and Treatment of Drug Dependency Act split the 1971 Act into two laws – the one dealing with criminal matters and the other seeking to 'decriminalize' the preventative and treatment aspects of drug dependence through 'a more humane medico-scientific preventative and treatment process' (*Hansard* 1992b, cols: 1013–14). As such, the move to liberalization/softening was coupled with harsher pro-minimum sentencing, drug and bail reforms, in terms of a type of bifurcated approach which intensified in the post-apartheid era.

Whereas in 1990, despite rising crime rates, the Department of Correctional Services had suggested shorter sentences and the greater use of parole as solutions to overpopulation, by 1993 parole was more difficult to obtain (Department of Correctional Services, 1993). This was partly in response to public anger over 'special remissions' of sentence.[5] The March 1993 White Paper abolished remission and provided that, in future, prisoners had to serve their whole sentence, albeit not necessarily in prison. The new credit system, introduced on the grounds that it was more due process-orientated, made it more difficult to obtain parole because it did away with automatic remission of sentences. The White Paper also introduced a new disciplinary system that did away with corporal punishment and dietary deprivation as penalties. Prison offences were now to be dealt with by the Institutional Committees in terms of a system based on 'natural justice'. Nevertheless, this very 'fairness' resulted in fewer releases, contributing to overcrowded prisons and widespread dissatisfaction amongst prisoners. Thus, ironically, with the advent of democracy, early release on parole became, with the greater regulation that ensued, more difficult to obtain and prisons became more overcrowded than under apartheid.

1994–2004 (Consolidating the 'New' South Africa)

Ubuntu and the Body

The Constitutional Court abolished the death penalty in a judgement delivered in 1995 in the case of *Makwanyane*.[6] It is a very important case not least because the judges drew a line between the past and the future in terms of the constitutional rupture. Davis and Le Roux (2009: 120) describe its significance as follows:

> Certain lawsuits transcend their facts and assume an importance far beyond the immediate dispute because of their significance for society at large. *State v Makwanyane* was such a case. Not only was it the first case chosen for hearing by the new Constitutional Court, but *Makwanyane* represented a foundational moment, a line drawn in the sands of South Africa's history marking the start of a new legal era.

The court, consisting of 11 judges, unanimously rejected the death penalty as being against South Africa's constitutional principles and in so doing it relied extensively on the notion of *ubuntu*.[7] Yet *ubuntu* is a type of slippery catch-all concept as evidenced by the slightly different nuances that each judge gave when interpreting and defining the concept.

5 Applied in the case of 'common law' offenders: by 31 December 1994, 27,511 prisoners had benefited from the special remission.

6 *S v T Makwanyane and M Mchunu* Case No. CCT/3/94, delivered on 6 June 1995.

7 See however Davis and Le Roux (2009), who criticize the judgement on the grounds that the judges relied more on consequentialist arguments that the death penalty was not effective rather than rendering it unconstitutional on the basis that offended against South Africa's basic values and the notion of *ubuntu*.

Judge Chaskalson stated that 'Retribution ought not to be given undue weight in the balancing process' (para 130) and specifically referred to the 'commitment' contained in the Interim Constitution that:

> The adoption of this Constitution lays the secure foundation for the people of South Africa to transcend the divisions and strife of the past, which generated gross violations of human rights, the transgression of humanitarian principles in violent conflicts and a legacy of hatred, fear, guilt and *revenge*. These can now be addressed on the basis that there is a need for understanding but *not for vengeance*, a need for reparation but *not for retaliation*, a need for *ubuntu* but *not for victimisation*. (Emphasis supplied) (para 130)

Mokgoro translated it as '*humaneness ... as personhood* and *morality*' (para 308), a type of Durkheimian metaphor for the collective conscience, of the 'rainbow heritage':

> While it envelops the key values of group solidarity, compassion, respect, human dignity, conformity to basic norms and collective unity, in its fundamental sense it denotes humanity and morality. Its spirit emphasises respect for human dignity, marking a shift from confrontation to conciliation.

Sachs traced out an African/indigenous jurisprudence that linked the principles of *ubuntu* with a humane justice system – one that did not endorse the use of death as a form of punishment. As he stated:

> It is a distressing fact that our law reports and legal textbooks contain few references to African sources as part of the general law of the country. (para 371)

Judge Langa described *ubuntu* as being a 'culture' which emphasized communality and regulated 'the exercise of rights by the emphasis it lays on sharing and co-responsibility' (para 224). He also regarded it as supporting a 'reformative theory' of punishment so 'that the person may, at a certain stage, become a normal law-abiding and useful member of the community once again' (para 242). Thus, a 'necessary consequence of its application' entailed that the offender had to be imprisoned for a long period for the purpose of rehabilitation', ceasing to be a 'danger to society' by 'treatment and training' (para 243). In this way then the Constitutional Court bought into the ideology of rehabilitation via imprisonment and perceived it as being consonant with *ubuntu*, albeit for the purposes of avoiding death. Thus, the effect of the Court's use of *ubuntu* has been to substitute, and indeed to justify, long prison sentences, instead of hanging by the neck until dead. A similar thing happened in the USA where the unintended consequence of the American rights revolution was that the courts started to impose longer sentences and became more willing to send offenders to prison, once they were perceived to be 'cleaner, safer and better administered' (Gottschalk 2006: 215).

As argued in the previous chapter the 1997 South African Law Commission 'Discussion Paper on *Community Dispute Resolution* allied *ubuntu* with *restorative justice*. Wilson critiques it for presenting the 'traditional' institutions of *ubuntu*, *makgotla*, *inkundla*, *ibunga* and *imbizos* 'in the populist terms of a relatively benign African nationalism', as 'always-already there' elements of a sanitized tribal past (quoted in Lenta 2001: 179). Yet African nationalism is not necessarily benign and neither are indigenous practices. Nor are 'indigenous' practices necessarily 'indigenous', having been superimposed by colonialism and reinterpreted and given a truth by cases such as *Makwanyane* and indeed the Truth and Reconciliation Commission itself.[8] The Constitutional Court in *S v Williams*[9] also gave credence to the notion of a shift from retribution to rehabilitation and a move towards greater humanism. In ruling that corporal punishment of juveniles was unconstitutional, it referred to the introduction of correctional supervision as being a 'milestone in the process of "humanising" the criminal justice system' which 'assisted in the shift of emphasis from retribution to rehabilitation' (para 67). The 1997 Abolition of Corporal Punishment Act abolished judicial corporal punishment and provided that any law which authorized corporal punishment by a court of law, including a court of traditional leaders, was repealed to the extent that it authorized such punishment.

Ubuntu thus legitimates the law in the 'new' South Africa, being evidence of its transformation, whilst at the same time being recognized and hailed, and brought into operation, by the law itself. Wilson (1996) states that *ubuntu* is a politically loaded 'polysemous ideological concept' rather than an 'accurate' historical construct (cited in Lenta 2001: 179). It also legitimates long term imprisonment by providing its justification insofar as it imbues it with an ethos of restorative justice. As such, it serves as a technology of bio-power in the sense that it has the potential to 'homogenise, normalise, elicit consensus and exclude' (Lenta 2001: 179). Foucault's (1979) observations about the increasing trend towards the abolition of the death penalty in Western societies being driven not by a drive to greater humanism, but as being a means to punish better, to be more effective, is thus also relevant in a non-Western context.

The Harsher Side of Democracy

Background noise Even in 1994, in the euphoric aftermath of the first democratic elections, when national discourse was peppered with restorative justice style words and phrases such as 'healing', 'reconciliation', 'reparation', 'transcending', 'restoring honor and dignity', 'regaining our humanity' and 'validation' (Skelton

8 See Sanders (2000), who writes about how the act of listening to victims was carefully structured by the Truth and Reconciliation Commission and how the 'truth' was judiciously withheld as a label for these voices.

9 S v Williams and Others (CCT20/94) [1995] ZACC 6; 1995 (3) SA 632; 1995 (7) BCLR 861 (CC) (9 June 1995).

2005: 375–6) all parties called for a tough approach to crime, from the far right Freedom Front, to the middle-of-the-road Democratic Party (DP) to the left-wing Pan African Congress (PAC).

By 1996 the ANC government was being accused of being incapable of governing on multiple fronts – not just crime – and the economy was also perceived to be lagging. Thus, for example on 1 March 1996 the South African Foundation (representing South Africa's 50 biggest companies) unveiled its 'Growth for All Plan', which called for a 'leaner government, anti-crime strategies, and privatization' (Johnson 2009: 73). This made the ANC government ultra-defensive: it had to show the public that it was doing something and that things were better than under apartheid.

It should be remembered that, thanks to the 'sunset' clause, Sydney Mufamadi, the first minister of Safety and Security, inherited 120,000 police from the old regime. These officials had no democratic tradition (Laufer 2001: 16–17) and were ineffective at controlling crime[10]. It should also not be forgotten that as a liberation movement the ANC had garnered experience in military and intelligence gathering (Laufer 2001: 15) but not in crime fighting.

There was a political backlash against the *Makwanyane* case and the spokesperson for the NP threatened to campaign for its reinstatement, stating that the decision gave out the wrong impression (Bae 2005: 60). It was claimed that the 'rights of murderers and rapists [were] being held in higher regard than those of their victims' and a radio talk show host stated that 'under the ANC, the message is that people can commit any crime and get away with it' (Bae 2005: 60).

There was also a backlash against the government's release policies and Mandela's mid-1998 release of 9,000 prisoners, as part of his birthday celebrations, met with widespread criticism. A Democratic Party MP stated that 'The government's response to the overcrowding crisis has been mindboggling in its shortsightedness and crass disregard for the victims of violent crime' (*Hansard* 1998b, col: 6183) and he blamed the increase in crime on the releases. The right-wing Freedom Front Party was also vocal in its critique:

> the Government is gambling with the safety of citizens by releasing these prisoners ... some of these released prisoners have now been re-arrested for the murder of the Greef couple of Hanover and Saul Damon of Malmesbury. There is also a strong suspicion that Andre Breytenbach of Soekmekaar, whose body was made a mockery of in a gruesome manner by having number plates and vehicle lights placed around it, are also among those released prisoners. (*Hansard* 1998b, col. 4925)

10 In fact, apartheid had not actually worked to control movement either but the pretense – via blitzes, raids and crackdowns – was there (Edwards and Hecht 2010).

According to Shubane (2001: 196) the new ANC government was too eager to 'present itself as distinct from its authoritarian predecessor' and thus sought to adopt a consensual and legitimatory approach to criminal justice (Shubane 2001: 196, Steinberg 2011). But in doing so it went too far and it was thus necessary to return to 'coercion' as a means to 'control crime' (Shubane 2001: 196).

Although the hard-line approach discussed below was clearly mired in the politics of the day, these policies should also be seen in the context of the ANC's poor track record in the camps. One only has to look at how it imposed discipline and order in the camps in order to gain some insight into the way that it adopted punitive penal policies soon after it gained power. The ANC already had a culture that predisposed it towards a crackdown on any form of deviance that threatened its hegemony. As Brown argues, past and current turns towards penal severity are specific techniques of governance to which modern states (and I would add, government's in the making – in the form of liberation movements) periodically make recourse (Brown 2002: 405). As such, penal severity/excess is a feature of rather than a threat to the modernizing process (Brown 2002: 419).

Since being punitive is an easy substitute for effectiveness (Garland 1996), the 'establishment of exclusionary rules' (Simon 2007: 195) became common. The prison, because it creates the illusion of 'total security' (Simon 2007: 164), is a graphic way to demonstrate loyalty to victims. As Garland (1996: 460) puts it:

> a willingness to deliver harsh punishments to convicted offenders magically compensates a failure to deliver security to the population at large' and 'it gives the impression that something is being done, here and now. It, like the waging of war, exemplifies the sovereign mode of state action.

Criminals Must Get the Message At the 1995 opening of Parliament the then President Nelson Mandela stated that

> We must take the war to the criminals and no longer allow the situation in which we are mere sitting ducks for those in our society who, for whatever reason, are bent on engaging in criminal and anti-social activities (Mandela, 1995).

He also stated that the country was at a 'crossroad' in respect of its 'approach to the combating of crime' and that:

> Because crime and violence are eroding the foundation of our democracy and the State is being pressurized into adopting a harsher approach … Some could argue that this trend infringes on fundamental rights, but it's obvious that terms and concepts such as democracy and human rights will become meaningless if we allow crime and the fear of crime to dominate our daily lives and to destroy the basic elements of our democracy. (Department of Safety and Security 1999: 9)

The 1995 Criminal Procedure 2nd Amendment Act, which provided that in the case of certain offences, the accused had to convince court that the interests of justice required release, was justified as seeking to 'establish certainty regarding the law of bail and … aimed at effective combating of crime' (Department of Justice 1995: 10). As ANC MP Hofmeyer stated:

> When we toughened the bail laws at the end of 1995, figures from the South African Institute of Race Relations indicated that the number of prisoners in jail who had not been granted bail increased from 23,000 to 30,000. This is an increase of over 50 per cent in just more than 18 months. I believe that the taking of all those criminals off the streets is one of those factors that led to the modest reduction in crime last year. (*Hansard* 1997a, col: 3024)

The 1997 Criminal Law Amendment Act introduced minimum sentences of 5, 7, 10, 15, 20, 25 years and life for a range of offences, including categories of theft, corruption, drug-dealing, assault, rape and murder. It obliged a magistrate and judge to impose the prescribed minimum sentence unless 'substantial and compelling' circumstances justified a lesser sentence. Its enactment was part of a backlash against the perceived lack of professionalism, skills and training amongst magistrates, prosecutors and judges, who were perceived as having too much discretion.[11] The Act was justified as an emergency measure to combat high crime levels and although the minimum sentence provisions were enacted on a temporary basis they have been consistently extended. In this way, then, the exceptional measure of mandatory minimum sentences has been normalized and routinized – even though it was initially introduced as a temporary measure. The result has been to increase the number of prisoners serving long and life sentences. Whereas in January 1998 (prior to the implementation of minimum sentencing) only 24 per cent of the sentenced prison population was serving a prison term of longer than ten years by 2004 this had increased to 48 per cent (Fagan 2004). Just as the sentences in the democratic South Africa lengthened so too did more sentencing categories emerge. The 2001–2002 Annual Report for the Department of Correctional Services broke the prison population statistics down in terms of sentenced, APOPS,[12] unsentenced, juveniles (under 21), male and female prisoners. Sentence categories and the number of prisoners per sentence group were broken down into 0–6 months, 6–12 months, 12–less than 24 months, 24 months–3

11 As is the case in the UK and the USA civil servants in South Africa are not protected by a 'sense of professional expertise' (Lacey 2008: 94) and are therefore vulnerable to being disciplined by government. There are numerous examples in South Africa where high profile prosecutors and investigating officers have been removed from their posts because they made politically controversial decisions.

12 Asset Procurement and Operating Partnership System – a private prison form (see p. 30).

years, 3–5 years, 5–7 years, 7–10 years,[13] 10–15 years, 15–20 years, more than 20 years, death, habitual criminal, life sentence, mental instability, reformatory, day parole,[14] ordered by court as dangerous and, periodic imprisonment (Department of Correctional Services 2002: 26).

According to the Minister of Safety and Security, the fact that prisons were overcrowded meant that the police were doing their job:

> If one goes to Pollsmoor Central and every other prison or holding cell in this country, one finds that they are bursting at the seams…Those people who are at Pollsmoor and other prisons did not take themselves to those prisons: they were arrested by the police. The police wake up every morning to do their job. This is why we are on top of the crime situation. It is not out of control. The South African crime situation is not out of control. The police are handling this situation and all what we need … is to fully rally behind the police and to declare that the fight against crime is our fight. (*Hansard* 2001b: col 2470)

The 1998 Judicial Matters Amendment Act increased the criminal jurisdiction of the lower courts: in the case of Regional Courts from 10 to 15 years and in respect of District Courts from one to three years' imprisonment. Researchers have observed that from that time the sentence categories which included three- and 15-year sentences increased markedly (Giffard and Muntingh 2006). Whilst admitting that 'these laws [were] drastic', Hofmeyer said, 'I do not believe that they are too harsh. They are all based on laws that are accepted in other democracies' (*Hansard* 1998a, col: 8054). He also stated that

> the new tough laws dealing with bail, parole and minimum sentences … clearly indicate that … this government is committed to fighting crime. The government has taken its gloves off in its fight against crime. (*Hansard* 1999b col: 2768)

Similarly, the launch of South Africa's first Closed Maximum Security Unit (CMAX)[15] at the Pretoria Maximum Prison at the end of 1997 was presented as a major breakthrough (in regard to the prevention of escapes and the housing of South Africa's most 'dangerous and hardened criminals'), as was the construction of electric perimeter fences at other 'vulnerable and high risk institutions' (Department of Correctional Services 1998).

Successful moral panics owe their appeal to their resonance with wider anxieties (Garland 2008) and South Africa was no exception where the anxiety about violent crime, perceived to be a result of the transition to democracy, resulted in

13 This category had the highest number of prisoners.

14 With only 21 people sentenced to day parole this category had the lowest number.

15 CMAX entailed isolation for 23 hours of the day, wire mesh ceilings and one hour of exercise, whilst handcuffed, in what one critic described as a 'small cage' (Duncan, quoted in Pete 2000: 6).

harsher penal policies. Although the particular moral panic(s) about violent crime committed by released prisoners may have died down, its effect – in view of the harsh government response to restrict parole considerably – was to result in rising prison numbers and the overuse of incarceration, long after the 'initial episode had run its course' (Garland 2008: 16). The restricting of parole was supported by all political parties and the 1998 Parole and Correctional Supervision Amendment Act met with no opposition.[16]

The fact that the Asset Procurement and Operating Partnership System (APOPS) – a way of building new prisons with the assistance of the private sector – was mentioned in the preface to the 1997 Annual Report as a solution to the problem of overcrowding is significant and in contradistinction to the old policies of providing alternatives to imprisonment. The APOPS for maximum security prisons was justified on the grounds of transferring the risks related to incarceration from the government to the private sector (Department of Correctional Services 2002: 38).

Private prisons were presented as a symbol of transformation and as part of an overall human rights discourse. Rehabilitation and prison privatization were linked insofar as the private sector was presented as being far more capable than the government of rehabilitating prisoners. As one official put it:

> We will be able to reduce costs, because the private sector comes with better methods of supervision. They are better at organizing, and we will learn from them. (*Hansard* 1998c, col: 1781)

Since rehabilitation could not take place in an overcrowded prison the solution was to build more prisons (*Hansard* 1997b, col: 1643–4). Apart from prison privatization the 1997 Annual Report also made mention of

> exploratory investigations … concerning more unconventional methods … such as using prison ships and the conversion of inner city buildings into prisons. (Department of Correctional Services 1998)

as a means of solving the overcrowding crisis.

---

16 A court which imposed a sentence of more than two years could now fix a non-parole period which could not exceed two thirds of the term of imprisonment or 25 years, whichever was shorter. In the case of a life sentence parole could not be obtained without having served at least 25 years of the sentence unless the prisoner turned 65 while in prison and had served at least 15 years of the sentence. The new legislation abolished the system of credits and gave the court which had imposed the initial sentence a direct say in the period served by a prisoner. Mandatory prison terms could not be reduced by the department – only the President could grant remission of mandatory terms and the department could apply remission to the non mandatory part as a 'reward for positive behavior and participation in rehabilitation programmes' (Department of Correctional Services 1997: 26).

The Reinvention of Rehabilitation

The official discourse of transformation in South Africa presented democracy and rehabilitation as being intertwined with each other, as mutually reinforcing concepts. The fact that prisons were no longer called 'prisons' but 'correctional centres' was significant at this discursive level because it connoted a shift from custody to correction. Yet by 1997 the narrative coherence or fit between what was going on inside the prison and how prison administrators and politicians justified the prison had totally broken down in the face of public pronouncements and widespread scepticism about rehabilitation. The following excerpt from a local newspaper is an example of this:

> Demoralised social psychologists working at Pollsmoor say rehabilitation is a "joke" … Head psychologist for the Western Cape Mr Fred Borchardt said that most of the prisoners up for parole had never seen a psychologist … Ms Petra Badenhorst, the only psychologist working in Pollsmoor's maximum security section, said she saw less than 10 prisoners a day, sometimes none … "Most of the prisoners leave here without a single day of evaluation and having had no rehabilitation at all," she said. On top of the heavy case loads, the psychologists worked in bad conditions for bad salaries. (*Cape Times*, 25 February 1997 quoted in Pete 1998: 27)

Despite this the ANC government justified making sentences tougher and its reliance on imprisonment as a means of punishment by virtue of its new vision of changing prisons into places of rehabilitation:

> It is the ANC that has the task of making sentences tougher, making bail harder to get and making parole conditions tighter. It is the ANC that is transforming our prisoners from hellholes that breed more hardened and dangerous criminals to institutions that will rehabilitate those who have strayed outside decent society into useful citizens who are able to contribute to a better SA. (*Hansard* 1998b, col: 6175)

In 2002, at the precise point in time when South Africa had the top incarceration rate in Africa and one of the highest in the world, a project called 'Gearing the Department of Correctional Services for Rehabilitation' was introduced. This followed on the 2001 launch of a restorative justice approach which 'aimed at facilitating the mediation and healing process between offenders, victims, family members and the community' (Department of Correctional Services, 2001: foreword). This 'major policy shift' (Department of Correctional Services 2002: 6–7) embraced a 'new prisons culture … a culture of corrections' where

> each member is … a rehabilitator, able to balance discipline and compliance with policy and the necessary security measures, with humanitarian commitment

> to correction of criminal behaviour and care for the offenders. (Department of Correctional Services 2002: 12)

In terms of a new 'security risk assessment system', which aligned the risk of escape with the need for rehabilitation, the prisoner's 'degree of cooperation' was presented as critical (Department of Correctional Services 2002: 81). The idea was that 'a comprehensive assessment tool' would identify an offenders 'needs' and that 'needs based rehabilitation programmes' would then be developed (Department of Correctional Services 2002: 81). This was presented as being 'at the heart of the shift', from a 'penal system that failed to recognize the human rights of offenders' to one which did. In this way then the department drew a distinct line between apartheid prisons and the prisons in the new South Africa and there was a noticeable discursive shift of focus from 'just incarceration', from focusing mainly on safe custody, to focusing 'both on safe custody and on rehabilitation' (Department of Correctional Services 2002: 80). All of this was couched in the framework of neoliberal penality with

> the reduction of re-offending through the enhancement of rehabilitation programmes … transforming our prisons from being … 'universities of crime' into effective rehabilitation centres that produce individuals who are trained in market-related skills and capable of successful reintegration into their communities as law-abiding citizens (Department of Correctional Services 2002: 6–7).

Standardization and definition were hallmarks of the new direction and 'for the first time in the history of the Department, rehabilitation within the context of corrections' (Department of Correctional Services, 2004: foreword) was being defined. The new motto was:

> From every official becoming a rehabilitator to every prison becoming a correctional centre – a place of new beginnings – to every offender becoming a nation-server through correction. (Department of Correctional Services, 2004: foreword)

This motto not only purported to serve as a 'rallying call to action for the staff, but also [sought] to inculcate a culture of social responsibility among the offenders' (Department of Correctional Services, 2004: foreword).

Yet the NP too had reinvented rehabilitation when it started to do away with petty apartheid, and black people and coloureds started to become the subjects and targets of the rehabilitation discourse. Thus none of this is entirely new, especially the institutional shortcomings in the way of rehabilitation. The figures speak for themselves: although there was a 14 per cent increase in expenditure under this programme, the prison population increased at the same time. As Hannah-Moffat's (1999: 84) work has shown, the language of needs is not one that is necessarily based on the provision of resources, but instead facilitates responsibilization and the concept of 'risk' is flexible and subjective, depending on who is doing the assessment and in what context it is taking place. According to Van Zyl Smit (1998: 418), despite the fact that the average cost of imprisoning a prisoner increased from R12 to R61 per day, when factoring in the declining value of the Rand, in real terms, the department was spending less than half of what it had 19 years previously. In 2003 there were 461 social workers and 63 psychologists employed by the department to service a total prison population of more than 185,000 prisoners ((*Hansard* 2003, col. 36: question 74).

The stress on 'reintegration' and the role of 'the community' that started under the Nationalist Party, in the context of a shift away from the white welfare state and racial Fordism, has continued and been given a new spin in the post apartheid era. As Robinson (2008: 435) points out the ability to accommodate an 'expressive rationality' has been key to the 'survival and evolution of rehabilitation' and the 'new rehabilitation' is characterized by a 'renewed interest in the moral consequences of offending'. In South Africa it has also been combined in a particular way with the anti-apartheid struggle and the construction of a post-apartheid morality. In terms of this 'new rehabilitationism' (Hudson, cited in Robinson 2008: 432) it is no longer offenders only who are presented as the main beneficiaries of rehabilitation but also communities and victims. Work on 'community projects' is presented as being 'empowering and useful', a way of 'helping communities to change their mindsets towards offenders, to help with a restorative justice approach and to incorporate offenders back into communities' (*Hansard* 2002b question 220, col: 4112).

Work is still of seminal importance in the prisons lexicon and the annual reports all reflect a constant refrain that the cultivation of a work ethic amongst prisoners will facilitate reintegration into the community. The 1995 Annual Report contained only a paragraph on social work whereas a few pages were written on training – all of it menial and gender stereotyped, with women trained to become hairdressers. The 1997 Annual Report stated that the purpose of prison labour was to 'promote productivity and combat idleness' (Department of Correctional Services 1997: 24). This was the case despite the fact that only 12,126 out of a total of 112,572 prisoners actually worked. Of these the vast majority were involved in agricultural services, i.e. highly unskilled and exploitative labour but in keeping with the neoliberal work ethic. As Goodman (2012) has pointed out, in the context of the USA, the work ethic is uncoupled from an actual set of work – this is as true of the situation inside the prisons, where very few prisoners actually work, as it is on the outside, where unemployment is endemic. Of equal importance is the aspect of responsibilization inherent in the promotion of a work ethic.

Conclusion

In apartheid South Africa the black body was an important site and symbol of punishment and in the post-apartheid era the state, in a show of force, has relied on the ferocity of its punishment power, via punitive laws, as a mode of showing that it is in control and is doing something about the crime problem. This is surprising because of its previous pronouncements on the causes of crime. On the other hand, given the history of Quatro, where human rights abuses were perpetrated against those accused of, and imprisoned for, committing treason and other offences against the movement, perhaps this was to be expected.

The prison in the 'new' South Africa serves more than one purpose: on the one hand it demonstrates the government's willingness to do something about crime and to punish criminals. On the other hand, in the context of the demise of the death penalty and corporal punishment, it is also a symbol of a humanizing shift in punishment, indicating the 'benevolence' or good intentions of the government – to strive towards fair, equitable and rehabilitational punishment in a democratic South Africa. Thus the ideal of the prison as a place where criminals are rehabilitated has remained constant since its inception, despite fact that the reality contradicts this (Ayers 1984: 83). As Foucault wrote:

> For a century and a half the prison had always been offered as its own remedy: the reactivation of the penitentiary techniques as the only means of overcoming their failure; the realization of the corrective project as the only method of overcoming the impossibility of implementing it. (Foucault 1977, 1995: 268)

Yet whereas Foucault saw prisons as expressions of the disciplinary impulse which swept over society – in South Africa prisons are an expression of a punitive impulse combined with a sense of powerlessness in the face of crime. What is particularly interesting in the 'new' South Africa is the mix of coercion and consensus, of retributive and restorative justice. Just as American republicanism, as observed by Tocqueville, produced both freedom and coercion (Ayers 1984: 71), so too has democratization in the 'new' South Africa been accompanied by an increase in long term imprisonment. The values that symbolize the ethos of post-apartheid South Africa – democracy, struggle morality, individualism, restorative justice, freedom, human rights – have also come to reinforce and underpin South Africa's simultaneous embracing of neoliberal ideology, responsibility, the government of the self, the transformative power of work, active citizenship and the necessity of good governance (in which crime control plays such a prominent part).[17] The crucial role that the prison plays in the penal complex of South Africa underpins the mutually reinforcing will to 'govern economically' and the 'will to govern democratically' (Cruikshank 2004: 8) in the context of a society which has one of the highest, if not the highest, rates of inequality in the world.

Penal discourse is as concerned with its image as it is with regulating actual institutional practices (Garland 1985) and the Department of Correctional Services in the 'new' South Africa is continuously trying to construct meaningful

17 See Ayers (1984: 71) in the context of how republicanism and capitalism reinforced each other in nineteenth century America.

accounts of itself, of what is being done in prison, 'how and with what effect' (Bright 1996: 14). Thus, because there are deep connections between politics, the ordering of things in the public sphere and the ordering of things inside the prison the justifications for imprisonment are constantly shifting, negotiated and renegotiated, contingent and contested (Bright 1996, O'Malley 1996, Simon 2000, Hannah-Moffat 2000, Robinson 2008).

Ironically, in the 'new' South Africa, the more people that are put in prison and the more chronic the overcrowding issue has become, the more the department has embraced the discursive manoeuvre of rehabilitation – how else could the ANC government, a former liberation movement, promoter of people's power, justify South Africa's heavily prisonized society? Yet the standard line of the department is that there has been a paradigm shift from the punitive, punishment-orientated prison regime of apartheid to the caring, rehabilitative prison of the 'new' South Africa. As such the South African state has deployed the concept of rehabilitation to justify the continued use of and revival of the prison and has sought to reinvent the prison through talk of restorative justice, self-help and a new regime of self-governance (Gillespie 2007). This chapter has shown how this talk is nothing terribly new. The Nationalist Party, too, spoke of a rehabilitative shift in the 1980s.

Punishment is socially integrative in the sense that it reinforces social solidarity and society's collective consciousness and in this sense it does play a functional role even though it does not eliminate crime in terms of a consequentialist or utilitarian argument (Durkheim 1982). It plays a positive role insofar as it reinforces social sentiments/solidarity and the punitive discourse against crime serves to re-cement society's moral core, to draw a line between the 'us' and the 'them'. It is therefore no coincidence that as apartheid was being dismantled so too did prison sentences lengthen – that long term imprisonment has replaced capital and corporal punishment – since there has always been a pool of people over whom the government could not establish hegemony, and therefore over whom it had to use its coercive power to punish.

Penality in post-apartheid South Africa, like everything else, was not constructed on a clean slate and Garland's (1985: 155) image of the social realm as a multi-layered mosaic, a

> product of layer upon layer of organisational forms, techniques and regulatory practices, each one partial in its operation, each one dealing with the residues and traces of previous strategies as well as its contemporary rivals and limitations

is useful. The prison as an institution and ideology is one that has been able to 'most easily absorb different elements and adapt' to various strategies of government – 'in contrast to capital and corporal punishment' (Garland, 1985: 155) because it can accommodate both liberal and authoritarian discourses. It has been justified both in terms of the punitive 'lock 'em up' rhetoric as well the more benign language of restorative justice and *ubuntu.* Perhaps this is because, as an institution, it has this seemingly endless capacity to reform (Foucault 1977, 1995,

Cruikshank 2004). Punishment was already reforming in the 'old' South Africa and the old government had started a liberalizing process back in the mid-1970s. The state in the 'new' South Africa continued this endless cycle of reforms, with the prison at its centre, even though the justifications and ideological underpinnings changed dramatically.

Just as the emergence of the penitentiary was a 'project constitutive of liberal democracy' (Dumm 1987: 6) in the early USA, so too has the prison in South Africa, reinvented (discursively at least) as the reintegrative prison, played a central role in the constituting of the newly democratizing and liberalizing South Africa. Yet there is a vast difference between democracy on paper and the vast inequalities that characterize many formally democratic countries and there is no getting away from the fact that the institution of the prison is one that is based on manifest unfreedom, no matter how empowering an institution it is represented to be and no matter how many times it is re-legitimated. It is also, as Foucault pointed out, a constantly failing project.

Epilogue and Concluding Thoughts

> We need to see things not in terms of the replacement of a society of sovereignty by a disciplinary society and the subsequent replacement of a disciplinary society by a society of government; in reality one has a triangle, sovereignty – discipline – government, which has as its primary target the population and its essential mechanism the apparatus of security. (Foucault 1991: 102)

The aim of this Epilogue is to observe, from the vantage point of the present moment, what this short history of official criminology has told us about governance in South Africa, about the broader debates on penality and neoliberalism, on prisons and democracy, and to reflect on recent developments.

Since I completed my research the fortunes of some of the political luminaries who spearheaded the various policies referred to in the book have waned dramatically. Thus, for example, Jackie Selebi, erstwhile National Commissioner of Police when the National Crime Combating Strategy, Prevention of Organised Crime Act, and other punitive policies were adopted, was found guilty of corruption in 2010 and sentenced to 15 years' imprisonment. He was granted medical parole in 2012. Selebi had been a staunch supporter and ally of President Thabo Mbeki, and although rumours about his corruption had circulated during Mbeki's presidency, it was only once Zuma became president and replaced Selebi with Cele[1] that Selebi was criminally charged. Indeed, Zuma himself has been the subject of multiple counts of fraud which were controversially withdrawn in April 2009, two weeks before the national elections which resulted in him becoming South Africa's new president. In other words, the point that I made at the start of the book, about the interconnections between politics and crime, at the very basic and obvious level of who gets charged and when, is a prominent part of South Africa's political landscape. The recent decision to charge Julius Malema[2] with money laundering – a week before the opening of ANC leadership nominations – is, as Jonathon Moyo cynically points out, 'a celebration of selective prosecution' (Butler 2012). Malema is loathed by most of the white middle classes for singing songs like 'kill the *boer*', and for calling for the nationalization of mines and return of land to the black masses. Despite his expulsion from the ANC in 2011 he still marshals support amongst South Africa's poor and downtrodden – as evidenced by his visits to the Marikana strikers and his encouraging of them to make the mines

1 Cele himself was suspended over allegations of corruption in 2011.

2 One-time president of the ANC Youth League and a powerful supporter of Zuma's presidency, until they fell out.

ungovernable until such time as their wage demands were met. He constituted a threat to Zuma's bid for re-election as head of the ANC in December 2012.

More of the Same

The debate about the crime statistics has remained largely the same – with criticism being levelled at the way the statistics are compiled and the fact that they are six months out of date (Institute for Security Studies 2012). The trend towards better numbers continues, with reports by the National Victims of Crime Surveys, the Medical Research Council, South African Insurance Association, South African Banking Risk and Information Centre, the Consumer Goods Council of South Africa and Grant Thornton International (Institute for Security Studies 2012), competing with the official crime statistics. Recent statistics reveal that murder has decreased by almost 54 per cent since 1994 but, even so, the concern is still that South Africa's murder rate is far too high. According to data collected by the World Health Organisation and United Nations Office on Drugs and Crime, South Africa's murder rate, at 17 per 100,000 is 4.5 times the global average and one of the highest in Africa (Institute for Security Studies 2012).

Other developments include the disbanding of the Scorpions and their replacement by the Hawks, the infamous 'shoot to kill' policy called for by police commissioners and high ranking government officials,[3] the tragedy of the Marikana massacre where 34 striking miners were shot dead by police in August 2012, the xenophobic killings, in particular the more than 60 people killed in 2008 and the re-emergence of macabre vigilante necklacings against suspected criminals in some of the Western Cape's black townships. Despite the fact that the government has consistently labelled the xenophobic violence as 'criminal' and not xenophobic, in 2009 it appointed a National Co-ordinator for Xenophobia and formed a specialized team to collect and collate information relating to crimes against foreign nationals (Polzer and Takabvirwa 2010). There has also been a spike in violent service delivery protests over the past few years and officially recorded instances of public violence increased dramatically in 2009. Although the latest crime statistics show that they have in fact dropped slightly since 2009, they are still 18.3 per cent higher than in 2004 (South African Police Service 2012). In fact, and once again in full homage to the ironic continuity with Nationalist Party (NP) government discourse and practice, the police claim that their crime combating resources are being drained by having to quell protests.[4]

---

3 In 2008 the Deputy Minister of Safety and Security instructed the police to to 'kill the bastards', referring to criminals. Police shootings resulted in the deaths of 1,080 people between April 2008 and 2010 (Van Wyk 2011).

4 Lieutenant General Mwazindile Petros, Gauteng Police Commissioner, quoted in *Cape Times*, 21 September 2012.

Overcrowding in South Africa's prisons stands at 136 per cent, with the majority (85,000) being imprisoned for 'aggressive crimes' (Republic of South Africa 2011: 11). Almost 48 per cent of awaiting trial prisoners have been held for longer than three months. The majority (50,205) of those incarcerated are serving sentences ranging from 20 years to life imprisonment. Between the years 2000 and 2010 the numbers of people serving life imprisonment rose from 1,436 to 9,651, representing an increase of 572 per cent. During this time the number of prisoners serving sentences of more then ten years increased by more than 128 per cent – from 23,702 in 2000 to 53,944 in 2010 (Republic of South Africa 2011: 14). As such, the trend towards the overpenalization of violent crime has continued.

At the same time communitization initiatives continue apace. Indeed the multiple sites of governing through crime are now more entrenched than ever, with new neighbourhood watches, community police forums, public private partnerships, environmental design, central improvement districts, urban renewal nodes, and car guards on every corner, being an ubiquitous fact of daily life.

This is on the one hand more of the same; on the other a sign that the hegemony of the ANC government is surely fracturing, that things are getting worse. The players and the details have changed – of course – but the themes remain the same. Clearly the dysfunctionalities wrought by apartheid have not been adequately addressed by the ANC. Thus, recourse to the inherently violent criminal law which was with varying intensity present during apartheid, as well in the culture of the ANC, has not disappeared in the post-apartheid era, especially when the government is faced, increasingly so, with its own lack of hegemony. At the same time the developmental, revolutionary and/or moral regeneration *ubuntuesque* discourse is invoked by politicians and supporters to prove that the ANC is pro-poor and pro 'the people'. This discourse has been adopted in tandem with neoliberalization policies such as GEAR, ASGISA (Accelerated and Shared Growth Initiative of South Africa) and deepening inequality.

Politicized Processes of Social Transformation

Instead of attributing the centrality of the prison to an increase in crime, and attributing the latter to the transition to democracy, I have argued that we should seek more grounded sociological explanations for why crime plays such an important role in governance in post-apartheid South Africa. I have not sought to answer the question of whether, objectively speaking, crime has increased in the post-1994 period, but there is no doubt that its form and content and the concern with it have changed dramatically over the years. As apartheid started to be dismantled in the 1980s the role that race played in criminalization and victimization patterns started to change. As likely offenders (poor black men) were no longer able to be kept away from likely victims (the whites), to the same extent as they had been under Verwoerdian apartheid, so too did criminalization and victimization patterns start to shift. These changes were deepened during and after the transition to democracy.

Not only were there more middle class white victims, but the emergence of a black middle class whose members also constituted attractive crime targets, as well a greater willingness on the side of poor blacks to lay criminal charges, resulted in crime's 'democratization'.

By 1995 the ANC had its back up against the wall and there were strong indications that things had got worse – certainly insofar as perceptions of the crime problem were concerned. With a ratcheting up of public anxiety, crime became a convenient anchor on which opposition parties and members of the public could attack the new government. Moral panics generated 'emotional energy and collective excitement' (Garland 2008: 18) and resulted in a disproportionate, angst-ridden reaction to crime, on the part of the public and opposition parties. There was also a change in the types of crime that were recorded in official statistics and the problem was subjected to ever more intensive measurement. As such, the high rates of imprisonment, the harsh laws and the resignification of the purpose of imprisonment should not be portrayed as a mere *response* to an objectively increasing crime rate but rather as a highly politicized process of social transformation which started in the 1970s and which I have described in this book.

Historic Residues

Although 1994 does represent a momentous change, in the sense that a black majority government replaced a white minority government, based on the historic first of the franchise being extended to everyone, on another level there is substantial continuity.

Crime in both the apartheid and ANC regimes was and is, partially at least, caused by socio-structural factors, but, for different reasons, both NP and ANC governments adopted versions of neoliberal market policies that worsened these structural processes. When the ANC became the ruling party in 1994 it faced a situation where neoliberalism had become doxic in the sense that it had 'established a broad hegemonic basis for its authority',[5] both within the NP and the liberal camp as well as in the international community. Apartheid rule had radically altered the social, economic and political terrain in South African society but instead of being able to reverse the deep structural inequalities caused by years of apartheid and colonial rule, the ANC's interpretation and implementation of their ideology of 'national democratic revolution' resulted in a deepening of inequality in 'post'-apartheid South Africa (Johnson 2009, Bond 2000, Everett 2010, Peet 2002, Terreblanche 2012). As such, the ruptures that occurred in 1994, albeit momentous, took place on a largely political level, rather than a deep socio-economic structural level, and resulted in an uneven distribution of the fruits of newly acquired citizenship.

---

5 This phrase is used by Hall (2003: 105) in relation to New Labour in Britain.

The coercive labour relations enforced by apartheid laws aimed to control the wage labour relations between whites and other races and after 1994 the consequent 'proletarianization of these recalcitrant recruits to the "free" labor market' (Lichtenstein 2001: 1987) remained a problem to be dealt with by the new government. The fact that intra-racial inequality has increased is evidence that Black Economic Empowerment has not solved the problems of the poor, and in fact has worsened them. Social inclusion is conflated with activity; thus labour in prison, outside of prison, on public works projects – all of these go into making South Africa's moral citizens. Yet the notion of employment in South Africa is also deeply divisive insofar as violent strikes, xenophobic acts of violence against those undocumented migrants who are perceived to be taking jobs away from South Africa's unemployed, the dividing line between insiders and outsiders, all centre around employment. Yet employment is itself a chimera, given the almost endemic nature of unemployment, coupled with the fact that work is not a guaranteed way out of poverty, as the shocking living conditions of the Marikana strikers tragically demonstrated.

In apartheid South Africa the criminal law was overtly used to uphold the power and status of a white minority and black and coloured males were disproportionately imprisoned. This criminalization and these apartheid policies have left historic residues which the new regime has not dealt with adequately. The politics behind crime, the root causes, the structural (and superstructural) conditions which the critical criminologists of the 1960s and 1970s drew our attention to, are markedly missing in official criminology as well as in the discourse of most political parties.

Although, on the face of it, the ANC represented an alternative set of social forces which one might have expected would have resulted in a fundamental counterweight to apartheid penality, it not only lacked a philosophical and policy framework on crime and punishment but had also, as a liberation movement, engaged in some distinctly punitive practices towards deviants. The prison, detention camp, execution and corporal punishment were all technologies that the ANC deployed to deal with disorder during the liberation struggle. Although its mentalities might have been grounded in socialist communitarianism, one should not assume that technologies, practices and mentalities are consistent – in fact they are contingent, contested and hybrid. The ethos of the ANC lay as much in some of the punitive technologies of order maintenance as it did in its politically correct mentalities on policing and prisons and perhaps punitive technologies were in fact 'embedded' in its ethos.

Not only did the ANC not pay sufficient attention to the problem of crime but so too were critical criminologists in the 'old' South Africa more concerned with political repression than the extent of the crime problem in the townships. Blaming crime on apartheid turned out to be an overly essentializing, political explanation which was also inadequate in the long run. By seeing crime as a function of ruling class and racial oppression the ANC and left-wing academics in South Africa made the mistake of viewing the apartheid era as being based on repression alone, when in fact there was also self-governance, liberalism and complexity within apartheid structures. The danger of oversimplifying issues resulted in the belief that implementing a system of human rights (the flipside of the repression) would automatically solve the problem of crime: because the left saw most criminality as being linked to politics and oppression, the discourse operated as if crime would cease once oppression was removed and a system of human rights was adopted. When this proved wrong and the public were baying for blood, it was a simple backwards somersault, that saw harsh laws being implemented alongside the restorative justice and more communitarian discourses.

Othering

In what Simon has described as 'governing through crime' the now increasingly fractured solidarity engendered by the notion of a 'rainbow nation' in the 'new' South Africa has centred around crime. Crime prevention is presented by the state as a moral undertaking that communities and individuals are responsible for and, together with a crackdown/hardline approach, which is as typical of 'third way/advanced liberal regimes' (Muehlebach, 2007: 296), as it is of 'developing' neoliberalizing regimes, the ANC government accommodates a very conservative, even draconian, approach to criminal justice, precisely because it claims to occupy the moral high ground. The fact that poorer communities support harsh law and order measures is often used as a justification for zero tolerance crime crackdowns in poor areas. Yet as Rowan (2011: 53), citing Lukes, points out, these communities might react punitively simply because, due to 'ideological conditioning … they could not imagine an alternative approach'.

The ANC government has vacillated in its responses, between denial that there is a problem, and panic, symptomized by knee-jerk reactions and rhetorical posturing about its intention to crack down on criminals. It has passed some harsh laws which provide for minimum sentences, restrict bail and criminalize gang membership. There has been a substantial increase in long-term imprisonment. As a governing party, unless it wants to commit political suicide, it has had to show that it is tough on crime but because it also wears the cloak of a liberation movement it simultaneously promotes a strong human rights and mass based populist discourse. Because of this it is easy to 'other' the criminal, to have a new enemy – the evil criminal – stripped of all claims to be acting within a socio-economic and political context. As discussed in Chapters Two and Five, the new South African government has been particularly unimaginative and conservative in the way that it has constructed the problem of crime and criminality and an in-depth discourse on the social foundations of offending is distinctively absent from official criminology.

Production of Identities

I have argued that official criminology is both constitutive of state building projects and also produced by them. It helps to shape the way that people think, feel and act. Both apartheid and post-apartheid practices of policing (such as pass law raids, raids on refugee centres, targeting illegal aliens, targeting gangs) resulted in the patterns of 'oversuspicion and underprotection' (Loader 2006: 212) that mark police relations with disadvantaged groups. Although repression was a fundamental aspect of apartheid rule it was not just about repression, and the production of identities was also a crucial mode of rule, one that remains in post-apartheid South Africa: the coloured prisoner, the *skollie*, the *tsotsi*, the 'lost generation', the gangster, the illegal alien, the undocumented migrant. Yet the categories of criminality that exist in the 'new' South Africa have emerged out of the subjectifications that occurred in the 'old' South Africa and there are continuities in technologies of rule between the two regimes. We know that politics is important in the construction of solutions for crime problems but how are these problems identified in the first place – who asks the questions and raises the issues? Whose voices are heard and what are the power relationships in these initial formulations? These are also the outcomes of (often unacknowledged) political struggles.

As Foucault observed, systems of rule differentiate between humans and power is exercised in relation to these differences. These differences, although constructed, assume a certain 'truth' and social meaning (Ashworth, 1990). This is why, even in democratic South Africa where citizens are constitutionally equal, there is still differentiation. As Ashworth (1990: 16–17) puts it: discrimination can be 'removed' or 'imposed' but differentiations always exist because they are a condition for the exercise of power. The separation of crime and politics in the 'new' South Africa has played a key role in this differentiation.

Flexible Eclecticism

The 'new' South Africa has seen a proliferation of strategy documents and white papers. These are technical, acronym ridden, glossy corporate-style publications where terms such as 'freedom', 'human rights', 'appeasement', 'inclusion', 'competition', 'racism', and 'black empowerment' are bandied about. The rhetoric draws on a wide array of ideologies and is used to justify an eclectic mix of policies. Yet policy-making is often a largely symbolic affair and, with implementation left to others further down the line, there is much room for mis/reinterpretation and resistance (Gilling 2010: 1150). In coupling managerialism with critical reform discourse, the engagement of reformers is rendered partially complicit. On the one hand there is the fiction that a restorative prison actually exists and on the other the punitive impulse to incarcerate as retribution for violent offences, in the face of substantive research that prisons do not work to solve the problem of crime or to rehabilitate.

Following Foucault's work on governmentality (1991) I have described the development of three forms of power in relation to penality: sovereign/repressive power as exemplified in spectacles such as the death penalty, corporal punishment, harsh policing techniques and torture. The second form is disciplinary power, which is present in techniques of rehabilitation and restorative justice, and thirdly governmental power, where the state seeks to 'act at a distance' – incorporating situational crime prevention, actuarialized forms of risk governance, community policing, managerialism and the like.

The various policies that the South African state has adopted to deal with crime are technologies used in the exercise of power. Yet power is not unidimensional or uniform. These forms of power co-exist precisely because power is relational (Foucault, 1982) – it is not something that can be handed over. I have argued that punishment, and the other technologies of rule associated with crime control (such as community based crime prevention, correctional supervision and other more 'holistic' initiatives) have been used in support of quite different political rationalities, such as apartheid, neoliberalism, neoconservatism, communitarianism, developmentalism and even people's power. Indeed, there are points of congruence between seemingly competing discourses – for example restorative justice and retributive justice both emphasize the notion of accountability. Similarly restorative justice and utilitarian approaches, such as situational crime prevention, are both consequentialist and seek to prevent future crime.

It is the unevenness and productive nature of 'neoliberal penality' that this book has been concerned to bring to the fore. One of the central tenets of my argument is that neoliberal ideology meshes well with other ideologies – thus it could be melded with apartheid rationalities of rule as well as those based on freedom and democracy in the 'new' South Africa. I have argued that penality, as an instance of neoliberal regulation in South Africa, is braided/uneven – discursively, in practice and spatially. Because neoliberal ideology meshes well with other ideologies it could be melded with apartheid rationalities of rule as well communitarian ones in the 'new' South Africa.

Although Wacquant (2009, 2001a, 2001b), Peck (2001, 2003, 2004), Peck and Tickel (2002), Samara (2003, 2005) and Gordon (1998, 2001, 2006) correctly identify the repressive aspects of neoliberal regimes they make the neoliberal project sound too much like a total onslaught of like-minded capitalists insofar as they tend to conflate neoliberalism with punitivism. In doing so they overlook the more benign practices, such as diversion programmes, social crime prevention, restorative justice initiatives, progressive child justice legislation, fines and the like which exist alongside punitive policies. Neoliberal ideology has an affinity with these practices insofar as it is premised on the empowered, active, responsibilized subject (or shall we say client) who is also the focal point of these discourses and practices. Thus whilst I do not argue that neoliberalism brought these practices into operation, this elective affinity, together with the flexible incoherence of 'actually existing neoliberalism' (Brenner and Theodore, 2002), has certainly made it difficult to unpick the configurations and strands that comprise the penal assemblage and the rationalities that underpin it.

Thus instead of mapping the evolution from one regime to another/from one political rationality (or technique of exercising power) to another, the purpose of my analysis has also been to analyse configurations and how crime policies are assembled (O'Malley 1996). Indeed, as Hannah-Moffat (2000: 529) points out in the Canadian context, the technologies of actuarialism, risk, responsibilization, compassion and restoration, what she refers to as the 'new forms of governing', exist within the context of the overtly repressive exercise of sovereign power, as evidenced by maximum-security prisons and punitive policies on privileges and release. These new techniques can coexist with older forms because the former are flexible and 'resonate with multiple and contradictory goals' (Hannah-Moffat 2000: 529). As Brown (2002: 405) points out, past and current turns towards penal severity are specific techniques of governance to which modern states periodically make recourse. According to Dubber this is due to the remaining traces of the police mentality which characterized pre-modern criminal justice systems, particularly those 'trained on the governance of the lower status members of society' (Lacey 2008: 100). Foucault (1995: 16) never stated that sovereign power would completely disappear; instead, he believed that 'traces of torture' remained in the modern system. As such the existence of privatized community crime control initiatives and other 'adaptive' responses side by side with a more punitive criminal justice system is not surprising.

We should not view these seemingly contradictory policies as diametric opposites: they exist because of each other and are in fact constitutive of each other. In fact penal discipline was and still is one of the hidden dimensions of democracy (Cruikshank 1999, Dumm 1987, Foucault 1995, Ignatieff 1978, Meranze 1996). In neoliberal/neoliberalizing/neoliberalesque regimes, such as the South African one, this becomes more marked because there is 'more freedom' and also lots of exclusion and a growing class of poor and unemployed who do not enjoy the fruits of democracy. As such, we should see things not in terms of a blanket 'replacement' (Foucault 1991: 102) of one political rationality (apartheid) by another (constitutionalism/ democracy), but rather in terms of a complex overlaying of various rationalities and governmental technologies that are configured in an unstable and fragmented way.

Appendix: List of Interviewees

Dennis Davis: A High Court Judge and Professor of Law at the University of Cape Town.

Peter Gastrow: Erstwhile director of the Cape Town Office of the Institute of Security Studies. He was the chairperson of the Interim Policing Board just before the 1994 elections and was part of the team that drafted the 1998 Prevention of Organised Crime Act.

Chris Giffard: A member of the Secretariat of the short-lived Transformation Forum on Correctional Services that was formed just after the April 1994 elections. He was incarcerated in Pollsmoor Prison for two years in the late 1980s, on charges of High Treason and Terrorism.

Nicholas Haysom: An ANC legal advisor during the early 1990s. He was integrally involved in policing reform during the period immediately preceding the 1994 elections and was part of the Constitutional Commission.

Sandra Hoffman: Former prison psychologist at Pollsmoor Correctional Centre, Department of Correctional Services.

Willie Hofmeyer: Former head of the Special Investigating Unit and head of the Asset Forfeiture Unit in the National Prosecution Authority. He was also a high profile political activist and part of the liberation movement in the 1980s and 1990s.

Lukas Muntingh: Coordinator of the Civil Society Prison Reform Initiative at the University of the Western Cape and previous Deputy National Director of the National Institute for Crime Prevention and the Reintegration of Offenders. He was involved in pre-trial diversion initiatives such as community service, during the 1990s.

Janine Rauch: One of the founders of the Policing Research Project at Wits University's Project for the Study of Violence in 1991. After the 1994 elections she became an adviser to the Ministry of Safety and Security and in 1996 was appointed Chief Director of Policy in the National Secretariat for Safety and Security. She coordinated the drafting of the National Crime Prevention Strategy.

Clifford Shearing: Director of the University of Cape Town's Institute of Criminology. He was invited to South Africa in 1991 by Dullah Omar to be involved in policing reform and work with the ANC's Constitutional Committee. Omar was to become the ANC's first Minister of Justice after the 1994 elections.

Graeme Simpson: Founder of the Centre for the Study of Violence and Reconciliation. He was one of the drafters of the National Crime Prevention Strategy and a member of the drafting team for the South African White Paper on Safety and Security.

Anne Skelton: Director of the Centre for Child Law at the University of Pretoria and one of the chief advocates of restorative justice in the sphere of juvenile justice. She was involved in child justice reform initiatives during the 1990s.

Julia Sloth-Nielson: Dean of the Law Faculty at the University of the Western Cape. She was involved in juvenile justice reform initiatives in the 1980s and 1990s.

Elrena van der Spuy: Associate Professor at the University of Cape Town's Institute of Criminology. She was involved in community policing initiatives during the transition period.

Bibliography

Books, Journal Articles and other Documentary Sources

Abel, R. 1982. The Politics of Informal Justice: Comparative Studies, Vol. 2. London: Academic Press.

Albrecht, H. 1999. Countries in transition: effects of political, social and economic change on crime and criminal justice – sanctions and their implementation. *European Journal of Crime, Criminal Law and Criminal Justice*, 7: 448–79.

Alence, R. 1999. The democratic transition and crime in South Africa, the record of the 1990s. *Nedbank ISS Crime Index*, 3: March–April.

Alence, R. and Pimstone, G. 1999. Crime and the 1999 election, perceptions of voters. *Nedbank ISS Crime Index*, 2: January–February.

Alexander, J. and Kynoch, G. 2011. Introduction: histories and legacies of punishment in Southern Africa. *Journal of Southern African Studies*, 37: 3.

Altbekker, A. 2007. *A Country at War with Itself, South Africa's Crisis of Crime*. Jeppestown: Jonathon Ball Publishers.

Ashworth, A. 1990. *The Politics of Official Discourse in Twentieth-Century South Africa*. Oxford: The Clarendon Press.

Auckerman, M. 2002. Extraordinary evil, ordinary crime: a framework for understanding transitional justice. *Harvard Human Rights Journal*, 15: 39.

Ayers, E. 1984. *Vengeance and Justice, Crime and Punishment in the 19th-Century American South*. Oxford: Oxford University Press.

Badroodien, A. 2000. A History of the Ottery School of Industries in Cape Town: Issues of Race, Welfare and Social Order in the Period 1937 to 1968. PhD dissertation, Faculty of Education, University of the Western Cape.

Bae, S. 2005. The right to life vs. the state's ultimate sanction: abolition of capital punishment in post-apartheid South Africa. *International Journal of Human Rights*, 9(1): 49–68.

Barchiesi, F. 2010. Informality and casualization as challenges to South Africa's industrial unionism: manufacturing workers in the East Rand/Ekurhuleni Region in the 1990s. *African Studies Quarterly*, 11(2 and 3): Spring.

Benit-Gbaffou, C. 2008. Unbundled security services and urban fragmentation in post-apartheid Johannesburg. *Geoforum*, 39: 1933–50.

Bond, P. 2000. *Elite Transition: from Apartheid to Neoliberalism in South Africa*. London: Pluto Press.

Bordieu, P. 1998. The essence of neoliberalism. What is neoliberalism? A programme for destroying collective structures which may impede the pure market logic. *Le Monde Diplomatique*, December.

Bosworth, M. and Guild, M. 2008. Governing through migration control. Security and citizenship in Britain. *British Journal of Criminology*, 48: 703–19, September.

Brenner, N. and Theodore, N. 2002. Cities and the geographies of actually existing neoliberalism. *Antipode*: 349–79.

Brenner, N., Peck, J. and Theodore. N. 2010a. Variegated neoliberalization: geographies, modalities, pathways. *Global Networks*, 10(2): 182–222.

Brenner, N., Peck, J. and Theodore, N. 2010b. After neoliberalization? *Globalizations*, 7.

Bright, C. 1996. *The Powers that Punish: Prison and Politics in the Era of the "Big House," 1920–1955*. Ann Arbor, MI: The University of Michigan Press.

Brogden, M. and Shearing, C. 1993. *Policing for a new South Africa*. London: Routledge.

Brown, M. 2002. The politics of penal excess and the echo of colonial penality. *Punishment and Society*, 4(4): 403–23.

Brown, S. 1984. A study of juvenile delinquency among Zulus in Natal, with particular reference to accounts and views of the delinquency. PhD dissertation, Durban: University of Natal.

Brown, S. 1985. Juvenile delinquency: some views among Zulus in Natal. *South African Journal of Criminal Law and Criminology (SACC)/Suid-Afrikaanse Tydskrif vir strafreg and Kriminologie (SASK)*, 9(1): April.

Bruce, D. 2007. The violent nature of crime in South Africa. A concept paper for the Justice, Crime Prevention and Security Cluster. The Centre for the Study of Violence and Reconciliation, 25 June.

Bruce, D. and Gould, C. 2009. The war against the causes of crime. Advocacy for social crime prevention in the face of tougher law enforcement. *SA Crime Quarterly*, No. 30, December.

Budlender, G. and Davis, D. 1984. Labour law, influx control and citizenship: the emerging policy conflict. *Acta Juridica*, 1: 141–72.

Buhrmann, M. 1980. The inner reality of the Black man and his criminal responsibility. *South African Medical Journal*, 58: 817–20.

Butana, K. and Hartley, A. 2012. Zille's army plan slammed. *IOL News*, 10 July, http://www.iol.co.za/news/crime-courts/zille-s-army-plan-slammed (accessed on 20 September 2012).

Butler, A. 2012. More than a hint of truth in Moyo's claims about South Africa. *Business Day*. 28 September 2012. http://www.bdlive.co.za/opinion/columnists/2012/09/28/more-than-a-hint-of-truth-in-moyos-claims-about-south-africa (accessed on 1 October 2012).

Buur, L. 2004. Introduction: vigilantism and the policing of everyday life in South Africa. *African Studies*, 63(2): December.

Buur, L. and Jensen, S. 2007. The South Africanisation of post-apartheid South Africa: nation-state building and consequences for mobile livelihoods, in: L. Buur, S. Jensen and F. Stepputat (eds.), *The Security-Development Nexus: Expressions of Sovereignty and Securitization in Southern Africa*. Pretoria: HSRC Press.

Caldeira, T. 2000. *City of Walls, Crime, Segregation, and Citizenship in Sao Paulo*. Berkeley, CA: University of California Press.
Calitz, J. 1988. Crime patterns as a basis for crime prevention strategies – a policing approach, in: C. Naude and R. Stevens, (eds.), *Crime Prevention Strategies*. Pretoria: De Jager-HAUM.
Carlen, P. 2006. Imprisonment and the penal body politic: the cancer of disciplinary governance, in: A. Liebling and S. Maruna (eds.), *The Effects of Imprisonment*. Cullompton, UK: Willan Publishing.
Carlen, P. 2010. Roundtable: a criminological imagination. Essays on justice, punishment, discourse. A roundtable discussion with Pat Carlen. *American Society of Criminology, Annual Meeting*. 17 November 2010.
Cassere, D. 1996. A harrowing week listening to the pain of our crime ravaged city. *Cape Times*, 23 August 1996, South African National Archives, Cape Town Records Centre.
Charney, C. 1983. Politics: National Party, *South African Review 1, Same Foundations New Facades*.
Cheliotis, L. and Xenakis, S. 2010. What's neoliberalism got to do with it? Towards a political economy of punishment in Greece. *Criminology and Criminal Justice*, 10: 353.
Chinkanda, E. and Maphatane, M. 1990. Juvenile delinquency: social work data, in: J. Lotter, L. Ndabandaba and R. Esterhuysen, (eds.), *Crime and its Impact: A Study in a Black Metropolitan area, Research Papers*. Pretoria: HSRC.
Chisholm, L. 1989. Reformatories and industrial schools in South Africa: a study in class, colour and gender, 1882–1932. PhD dissertation, Johannesburg: University of the Witwatersrand.
Clear, T. 2008. Mindful punishment: what to do about the South African penal system, and why. *South Africa Crime Quarterly*, 23(1–6): March.
Clinard, M. and Abbott, D. 1973. *Crime in Developing Countries, A Comparative Perspective*. New York: Wiley.
Cloete, M. 1979. Some elements of negative assimilation in the closed prison society. *South African Journal of Criminal Law and Criminology (SACC)/ Suid-Afrikaanse Tydskrif vir Strafreg and Kriminologie* (SASK), 3(3): November.
Cloete, N. and Muller, J. 1991. Human sciences research council incorporated (Pty) Ltd: social science research, markets and accountability in South Africa, in: J. Jansen (ed.), *Knowledge and Power in South Africa: Critical Perspectives Across the Disciplines*. Johannesburg: Skotaville.
Cohen, S. 1985. *Visions of Social Control: Crime, Punishment and Classification*, Cambridge: Polity Press.
Comaroff, J. and Comaroff, J. 2006. Figuring crime: quantifacts and the production of the un/real. *Public Culture*, 18: 209–47.
Corpun 1985. Judicial corporal punishment in South Africa. *World Corporal Punishment Research*, http://www.corpun.com/jcpza2.htm (accessed on 12 January 2010).

Cronje, G.1982. *The Delinquent as a Personality: The Concept of Bio-Sociocriminological Causality*, Part 1. Pretoria: UNISA.

Cruikshank, B. 1999. *The Will to Empower. Democratic Citizens and Other Subjects*. Ithaca: Cornell University Press.

Cruikshank, B. 2004. Neopolitics: policy decentralization and governmentality. Paper presented at the conference on Professionals between Policy and People, Amsterdam/Utrecht, 7–8 October 2004.

Crush, J. and McDonald, D. 2001. Introduction to special issue: evaluating South African immigration policy after apartheid. *Africa Today*, 48(3): Fall.

Crush, J. and Williams, V. 2003. Criminal Tendencies: Immigrants and Illegality in South Africa, Southern Africa Migration Project, Migration Policy Brief No. 10, Cape Town.

Davis, D. 1985. Introduction: criminology and South Africa, in: D. Davis and M. Slabbert (eds.), *Crime and Power in South Africa.* Cape Town: David Philip.

Davis, D. and le Roux, M. 2009. *Precedent and Possibility. The (Ab)use of Law in South Africa.* Cape Town: Double Story.

De Giorgi, A. 2006. *Rethinking the Political Economy of Punishment: Perspectives on Post-Fordism and Penal Politics.* Aldershot: Ashgate.

De Minnaar, A. and Esterhuysen, R. 1990. The community and its people, in: J. Lotter, L. Ndabandaba, R. Esterhuysen (eds.), *Crime and its Impact: A Study in a Black Metropolitan Area, Research Papers*. Pretoria: HSRC.

De Olieveira, J. and De Olieveira, S. 1983. Corporal punishment. *The Magistrate*, 91–202.

De Tocqueville, A. 1864. *Democracy in America*, transl. H. Reeve. Cambridge: Sever and Francis.

Devenish, G. 1992. The death penalty in South Africa and its relationship with constitutional and political reform. *South African Journal of Criminal Justice* 5(1): 1.

Dixon, B. 2000. *The Globalisation of Democratic Policing: Sector Policing and Zero Tolerance in the New South Africa*. Cape Town: Institute of Criminology.

Dixon, B. 2004a. Cosmetic crime prevention, in: B. Dixon and E. Van der Spuy (eds.), *Justice Gained? Crime and Crime Control in South Africa's Transition.* Cape Town/Cullompton, UK: UCT Press/Willan.

Dixon, B. 2004b. In search of interactive globalization: critical criminology in South Africa's transition. *Crime, Law and Social Change*, 41: 359–84.

Dixon, B. 2004c. Justice gained? Crime, crime control and criminology in transition, in: B. Dixon and E. Van der Spuy (eds.), *Justice Gained? Crime and Crime Control in South Africa's Transition*. Cape Town/Cullompton, UK: UCT Press/Willan.

Dixon, B. 2006. Development, crime prevention and social policy in post-apartheid South Africa. *Critical Social Policy*, 26: 169.

Dolley, C. 2011. Mountain Knife Attack. *Cape Times*, 21 November 2011.

Donzelot, J. 1979. *The Policing of Families*, trans. Robert Hurley. New York: Pantheon.

Dubow, S. 1995. *Illicit Union: Scientific Racism in Modern SA*. Cambridge: Cambridge University Press.

Dugard, J. 2001. Drive on? Taxi wars in South Africa, in: Steinberg, J. (ed.), *Crime Wave*. Johannesburg: Wits University Press.

Dumm, T. 1987. *Democracy and Punishment: Disciplinary Origins of the United States*. Madison, WI: University of Wisconsin Press, 1987.

Du Plessis, A. and Louw, A. 2005. The tide is turning, the 2003/2004 SAPS crime statistics. *Crime Quarterly*, 12.

Du Preez, G. 1992. Police and policing in the new South Africa, paper presented at Conference on Policing in the New SA, Durban 19–21 September, AK 2915 CALS C3 Conferences C3.4.b C 3.5.1–2, South African History Archive, University of the Witwatersrand.

Durkheim, E. 1982. *The Rules of Sociological Method*. New York: The Free Press.

Duwenhage, S. 1975. Permissiwiteit as grooibodem vir misdaad, in: P. Van de Walt (ed.), *Misdaad in die Gemeenskap/Crime and Society*. Pretoria: UNISA.

Edwards, P. and Hecht, G. 2010. History and the technopolitics of identity: the case of apartheid South Africa. *Journal of Southern African Studies*, 36(3): 619–39.

Everett, L. 2010. Inequalities keep us apart from each other. *Cape Times*, 13 January.

Fagan, H. 2004. Curb the vengeance, laws on minimum sentencing and parole spell worsening prison conditions. *SA Crime Quarterly*, No 10.

Feeley, M. and Simon, J. 1992. The New Penology: Notes on the emerging strategy of corrections and its implications. *Criminology*, 30(4): 449–74.

Feld, B. 1999. *Bad Kids, Race and the Transformation of the Juvenile Court*. New York: Oxford University Press.

Ferrinho, H. 1979. Interpreting crime in South Africa. *South African Journal of Criminal Law and Criminology (SACC)/Suid-Afrikaanse Tydskrif vir Strafreg and Kriminologie (SASK)*, 3(1): April, 37–42.

Filippi, N. 2011. Deviance, punishment and logics of subjectification during apartheid: insane, political and common-law prisoners in a South African gaol. *Journal of Southern African Studies*, 37(3): September, 627–43.

Foster, D., Haupt, P., de Beer, M. 1998. *The Theatre of Violence: Narratives of Protagonists in the South African Conflict*. Pretoria: HSRC Press.

Foucault, M. 1980. *The History of Sexuality*, Vol.1, transl. Robert Hurley. New York: Random House.

Foucault, M. 1982. The subject and power. Published as the Afterword to H. Dreyfus and P. Rabinow, *Michel Foucault: Beyond Structuralism and Hermeneutics*. Brighton/Chicago: Harvester/Chicago University Press, 208–26.

Foucault, M. 1991. Governmentality, in: Burchell, G., Gordon, C. and Miller, P. (eds.), *The Foucault Effect, Studies in Governmentality*. Chicago, IL: The University of Chicago Press.

Foucault, M. 1977, 1995. *Discipline and Punish: The Birth of the Prison*, Transl. Alan Sheridan. New York: Vintage Books.

Foucault, M. 2000. Power, in: J. Faubion (ed.), *Essential Works of Foucault, 1954–1984*, Vol. 3. New York: New Press.

Frank, C. 2007. Quality services guaranteed, a review of victim services in South Africa, *ISS Monograph Series*, Monograph No. 137, July. Pretoria: Institute for Security Studies.

Garland, D. An Introduction to the "Governmentality Literature", unpublished, on file with the author.

Garland, D. 1985. *Punishment and Welfare, A History of Penal Strategies*. Aldershot: Gower.

Garland, D. 1990. *Punishment and modern society: a study in social theory*. Chicago/Oxford: University of Chicago Press/Oxford University Press.

Garland, D. 1996. The limits of the sovereign state: strategies of crime control in contemporary society. *British Journal of Criminology*, 36(4): 445–71.

Garland, D. 2001. *The Culture of Control. Crime Control and Social Order in Contemporary Society*. Oxford: Oxford University Press.

Garland, D. 2003. Penal modernism and postmodernism, in: S. Cohen and T.Blomberg (eds.), *Punishment and Social Control*. New York: Aldine de Gruyter.

Garland, D. 2008. On the concept of moral panic. *Crime, Media, Culture*, 4(1): 9–30.

Garland, D. 2010. Critic on panel of author meets critics: Prisons of Poverty. *American Society of Criminology, Annual Meeting*, 18 November 2010.

Gelb, S. 1991. South Africa's economic crisis: an overview, in: S. Gelb (ed.), *South Africa's Economic Crisis*. Cape Town/New Jersey: David Philip/Zed Books.

Giffard, C. (1997). Out of step?: The transformation process in the South African Department of Correctional Services. Unpublished MSc dissertation, Scarman Centre for the Study of Public Order, University of Leicester.

Giffard, C. and Muntingh, L. 2006. The effect of sentencing on the size of the South African prison population. Open Society Foundation, http://www.osf.org.za/Publications/default.asp?PubCatID=30&offset=15 (accessed on 11 September 2006).

Gillespie, K. 2007. Criminal Abstractions and the Post-Apartheid Prison. PhD dissertation, Anthropology Department, University of Chicago.

Gillespie, K. 2008. Moralizing security: 'corrections' and the post-apartheid prison. *Race/Ethnicity: Multidisciplinary Global Perspectives*, 2(1): Autumn, 69–87.

Gillespie, K. 2011. Containing the 'wandering native': racial jurisdiction and the liberal politics of prison reform in 1940s South Africa. *Journal of Southern African Studies*, 37(3): 499–515.

Gilling, D. 2010. Crime control and due process in confidence-building strategies, a governmentality perspective. *British Journal of Criminology*, 50: 1136–54.

Glanz, L. 1989. *Coping with Crime: The South African Public's Perceptions of and Reactions to Crime*. Pretoria: HSRC.

Glanz, L. 1990. Juvenile delinquency and self-report data, in: J. Lotter, L. Ndabandaba, R. Esterhuysen (eds.), *Crime and its Impact: A Study in a Black Metropolitan Area, Research Papers*. Pretoria: HSRC.

Glaser, C. 1998. We must infiltrate the Tsotsis: School politics and youth gangs in Soweto, 1968–1976. *Journal of Southern African Studies*, 14: June.

Goodman, P. 2012. Hero and inmate: work, prisons, and punishment in California's fire camps. *Special issue (Labor and the Political Economy of Punishment)* of *Working USA: The Journal of Labor and Society*, 15(3): 353–76.

Gordon, D.1998. Crime in the new South Africa. *The Nation*, 9 November.

Gordon, D. 2001. Side by side: neoliberalism and crime control in post-apartheid South Africa. *Social Justice*, 28(3): 141–88.

Gordon, D. 2006. *Transformation and Trouble: Crime, Justice and Participation in Democratic South Africa*. Ann Arbor, MI: University of Michigan Press.

Gottschalk, M. 2006. *The Prison and the Gallows, The Politics of Mass Incarceration in America*. New York: Cambridge University Press

Gould, C. 2009. Editorial. *South African Crime Quarterly*, 27: March.

Gould, C. 2012. Fear, anger and avarice: how not to craft solutions to violence. *Institute for Security Studies*, 30 August. http://www.issafrica.org/iss_today.php?ID=1537&utm_source=ISS%2BWeekly%2B34&utm_medium=Email&utm_campaign=ISS%2BWeekly (accessed on 30 August 2012).

Graser, R. 1985. Parole in South Africa: attitudes and opinions of judicial officers, prison personnel and aftercare social workers. *South African Journal of Criminal Law and Criminology (SACC)/Suid-Afrikaanse Tydskrif vir Strafreg and Kriminologie (SASK)*, 28(3): April, 28–38.

Guetzkow, J. 2006. Constructing welfare and criminal justice policies, Paper presented at American Sociological Association annual meeting.

Hacking, I. 1986. Making up people, in: T. Heller, M. Sosna and D. Wellbery (eds.), *Reconstructing Individualism*. Stanford: Stanford University Press.

Hacking, I. 1999. *The Social Construction of What*. Cambridge: Harvard University Press.

Hall, S. 2003. New Labour's double shuffle. *Soundings*, 24: 10–24.

Hannah-Moffat, K. 1999. Moral agent or actuarial subject: risk and Canadian women's imprisonment. *Theoretical Criminology*, 3(1): 71–94.

Hannah-Moffat, K. 2000. Prisons that empower: neoliberal governance in Canadian women's prisons. *British Journal of Criminology*, 40: 510–31.

Hannah-Moffat, K. 2005. Criminogenic needs and the transformative risk subject. Hybridizations of risk/need in penality. *Punishment and Society*, 7(1): 29–51.

Harcourt-Baldwin, J. 1981. Sentencing in South African juvenile courts. *Natal University Law Review*, 2: 479.

Hay, C. 1996. *Re-stating Social and Political Change*. Milton Keynes: Open University Press.

Hay, D. 1976. Property, authority and the criminal law, in: D. Hay, P. Linebaugh and E.P. Thompson (eds.), *Albion's Fatal Tree: Crime and Society in Eighteenth Century England*. London: Allen Lane.

Haysom, N. 1981. *Towards an Understanding of Prison Gangs*. Cape Town: Institute of Criminology, University of Cape Town.

Hirsch, L. 1992. *The Rise of the Penitentiary Prisons and Punishment in Early America*. Yale Historical Publications.

Holt, N. 1989. Human rights and capital punishment: the case of South Africa. *Virginia Journal of International Law*, 30.

Hudson, B. 1987. *Justice Through Punishment: A Critique of the "Justice" Model of Correction*. New York: St Martin's Press.

Humphries, R. 2000. Crime and confidence: voter's perceptions of crime. *Nedbank ISS Crime Index*, 2(4), March–April.

Human Rights Watch 1997. Prohibited persons: abuse of undocumented migrants, asylum seekers and refugees in South Africa.

Hunt, A. 2003. Risk and moralization in everyday life, in: R. Ericson and A. Doyle (eds.), *Risk and Morality*. Toronto: University of Toronto Press, pp. 165–92.

Hutchinson, S. 2006. Countering catastrophic criminology, reform, punishment and the modern liberal compromise. *Punishment and Society*, 8(4): 443–67.

Ignatieff, M. 1978. *A Just Measure of Pain: The Penitentiary in the Industrial Revolution, 1750–1850*. New York: Pantheon Books.

Institute for Security Studies, 2012. Fact sheet: explaining the official crime statistics for 2011/12. 20 September 2012. http://www.issafrica.org/crimehub/system/components/blog/files/2012_Crime_Stats_Factsheet.pdf (accessed on 1 October 2012).

Jensen, S. 200. The South African transition: from development to security? *Development and Change*, 36(3): 551–70.

Jensen, S. 2008. *Gangs, Politics and Dignity in Cape Town*. Oxford/Chicago/Johannesburg: James Curry, The University of Chicago Press, Wits University Press.

Johnson, R. 2009. *South Africa's Brave New World: The Beloved Country since the End of Apartheid*. London: Penguin.

Katzin, K. 1977. Crime soars as politics, poverty gnaw at morale. *Cape Times*, 25 September, Cape Times: file X147471977, National Archives of South Africa, Cape Town.

Kelling, G. and Coles, C. 1996. *Fixing Broken Windows: Restoring Order and Reducing Crime in Our Communities*. New York: The Free Press.

King, D. 1999. *In the Name of Liberalism: Illiberal Social Policy in the USA and Britain*. Oxford: Oxford University Press.

Kinnes, 1. 2000. From urban street gangs to criminal empires: the changing face of gangs in the Western Cape. *ISS Monograph Series*, no. 48. Pretoria: Institute for Security Studies.

Klaaren, J. and Ramji, J. 2001. Inside illegality: migration policing in South Africa after apartheid. *Africa Today*, 48(3): Fall.

Kneen, D. 199. Siege of the suburbs. *The Argus*, 30 November 91, 63687 May–December 1991, South African National Archives, Cape Town Records Centre.

KPMG and TRL (2009). Department of Community Safety. 10 Safety Audits. Final Report on Khayelitsha Police Station, 30 March 2009, R2903-6468, KPMG (Pty) Ltd.

Kynoch, G. 2005. Crime, conflict and politics in transition-era South Africa. *African Affairs*, 104: 416.

Kynoch, G. 2008. Violence in colonial Africa: a case for South African exceptionalism. *Journal of Southern African Studies*, 34: 3.

Kynoch, G. 2011. Of compounds and cellblocks: the foundations of violence in Johannesburg, 1890s–1950s. *Journal of Southern African Studies*, 37(3): 463–77.

Labuschagne, J. 1975. Law enforcement and permissiveness, in: P. Van Der Walt (ed.), *Misdaad in die Gemeenskap/Crime and Society*. Pretoria: UNISA.

Lacey. N. 2008. *The Prisoners' Dilemma, Political Economy and Punishment in Contemporary Democracies*. Cambridge: Cambridge University Press.

Lacey, N. and Zedner, L. 1995. Discourses of community in criminal justice. *Journal of Law and Society*, 22(3): September, 301–25.

Landau, L. 2005. Transplants and transients: nativism, nationalism and migration in inner-city Johannesburg. Forced Migration Studies Programme. Working paper #19, Johannesburg.

Landau, L. 2011. Introducing the demons, in: Landau (ed.), *Exorcising the Demons Within. Xenophobia. Violence and Statecraft in Contemporary South Africa.* Johannesburg: Wits University Press.

Larner, W. 2000. Neo-liberalism: policy, ideology, governmentality. *Studies in Political Economy*, 63: 5–25.

Larner, W. 2009. Neoliberalism, Mike Moore and the WTO. *Environment and Planning A*, 41: 1576–93.

Laufer, S. 2001. The politics of fighting crime in South Africa since 1994, in: J. Steinberg (ed.), *Crime Wave.* Johannesburg: Wits University Press.

Leggett, T. 1999. For better or worse? Criminal legislation in 1998. *Crime and Conflict*, (15), Autumn.

Leggett, T. 2003. Rainbow tenement: crime and policing in inner Johannesburg, Monograph No. 78. Pretoria: Institute for Security Studies.

Leggett, T. 2004. Crime in the Coloured community, 7 *SA Crime Quarterly*. Pretoria: Institute for Security Studies.

Leibbrandt, M., Woolard, I., Finn, A. and Argent, J. 2010. Trends in South African Income Distribution and Poverty since the Fall of Apartheid. *OECD Social, Employment and Migration Working papers No. 101*. OECD Publishing, doi:10.1787/5kmms0t7p1ms-en.

Lenta, P. 2001. Just gaming? The case for post-modernism in South African legal theory. *South African Journal on Human Rights*, 17: 173.

Le Roux, J. 1996. Street children in South Africa: findings from interviews on the background of street children in Pretoria, South Africa. *Adolescence*, Summer.

Lichtenstein, A. 1996. *Twice the Work of Free Labor, the Political Economy of Convict Labor in the New South.* New York, London: Verso.

Loader, I. 2006. Policing, recognition and belonging. 605 *Annals, The American Academy of Political and Social Science*, 605: May, 202–21.

Loader, I. and Sparks, R. 2010. Wacquant and civic sociology: 'formative intentions' and formative experiences. *Criminology and Criminal Justice*, 10: 405.

Loening, W. 1981. Child abuse among the Zulus: a people in cultural transition. *Child Abuse and Neglect*, 5: 3.

Los, M. 2002. Post-communist fear of crime and the commercialization of security. *Theoretical Criminology*, 6: 165–88.

Lotter J. and Schurink, W. 1986. *Gevangenisbendes: 'n ondersoek met spesiale verwysing na nommerbendes onder kleurlinggevangenes*, Pretoria: Raad vir Geestesnavorsing, Verslag S-115.

Lotter, J. and Ndabandaba, G. 1990. Orientation, in: J. Lotter, L Ndabandaba; R Esterhuysen (eds.), *Crime and its Impact: A Study in a Black Metropolitan Area, Research Papers*. Pretoria: HSRC.

Louw, A. and Schonteich, M. 2001. Playing the numbers game: promises, policing and crime statistics, in: Steinberg, J. (ed.), *Crime Wave*. Johannesburg: Wits University Press.

Mabin, A. 1998. Social geography of divided cities/urban division, presented at the International Centre for Advanced Studies, Project on Cities and Urban Knowledges, New York University (18–26 February).

Makhubu, N. 2011. Children die in desperate search for food. *Cape Times*, 21 November.

Machava, L. 2011. State discourse on internal security and the politics of punishment in post-independence Mozambique. *Journal of Southern African Studies*, 37(3): 593–609.

Mandela, N. 1995. Address on the occasion of the opening of the second session of the democratic parliament Cape Town, 17 February 1995, www.info.gov.za/speeches/1995/170595001.htm (accessed on 12 January 2007).

Mandela, N. 1998. Address at the closing of parliament, 6 February 1998, http://www.anc.org.za/ancdocs/history/mandela/1998/sp980206.html (accessed on 12 January 2007).

Marais, H. 2001. *South Africa: Limits to Change: the Political Economy of Transition*. Cape Town/London: UCT Press/Zed Press.

Marais, H. 2011. *South Africa. Pushed to the Limit, The Political Economy of Change*. Cape Town: UCT Press.

Martel, J., Brassard, R. and Jaccoud, M. 2011. When two worlds collide: Aboriginal risk management in Canadian Corrections. *British Journal of Criminology*, 51(2): March, 235–55.

McClellan, R. 2008. *The Crisis of Imprisonment. Protest, Politics, and the Making of the American Penal State, 1776–1941*. New York: Cambridge University Press.

Mbeki, T. 2004. Address of the President of South Africa, Thabo Mbeki at the Opening Ceremony of the 16 Days of Activism Campaign. Motherwell, 25

November, www.dfa.gov.za/docs/speeches/2004/mbek1126.htm (accessed on 14 August 2007).

Mbeki, T. 2006. State of the Nation Address, http://www.info.gov.za/speeches/2006/06020310531001.htm (accessed on 14 August 2007).

McCord, A. 2007. Expanded public works programme delivers only short-term benefits, steps to address poverty fall far short of mark. *Cape Times*, 8 March.

McDonald, D. 2002. No Money, No Service. South Africa's poorest citizens out under attempts to recover service costs for water and power. *Alternatives Journal*, 28(2): 16–20.

Mclachlan, F. 1986. *Children in Prison.* Cape Town: Institute of Criminology, University of Cape Town.

Media Tenor 2008. Lessons in the rear-view mirror: the part the South African media have played in stoking xenophobic sentiments. *Media Tenor Newsletter*, 4 June.

Meranze, M. 1996. *Laboratories of Virtue: Punishment, Revolution, and Authority in Philadelphia, 1760–1835*. Chapel Hill: University of North Carolina Press.

Midgley, J. 1977. Crime in South Africa: a comparative analysis. *South African Journal of Criminal Law and Criminology*, 1: 71–92.

Midgley, J. 1982. Corporal punishment and penal policy: Notes on the continued use of corporal punishment with reference to South Africa. *The Journal of Criminal Law and Criminology*, 73(1): 388–403.

Muehlebach, A. 2007. The moral neoliberal: welfare state and ethical citizenship in contemporary Italy. PhD dissertation, Department of Anthropology, University of Chicago.

Nash, M. 1976. Why they burn their schools, *Cape Times*, 22 June 1976, Cape Times file: x14746, South African National Archives, Cape Town.

Nathan, L. and Collin, S. 1993. From Police Force to Service. *Track Two*, 2(4): November.

Nattrass, N. 1999. Gambling on investment: Competing economic strategies in South Africa, in: G. Maharaj (ed.), *Essays on Nation-Building in Post-Apartheid South Africa, Between Unity and Diversity*. Cape Town: David Philip Publishers.

Naude, C. 1988a. Approaches to prevention, in: C. Naude and R. Stevens (eds.), *Crime Prevention Strategies*. Pretoria: De Jager-HAUM.

Naude, C. 1988b. Prison treatment programmes for crime prevention, in: C. Naude and R. Stevens (eds.), *Crime Prevention Strategies*. Pretoria: De Jager-HAUM.

Ndabandaba, G.1987. *Crimes of Violence in Black Townships*. Durban: Butterworths.

Ndabandaba, G. 1990a. Faction Fights, in: J. Lotter, L. Ndabandaba and R. Esterhuysen (eds.), *Crime and Its Impact: A Study in a Black Metropolitan Area, Research Papers.* Pretoria: HSRC.

Ndabandaba, G. 1990b. Juvenile gangs, in: J. Lotter, L. Ndabandaba and R. Esterhuysen (eds.), *Crime and Its Impact: A Study in a Black Metropolitan Area, Research Papers.* Pretoria: HSRC.

Ngculu, J. 2009. *The Honour to Serve, Recollections of an Umkhonto Soldier*. Johannesburg: David Philip.

Nelken, D. 2010. Denouncing the penal state. *Criminology and Criminal Justice*, 10: 331.

Newburn T. 2010. Diffusion, differentiation and resistance in comparative penality, *Criminology and Criminal Justice*, 10: 341.

Olsen, T. 1976. Tsotsis blamed for vandalism. *Cape Times*,1 July 1976, file: x14746, South African National Archives, Cape Town.

Olsen, T. 1976. A year marked by a rash of lawlessness. *Cape Times*, 30 December 1976 file: x14746, South African National Archives, Cape Town.

Olmesdahl, M. 1982. Predicting the death sentence. *South African Journal of Criminal Law and Criminology (SACC)/Suid-Afrikaanse Tydskrif vir Strafreg and Kriminologie (SASK)*, 6(3): 201–18.

O'Malley, P. 1992. Risk, power and crime prevention. *Economy and Society*, 21(3): August.

O'Malley, P. 1996. Post social criminologies, some implications of current political trends for criminological theory and practice. *Current Issues in Criminal Justice*, July.

O'Malley, P. 1999. Volatile and contradictory punishment. *Theoretical Criminology*, 3(2): 175–96.

O'Malley, P. 2004a. *Risk, Uncertainty and Government*. Portland, OR: Cavendish Publishing.

O'Malley, P. 2004b. Penal policies and contemporary politics in: Sumner, C. (ed.), *The Blackwell Companion to Criminology*. Oxford: Blackwell.

Parenti, C. 1999. *Lockdown America: Police and Prisons in the Age of Crisis*. London: Verso.

Peck, J. 2001. Neoliberalizing states: thin policies/hard outcomes. *Progress in Human Geography*, 25(3): 445–55.

Peck, J. 2003. Geography and public policy: mapping the penal state. *Progress in Human Geography*, 27(2): 222–32.

Peck, J. 2004. Geography and public policy: constructions of neoliberalism. *Progress in Human Geography*, 28: 392.

Peck, J. and Tickel, A. 2002. Neoliberalizing space. *Antipode*, 380–404.

Peck, J., Theodore, N. and Brenner, N. 2009. Postneoliberalism and its malcontents. *Antipode*. 41(s1): 94–116.

Peet, R. 2002. Ideology, discourse and the geography of hegemony: from socialist to neoliberal development in postapartheid South Africa. *Antipode*, 54–84.

Pete, S. 1998. The politics of imprisonment in the aftermath of South Africa's first democratic election. *South African Journal of Criminal Justice*, 11: 51–83.

Pete, S. 2000. The good, the bad and the warehoused: the politics of imprisonment in the run-up to South Africa's second democratic elections. *South African Journal of Criminal Justice*, 13.

Pelser, E. 2000. Operation Crackdown: the new policing strategy. *Nedbank ISS Crime Index*, 4(2): March–April.

Pelser, E. and Louw A. 2002. Lessons from practice, in: E. Pelser (ed.), *Crime Prevention Partnerships: Lessons from Practice*. Pretoria: Institute for Security Studies.

Phillips, S. 2004.The Expanded Public Works Programme (EPWP): overcoming underdevelopment in South Africa's second economy, http://www.sarpn.org.za/documents/d0000986/P1102-Phillips_Public_Works_Oct2004.pdf (accessed on 25 June 2007).

Platt, A. 1969. *The Child Savers: the Invention of Delinquency*. Chicago, IL: University of Chicago.

Polzer, T. and Takabvirwa, K. 2010. Just crime? Violence, xenophobia and crime: discourse and practice. *South African Crime Quarterly* 33, 2–10 September, Institute for Security Studies.

Posel, D. 1984. Language, legitimation and control: the South African State after 1978. *Social Dynamics*, 10(1): 1–16.

Power, M. 1994. The Audit Explosion, Paper No. 7. London: Demos.

Power, M. 1997. From risk society to audit society. *Soziale Systeme*, 3: 3–21.

Pratt, J. 2000. The return of the wheelbarrow men or; the arrival of postmodern penality. *British Journal of Criminology*, 40: 127–45.

Pridemore, W. and Sang-weon K. 2006. Democratization and political change as threats to collective sentiments: testing Durkheim in Russia. *Annals, American Academy of Political and Social Science*, 605: May.

Rauch, J. 2002. Changing step: crime prevention policy in South Africa, in: E. Pelser (ed.), *Crime Prevention Partnerships: Lessons from Practice*. Pretoria: Institute for Security Studies.

Rauch, J. 2005. Crime prevention and morality, the campaign for Moral Regeneration in South Africa, *ISS Monograph Series* No. 114, April. Pretoria: Institute for Security Studies.

Rauch, J. 2007. Criminal justice after apartheid, in: C. Call (ed.), *Constructing Justice and Security after War*. Washington, DC: United States Institute of Peace Press.

Retief, G. 1968. *Die Bantoe in die Stad: Misdaad*. Pretoria: SABRA.

Robinson, G. 2008. Late-modern rehabilitation: the evolution of a penal strategy. Punishment and Society, 10: 429.

Rocha, S. (1983). *Die Meting van Alkohol inname in die Kleurling Woonbeurt Eersterus-'n Toepassing van die Khavafri Alkohol Toets*. RGN Uitgewers.

Rose, N. 1996. The death of the social? Re-figuring the territory of government, *Economy and Society*, 25(3): August, 327–56.

Rose, N. 1999. *Powers of Freedom, Reframing Political Thought*. Cambridge: Cambridge University Press.

Rose, N. 2000. Government and control. *British Journal of Criminology*, 40: 321–39.

Roux, J. 1975. The treatment of offenders. *Crime, Punishment and Corrections*, 4(2), June, 16–27.

Rowan, M. 2011. Democracy and punishment: a radical view. *Theoretical Criminology*, 16(1): 43–62.
Sachs, A. 1986. The people's courts and people's justice. Some discussion notes, 30 July, A Sachs Box MCH 91, Mayibuye Archives, University of the Western Cape.
Samara, T. 2003. State security in transition: the war on crime in post-apartheid South Africa. *Social Identities: Journal for the Study of Race, Nation and Culture*, 9(2).
Samara, T. 2005. Youth, crime and urban renewal in the Western Cape. *Journal of Southern African Studies*, 31(1): March, 209–27.
Samara, T. 2011. *Cape Town after Apartheid. Crime and Governance in the Divided City.* London, Minneapolis: University of Minnesota Press.
Sampson, R. 1995. The community, in: J. Wilson and J. Petersilia (eds.), *Crime*. San Francisco, CA: Institute for Contemporary Studies.
Sanders, M. 2000. Truth, telling, questioning: the Truth and Reconciliation Commission, Antjie Krog's Country of My Skull, and literature after apartheid. *Modern Fiction Studies*, 46(1): Spring, 13–41.
Scharf, W.1990. The resurgence of urban street gangs and community responses in Cape Town during the late eighties, in: D. Hansson and D. Van Zyl Smit (eds.), *Towards Justice? Crime and State Control in South Africa*. Cape Town: Oxford University Press.
Scheingold, S. 1998. Constructing the new political criminology: power, authority and the post liberal state. *Law and Social Inquiry*, 23(4): 853–95.
Schinkel, W. 2002. The modernist myth in criminology. *Theoretical Criminology*, 6(2): 123–44.
Schmidt, J. 1976. The use of alcohol and tobacco among Blacks, S-N-97. Pretoria: HSRC.
Schonteich, M. 1999a. Assessing the crime fighters: the ability of the criminal justice system to solve and prosecute crime, *Occasional Paper No. 40*, September. Pretoria: Institute for Security Studies.
Schonteich, M. 1999b. Age and aids: South Africa's crime time bomb. *African Security Review*, 8(4).
Schonteich, M. 2001a. The South African Prosecution Service, in: Steinberg, J. (ed.), *Crime Wave.* Johannesburg: Wits University Press.
Schonteich, M. 2001b. Crime trends: a turning point? *SA Crime Quarterly*, 1 July 2002.
Schonteich, M. and Louw, A. 2001. Crime in South Africa: a countries and cities profile, *Occasional Paper No. 49*. Pretoria: Institute for Security Studies.
Schonteich, M. 2002. Making courts work, Pretoria: Institute for Security Studies, Monograph No. 75, October.
Schurink, W. 1982. Prostitution in Johannesburg: preliminary findings. *South African Journal of Criminal Law and Criminology (SACC)/Suid-Afrikaanse Tydskrif vir strafreg and Kriminologie (SASK)*, 6(1): March.

Schurink, W. and Lotter, J. 1975. Class-based sociological theories of deviancy and relevant ecological patterns in Pretoria, *Research finding S-N-70*. Pretoria: HSRC, Institute for Sociological, Demographic and Criminological Research.

Schurink, W. and Strijdom, M. 1976a. Class-based sociological theories of deviancy and relevant ecological patterns in Pretoria, S-N-70. Pretoria: HSRC.

Schurink, W. and Strijdom, M. 1976b. Research finding, data on primary victimization in Soweto, HSRC. *Research finding S-N-79*. Institute for Sociological, Demographic and Criminological Research.

Schurink, W. and Kerr, M. 1986. Paradigms in criminology, in: Schurink and Lotter, W. (eds.), *Research Methodology in criminology: Navorsings Metodologie in die Kriminologie*. Pretoria: HSRC.

Seale, T. 1993. Reeling under crime wave. *Cape Argus*, 27 February, January–July 1993, file 63690, South African National Archives, Cape Town.

Seekings, J. 1995. The 'Lost Generation': South Africa's 'Youth Problem' in the early 1990s. *Transformation*: 29.

Seekings, J. and Nattrass, N. 2005. *Class, Race, and Inequality in South Africa: The Changing Nature of Inequality in South Africa*. New Haven, CT: Yale University Press.

Shaw, M. 1995. 'Partners in Crime'? Crime, political transition and changing forms of policing control, *Transition Series*, Research Report no 39, June. Johannesburg: Centre for Policy Studies.

Shaw, M. 1996. Crime, political transition and changing forms of policing control, in *Policing the Transformation*, Monograph 3, April. Pretoria: Institute for Security Studies.

Shaw, M. 1997. Crime in transition, in: M. Shaw, L. Camerer, D. Mistry, S. Oppler and L. Muntingh, (eds.), *Policing the Transformation: Further Issues in South Africa's Crime Debate*, Monograph 12. Pretoria: Institute for Security Studies.

Shaw, M. 2002. *Crime and Policing in Post-Apartheid South Africa: Transforming under Fire*. London: Hurst.

Shaw, M. and Gastrow, P. 2001. Stealing the show? Crime and its impact in post-apartheid South Africa. *Daedalus, Journal of the American Academy of Science and Arts, Why South Africa Matters*, 130: 237.

Shearing, C. 1991. Policing the transformation. *Work in Progress*, 79 (December): 22.

Shearing, C. 1992. The relation between public and private policing. *Crime and Justice*, 15: 399–434.

Shearing, C. 2001. Punishment and the changing face of governance. *Punishment and Society*, 3(2): 203–20.

Shearing, C. and Stenning, P. 1981. Modern private security: its growth and implications, in: M. Tonry and N. Morris, (eds.), *Crime and Justice – An Annual Review of Research*, vol. 3, pp. 193–245. Chicago, IL: University of Chicago Press.

Sher, M. 1985. Legal control of migrant labour, in: D. Davis and M. Slabbert (eds.), *Crime and Power in South Africa*. Cape Town: David Philip.

Shubane, K. 2001. A question of balance: crime-fighting in a new democracy, in: Steinberg, J. (ed.), *Crime Wave*. Johannesburg: Wits University Press.

Silber, G. and Geffen, N. 2009. Race, class and violent crime in South Africa. *SA Crime Quarterly*, 30 (December): 35–43.

Simon, J. 1993. *Poor Discipline: Parole and the Social Control of the Underclass, 1890–1990*. Chicago, IL: The University of Chicago Press.

Simon, J. 1997. Governing through Crime, in: L. Friedman and G. Fisher (eds.), *The Crime Conundrum: Essays on Criminal Justice*. Boulder, CO: Westview Press.

Simon, J. 2000. From the Big House to the Warehouse: Rethinking prisons and state government in the 20th century. *Punishment and Society*, 2: 213–35.

Simon, J. 2001. Sanctioning government: explaining America's severity revolution. *University of Miami Law Review*, 56: 217–54.

Simon, J. 2007. *How the War on Crime Transformed American Democracy and Created a Culture of Fear*, Studies in Crime and Public Policy. Oxford: Oxford University Press.

Simpson, G. 2001. Shock troops and bandits: youth, crime and politics, in: J. Steinberg (ed.), *Crime Wave*. Johannesburg: Wits University Press.

Simpson, G. 2004. A Snake Gives Birth to a Snake, Politics and Crime in the Transition to Democracy in South Africa, in: B. Dixon and E. Van der Spuy (eds.), *Justice Gained, Crime and Crime Control in South Africa's Transition*. Cape Town/Cullompton, UK: UCT Press/Willan Publishing.

Singh, A. 1999. Changing the soul of the nation? South Africa's National Crime Prevention Strategy. *The British Criminology Conferences, Selected Proceedings*, Vol. 2.

Singh, A. 2005a. Private security and crime control, *Theoretical Criminology*, 9(2): 153–74.

Singh, A. 2005b. Some critical reflections on the governance of crime in post-apartheid South Africa. *Transnational and Comparative Criminology*, 1(3): 135–56.

Singh, A. 2008. *Policing and Crime Control in Post-Apartheid South Africa*. Aldershot: Ashgate.

Sisulu, W. 1986. Keynote address at the NECC (National Education Crisis Committee) Conference, Durban, 27–28 March 1986 (AK 2915 CALS A1.3), South African History Archives, University of the Witwatersrand.

Skelton, A. 2005. The influence of the theory and practice of restorative justice in South Africa with special reference to child justice, LL.D. dissertation, Faculty of Law, University of Pretoria.

Skweyiya, A.T.L., Mabandla B., Marcus, A G.J. 1992. Skweyiya Commission Report.

Report of the Commission of Enquiry into Complaints by former African National Congress Prisoners and Detainees, http://www.anc.org.za/show.php?id=95 (accessed on 10 January 2011).

Sloth-Nielson, J. 1986. A matter of social justice: a review of parole. *SA Journal of Criminal Law and Criminology*, 1 (April): 29.

South African Comrades for the Encounter 1997. Resistance to neoliberalism: a view from South Africa. *Contribution to the Second Intercontinental Encounter for Humanity and Against Neoliberalism*, http://www.geocities.com/CapitolHill/3849/safrica_paper.html (accessed on 22 February, 2004).

South African Human Rights Commission 1999. Report into the arrest and detention of suspected undocumented migrants. March. Johannesburg, http://www.sahrc.org.za/home/21/files/Reports/Report%20into%20the%20Arrest%20and%20Detention%20of%20suspected%20migrants19.pdf (accessed on 5 March 2008).

South African Law Commission 1997. Discussion paper on community dispute resolution structures, Discussion Paper 87, Project 9.

South African Law Commission 2000. A New Sentencing Framework, Project 82, November.

South African Police Service 2012. Crime statistics overview RSA 2011/2012, http://www.saps.gov.za/statistics/reports/crimestats/2012/downloads/crime_statistics_presentation.pdf (accessed on 28 September 2012).

Sparks, R. 2000. Perspectives on risk and penal politics, in: T. Hope and R. Sparks (eds.), *Crime, Risk and Insecurity: Law and Order in Everyday Life and Political Discourse*. Oxon: Routledge.

Sparks, R. 2003. State punishment in advanced capitalist countries, in: S.Cohen and T. Blomberg (eds.), *Punishment and Social Control*. New York: Aldine de Gruyter.

Standing, A. 2003. *Rival views of organised crime*, Monograph 77. Pretoria: Institute for Security Studies.

Standing, A. 2006. *Organised Crime, A Study from the Cape Flats*. Pretoria: Institute for Security Studies.

Steinberg, J. 2004. *The Number, One Man's Search for Identity in the Cape Underworld and Prison Gangs*. Johannesburg: Jonathan Ball Publishing.

Steinberg, J. 2008. *Thin Blue, The Unwritten Rules of Policing in South Africa*. Johannesburg: Jonathon Ball Publishing.

Steinberg, J. 2011. Crime prevention goes abroad: Policy transfer and policing in post-apartheid South Africa. *Theoretical Criminology*, 15(4): 349–64.

Steinberg, J. 2012. Security and disappointment. *The British Journal of Criminology*, 52(2): 345–60.

Stenson, K. 2001. The new politics of crime control, in: K. Stenson and R. Sullivan (eds.), *Crime, Risk and Justice, The Politics of Crime Control in Liberal Democracies*. Cullompton, UK: Willan.

Stevens, R. 1983, 1987. *Introduction to Criminology*. Johannesburg: Macmillan.

Stevens, R. 1988. The Prevention of crimes against the person, in: C. Naude and R. Stevens (eds.), *Crime Prevention Strategies*. Pretoria: De Jager-HAUM.

Steytler, N. 1983. Justice report 1981/82, Record. *South African Journal of Criminal Law and Criminology (SACC)/Suid-Afrikaanse Tydskrif vir Strafreg and Kriminologie (SASK)SACC*, 7(2): July.

Steytler, N. 1992. Reform of the South African Police. *Legal Studies Forum*, Vl XVI (2).

Sumner, C. 1982. *Crime, Justi*ce *and Underdevelopment*. London: Heinemann.

Super, G. 2010. The spectacle of crime in the 'new' South Africa: a historical perspective (1976–2004). *British Journal of Criminology*, 50(2): March.

Super, G. 2011a. 'Like Some Rough Beast Slouching Towards Bethlehem to be Born': A historical perspective on the institution of the prison in South Africa, 1976–2004. *British Journal of Criminology*, 51(1): January, 201–21.

Super, G. 2011b. Punishment and the body in the 'old' and 'new' South Africa, a story of punitive humanism. *Theoretical Criminology*, 15(4): 427–43.

Suttner, R. 1990. From the Freedom Charter to a new constitution. *The Road To Peace, Resource Material on Negotiations*. ANC Department of Political Education, June 1990, Marshaltown, Johannesburg, AK215 CALS N2 Negotiations N2 a b, South African History Archives, University of the Witwatersrand.

Suttner, R. and Cronin, J. 1986. *30 Years of the Freedom Charter*, Johannesburg: Ravan Press.

Swart, D. and Naude, C. 1994. A proposed structure for the reintegration of released offenders in the RSA. *Acta Criminologica*, 7(1).

Terreblanche, S. 2012. *Lost in Transformation. South Africa's Search for a New Future since 1986.* Johannesburg: KMM Review Publishing Company.

Thamm, M. 2000. Crime at an all-time high. *Cape Times*, 2 November 2000, South African National Archives, Cape Town branch.

Theron, F. 1979. Towards radicalism in criminology: a review. *South African Journal of Criminal Law and Criminology (SACC)/Suid-Afrikaanse Tydskrif vir strafreg and Kriminologie (SASK)SACC*, 21.

Thompson, E. 1975. *Whigs and Hunters: The Origin of the Black Act*. London: Allen Lane.

Tikly, L. 2003. Governmentality and the study of education policy in South Africa. *Journal of Education Policy*, 18(2): 161–74.

Tonry, M. 2009. *Thinking about Punishment. Penal Policy across Space, Time and Discipline.* Farnham: Ashgate.

Toups, T. 1985. Inside South Africa's burning townships (with the S.A. Police). *Servamus*, November.

Turrel, R. 2004. Murder and capital punishment after apartheid, in: B. Dixon and E. Van der Spuy (eds.), *Justice Gained? Crime and Crime Control in South Africa's Transition.* Cape Town/Cullompton, UK: UCT Press/Willan.

United Nations Office on Drugs and Crime 2005. Why fighting crime can assist development in Africa, rule of law and the protection of the most vulnerable, www.unodc.org. (accessed on 9 September 2007).

Valverde, M. 2003.Targeted governance and the problem of desire, in: R. Ericson and K. Haggerty (eds.), *Risk and Morality*. Toronto: University of Toronto Press.

Van der Berg, A. 2007. Summary and comment on the Final Report of the Judicial Commission of Inquiry into Allegations of Corruption, Maladministration and

Violence in the Department of Correctional Services – 'the Jali Commission'. Civil Society Prison Reform Initiative, Research Report No. 13. Cape Town: University of the Western Cape.

Van der Burgh, C. and De Beer, F. 1977. The Attitude of Urban Black Ethnic Units Towards the Law, Crime and Aspects of the Criminal Justice System. Pretoria: HSRC.

Van der Burgh, C. 1984. *The Drug-Using Behavior and View on Illicit Drug Use of Post-School White Male South Africans*. Pretoria: HSRC.

Van Der Spuy, E., Scharf, W. and Lever, J. 2004. The politics of youth crime and justice in South Africa, in: Sumner, C. (ed.), *The Blackwell Companion to Criminology*. Oxford: Blackwell.

Van der Walt, P. 1975. *Misdaad in die Gemeenskap/Crime and Society*. Pretoria: UNISA.

Van Der Walt, P., Cronje, G. and Smit, B. 1982. *Kriminologie: 'n inleiding*. Pretoria: Haum

Van Wyk, E. 2011. Deaths escalate after Shabangu says shoot to kill. *City Press*, http://m.news24.com/citypress/SouthAfrica/News/Deaths-escalate-after-Shabangu-says-shoot-to-kill-20110507 (accessed on 20 September 2012).

Van Zilla, C. and Stead, G. 1997. 4000 Cape parolees escape supervision. *Cape Times*, 5 June 1997,Crime Cape Town June–October 1997 Cape Argus (69888), National Archives of South Africa, Cape Town.

Van Zyl Smit, D. 1984. Public policy and the punishment of crime in South Africa. *Crime and Social Justice*, 146.

Van Zyl Smit, D. 1989. Adopting and adapting criminological ideas: criminology and Afrikaner Nationalism in South Africa. *Contemporary Crises*, 13: 227–51.

Van Zyl Smit, D. 1990. Introduction: Contextualising criminology in contemporary South Africa, in: D. Hansson and D. Van Zyl Smit (eds.), *Towards Justice? Crime and State Control in South Africa*. Oxford University Press: Cape Town.

Van Zyl Smit, D. 1998. Change and Continuity in South African Prisons, in: R. Weiss and N. South (eds.), *Comparing Prison Systems. Towards a Comparative and International Penology*. Amsterdam: Gordon and Breach Publishers.

Van Zyl Smit, D. 2004. Swimming against the tide, in: B. Dixon and E. Van der Spuy (eds.), *Justice Gained? Crime and Crime Control in South Africa's Transition*. UCT/Willan: Cape Town/Cullompton, UK.

Van Zyl Smit, D. and Van der Spuy, E. 2004. Importing criminological ideas in a new democracy: recent South African experiences, in: T. Newburn and R. Sparks (eds.), *Criminal Justice and Political Cultures, National and International Dimensions of Crime Control*. Cullompton, UK: Willan.

Venter, H. 1972. *Kriminologie: 'n Handleiding vir Studente in die Kriminologie*. Pretoria: Published privately.

Vetten, L. and Bhana, K. 2005. The justice for women campaign: incarcerated domestic violence survivors in post-apartheid South Africa, in: J. Sudbury (ed.), *Global Lockdown, Race, Gender and the Prison–Industrial Complex*. New York: Routledge.

Vigneswaran, D. and Hlalambelo, T. 2008. Border crimes. *The Wiser Review*, 3.

Wacquant, L. 2001a. Deadly symbiosis: When ghetto and prison meet and mesh. *Punishment and Society*, 3(1): 95–132.

Wacquant, L. 2001b. The penalisation of poverty and the rise of neoliberalism. *European Journal on Criminal Policy and Research*, 9(4), special issue on Criminal Justice and Social Policy.

Wacquant, L. 2007. *Urban Outcasts, A Comparative Sociology of Advanced Marginality*. Malden, MA: Polity.

Wacquant, L. 2009. *Punishing the Poor: The Neoliberal Government of Social Insecurity*. Durham, NC: Duke University Press.

Williamson, C. 1984. Wet, orde en staatsveiligheid: die uitdaging vir die Suid-Afrikaanse Polisie en die Wet en Ordegemeenskap. *South African Journal of Criminal Law and Criminology (SACC)/Suid-Afrikaanse Tydskrif vir strafreg and Kriminologie (SASK)*.

Wilson, J. and Kelling, G. 1982. Broken windows, the police and neighbourhood safety. *Atlantic Magazine*, March.

Wolfgang, M. and Ferracuti, F. 1982. *The Subculture of Violence: Towards an Integrated Theory in Criminology*. Beverly Hills, CA: Sage.

Woodiwiss, M. and Hobbs, D. 2009. Organized evil and the Atlantic Alliance. Moral panics and the rhetoric of organized crime policing in America and Britain. *British Journal of Criminology*, 49: 106–28.

Young, J. 1999. *The Exclusive Society: Social Exclusion, Crime and Difference in Late Modernity*. London: Sage.

Zuern, E. 2006. The contentious poor – marginalization in an era of constitutional democracy. *Politique Africaine*, 103.

Hansards

Hansard, 1977a. Motion on Economic System of Free Enterprise. 4 February, Vol. 66, cols 1–2848.

Hansard, 1977b. Criminal Procedure bill. 7 March–15 April, Vol. 67, cols 2841–5392.

Hansard, 1977c. Liquor Amendment bill, Second reading. 8 February 1977, 21 January–4 March, Vol. 66, cols 1–2848.

Hansard, 1977d. Abuse of Dependence Producing Substances and Rehabilitation Centres Amendment Bill. Wednesday 2 March, Vol. 66 cols 1–2848.

Hansard, 1977e. Prevention of Illegal Squatting Amendment bill. Wednesday 27 April, Vol. 68, cols 5393–8112.

Hansard, 1977f. Prisons Appropriation bill. 6 June, Vol. 69, cols 8113–11152.

Hansard, 1977g. Community Councils bill, second reading. 23 May–24 June, Vol. 69, cols 8113–11512.

Hansard, 1977h. Interpellations, Questions and Replies. 2 February–22 June, Vol. 21.

Hansard, 1978a. Abuse of Dependence Producing Substances and Rehabilitation Centres Amendment bill. 8 May–16 June, Vol. 74, cols 6297–9848.

Hansard, 1978b. National Welfare Amendment bill. 8 May–16 June, Vol. 74, cols 6297–9848.

Hansard, 1978c. Prisons Appropriation Vote. Vol. 74.

Hansard, 1978d. Appropriation bill. Friday 28 April, Vol. 73 cols 3265–6296.

Hansard, 1979a. State President's speech to opening of parliament. Vol. 79 cols 1–3252.

Hansard, 1979b. Appropriation bill. 12 April–5 May, Vol. 11, cols 5185–7912.

Hansard, 1979c. Appropriation bill police. Vol. 79, cols 1–3252.

Hansard, 1980a. Appropriation bill, vote 23 Police. Friday 9 May, Vol. 86, cols 3323–6572.

Hansard, 1980b. Appropriation bill, vote 24 Prisons. Friday 9 May, Vol. 86, cols 3325–6572, 24 March–16 May.

Hansard, 1981a. Appropriation bill, Justice, Vote 22. 7 September–9 October, Vol. 95, cols 3001–6406.

Hansard, 1981b. Interpellations, Questions and Replies. 23 January–26 February Vol. 92(1).

Hansard, 1981c. Debate on Liquor Amendment Bill, second session, 7 September–9 October, Vol. 95, cols 3001–6406.

Hansard, 1981d. Prisons Amendment bill. 23 January–26 February, Vol. 91, cols 1–2626.

Hansard, 1982a. Interpellations, Questions and Replies. 29 January–11 June, Vol. 103.

Hansard, 1982b. Opening Address of State President. 29 January–19 March, Vol. 99 cols 1–3380.

Hansard, 1982c. Motion on Promotion of Free Market System in South Africa. 22 March–7 May, Vol. 100, cols 3381–6424

Hansard, 1982d. Debates on Standing Committee on Appropriation bill. votes 22 and 23, 1982, Vol. 102.

Hansard, 1982e. Prisons Amendment bill, 22 March–7 May, Vol. 100, cols 3381–6424.

Hansard, 1982f. Standing Committee on Appropriation bill. Votes 22 and 23, Justice and Prisons, Vol. 102, Debates of the Standing Committees.

Hansard, 1983. Criminal Law Amendment bill, Vol. 106, cols 3489–7044.

Hansard, 1984. Liquor Amendment bill, Vol. 113, cols 2717–5396, 12 March–27 April.

Hansard, 1985a. Human Sciences Research Council Amendment bill, Vol. 3, cols 2665–5368, 25 March–10 May.

Hansard, 1985b. Interpellations, Questions and Replies. Vol 5, 25 January–19 June.

Hansard, 1986a. Debate on abolition of influx control. Vol. 10, cols 7045–9368, 2 June–21 June.

Hansard, 1986b. Interpellations, Questions and Replies. Vol. 12, 31 January–5 September.

Hansard, 1986c. Debate on the Abuse of Dependence Producing Substances and Rehabilitation Centres Amendment bill. 23 June 1986–23 January. 1987, Vol. 11, cols 9369–11698.

Hansard, 1986–87. Probation Services Amendment bill. 23 June 1986–26 January 1987, Vol. 11, cols 9369–11698.

Hansard, 1987a. Appropriation bill. Vote 15, Justice. 27 July–28 August, Vol. 18, cols 2381–4876.

Hansard, 1987b. Appropriation bill. Vote 16 Prisons. 27 July–28 August, Vol. 18, cols 2381–4876.

Hansard, 1987c. Interpellations, Questions and Replies. 18 May–2 February, Vol. 20.

Hansard, 1988a. Interpellations, Questions and Replies. 5 February–30 September, Vol. 7.

Hansard, 1988b. Debate on the Transport Deregulation bill. Vol. 5, cols 11905–14544, 27 May–20 June.

Hansard, 1990a. Interpellations, Questions and Replies. 2 February–22 June, Vol. 21.

Hansard, 1990b. Prevention of Illegal Squatting Amendment bill. 4 April–4 May, Vol. 18, cols 5433–8104.

Hansard, 1990c. Criminal Law Amendment bill. 4 June–22 June, Vol. 20, cols 10625–12928.

Hansard, 1990d. Abuse of Dependence Producing Substances bill. Vol. 20, cols 10625–12928, 4 June–22 June.

Hansard, 1990e. Prisons Amendment bill. 4 June–22 June, Vol. 20, cols 10625–12928.

Hansard, 1991a. Interpellations, Questions and Replies. Vol. 29, 1 February–21 February.

Hansard, 1991b. Appropriation bill. Vote 9 Justice and Vote 18 Police, cols: 7537–9664, Vol. 26.

Hansard, 1991c. Decriminalisation bill. Vol. 26, cols 7537–9664, 6 May–21 May.

Hansard, 1991d. Probation Services Amendment bill. Vol. 28, 5 June–21 June, cols 11585–13760.

Hansard, 1992a. Appropriation bill. Vote No. 8, Justice. 27 April–12 May, Vol. 33, cols 5313–7689.

Hansard, 1992b. Prevention and Treatment of Drug Dependency bill. 22 January–20 March, Vol. 31, cols 1–2768.

Hansard, 1992c. Interpellations, Questions and Replies. 22 January–21 October, Vol. 13.

Hansard, 1992d. Interpellations, Questions and Replies, Vol. 36, 22 January–21 October.

Hansard, 1992e. House of Delegates, Interpellations, Questions and Replies, Wednesday 19 February.

Hansard, 1992f. Drugs and Drug Trafficking bill. Vol. 35, cols 10417–12840, 8 June–21 October.

Hansard, 1993–94a. Criminal Matters Amendment bill. 1 June–24 June, 1993, Vol. 42, cols 9649–12304.
Hansard, 1993–94b. Correctional Services Amendment bill. 19 April–6 May 1993, Vol. 40, cols 5297–7288.
Hansard, 1994. Appropriation bill, debate on Vote No. 6. Justice, Vol. 1, cols 1–2304.
Hansard, 1995a. Interpellations, Questions and Replies. 1 March–14 September, Vol. 7.
Hansard, 1995b. Debate on Vote 24, Police services. 6 June–11 October, Vol. 6, cols 2125–4478.
Hansard, 1996. Debate on International Co-operation in Criminal Matters bill; Proceeds of Crime bill; Criminal Procedure Amendment bill. 10 June–7 November, Vol. 10, cols 2509–5456.
Hansard, 1997a. Debate on Parole and Correctional Supervision Amendment bill. 5 May–4 June, Vol. 14, cols 2043–4130.
Hansard, 1997b. Appropriation bill, debate on vote 10, Correctional Services. 6 February–25 April, Vol. 13, cols 1–2072.
Hansard, 1998a. Prevention of Organised Crime bill. Vol. 21, col: 6201–8092, 14 September–6 November.
Hansard, 1998b. Debate on Correctional Services bill. Vol. 20, 22 July–11 September, cols 4413–6200.
Hansard, 1998c. Appropriation bill, debate on Vote 10, Correctional Services. Vol. 18, cols 1–2022, 10 February–8 May.
Hansard, 1999a. Interpellations, Questions and Replies. Vol. 30, cols 1–2306.
Hansard, 1999b. Appropriation bill, debate on vote 20, Justice. Vol. 25, cols 1747–3494, 10 March–25 March.
Hansard, 1999c. Interpellations, Questions and Replies. Vol. 30, 18 August–3 December.
Hansard, 2000a. Interpellations, Questions and Replies. 17 April–8 September, Vol. 36b, cols 1285–3076.
Hansard, 2000b. Interpellations, Questions and Replies. 2 February–14 April, Vol. 36A, cols 1–1284.
Hansard, 2000c. National Prosecuting Authority Amendment bill. Vol. 35, 19 September–3 November, cols 5703–7532.
Hansard, 2000d. Appropriation bill, debate on Vote 6, Correctional Services. 4 April–26 May, Vol. 33, cols 1849–3879.
Hansard, 2001a. Discussion on alarming incidence of child rape and abuse. Vol. 41, cols 6413–8290, 9 October–16 November.
Hansard, 2001b. Interpellations, Questions and Replies. Vol. 42, 15 February–28 June, cols 1–2690.
Hansard, 2001c. Interpellations, Questions and Replies. Vol. 43B, 15 October–16 November, cols 4209–5840.
Hansard, 2001d. Appropriation bill. Debate on Vote 19, Correctional Services. Vol. 39, 8 May–14 June, cols 2321–4772.

Hansard, 2002a. Moral Regeneration: A call on South Africans to work together to restore the social fabric. Vol. 50, cols 6941–8048, 21 August–22 October.

Hansard, 2002b. Interpellations, Questions and Replies. Vol. 54, cols 2973–4420.

Hansard, 2003. Interpellations, Questions and Replies. Vol. 48, cols 4655–3834, 12 June–20 June.

Hansard, 2004a. Debate on Vote 24, Justice and Constitutional Development. 17 June–25 June, Vol. 72.

Hansard, 2004b. Appropriation bill. Debate on Vote 21, Correctional Services. Vol. 71.

Hansard, 2004c. Interpellations, Questions and Replies. 3 June–3 September, Vol. 76, cols 1–802.

Hansard, 2004d. Interpellations, Questions and Replies. Vol. 77, 6 September–29 October, cols 803–1628.

Government Documents

Department of Constitutional Development and Planning 1985. Report on Investigation into the Present Welfare Policy in the RSA.

Department of Correctional Services 1992. Report 1 July 1990–30 June 1991, RP 36-1992, ISBN 0-621-14340-5.

Department of Correctional Services 1993. Annual Report 1 July 1991–31 December 1992. RP 64-1993 ISBN 0-621-15419-9.

Department of Correctional Services 1995. Annual Report 1 January–31 December 1994, S5199, RP 146-1995, ISBN 0-621-16826-2.

Department of Correctional Services 1996. Annual Report of the Department of Correctional Services for the period 1 January 1995–31 December 1995, RP 88-1996.

Department of Correctional Services 1997. Annual Report of the Department of Correctional Services for the period 1 January 1996–31 December 1996. RP 71-1997, s 5199.

Department of Correctional Services 1998. Annual Report of the Department of Correctional Services for the period 1 January–31 December 1997.

Department of Correctional Services 1999. Department of Correctional Services Annual Report 1998.

Department of Correctional Services 2001. Department of Correctional Services Annual Report, 1 January 2000–21 March 2001.

Department of Correctional Services 2002. Department of Correctional Services Annual Report, 1 April 2001–31 March 2002.

Department of Correctional Services 2003. Department of Correctional Services Annual Report, 1 April 2002–31 March 2003.

Department of Correctional Services 2004. Department of Correctional Services Annual Report, 1 April 2003–31 March 2004.

Ministry of Finance 1996. Growth, Employment and Redistribution, A Macroeconomic Strategy. http://www.treasury.gov.za/documents/gear/chapter.pdf (accessed on 19 November 2008).

Department of Health and Welfare 1984. Annual Report for Department of Health and Welfare.

Department of Health and Welfare 1985. Report on Investigation into the Present Welfare Policy.

Department of Health and Welfare 1991. Annual Report for the Department of Welfare 1991.

Department of Health and Welfare 1992. Annual Report for the Department of Welfare 1992.

Department of Health Services and Welfare Administration 1990. Annual Report for the Health Services and Welfare Administration, House of Assembly 1990.

Department of Justice 1981. Annual Report Commissioner of Prisons, 1979–80.

Department of Justice 1982a. Annual Report Commissioner of Prisons, 1980–1981.

Department of Justice 1982b. Department of Justice Report for 1 July 1980–30 June 1981. Parliamentary Annexures no. 108–127.

Department of Justice 1984a. Department of Justice Annual Report 1 July 1982–30 June 1983. Parliamentary Annexures no. 110–123.

Department of Justice 1984b. Annual Report of the South African Prisons Service 1982–1983.

Department of Justice 1987. Annual Report 1 July 1985–30 June 1986. Parliamentary Annexures no. 47–66.

Department of Justice 1991a. Annual Report 1 July 1989–30 June 1990. Parliamentary Annexures no. 218–240, 1991.

Department of Justice 1991b. Report of SA Prisons Service 1 July 1989–30 June 1990. Parliamentary Annexures no. 218–240, 1991.

Department of Justice 1992. Annual Report 1 July 1991–30 June 1992.

Department of Justice 1995. Annual Report 1 July 1994–30 June 1995.

Department of Justice, Police and Prisons 1977. Annual Report of the Commissioner of the South African Police for the period 1 July 1975–30 June 1976. RP 45-1977.

Department of Justice, Police and Prisons 1978a. Annual Report of the Commissioner of the South African Police for the period 1 July 1976–30 June 1977. RP 15-1978.

Department of Justice, Police and Prisons 1978b. Report of Commissioner of Prisons, 1 July 1976–30 June 1977, RP 44-1978. Parliamentary Annexures, 126–144.

Department of Law and Order 1986. Annual Report of the Commissioner of the South African Police for the period 1 July 1984–30 June 1985. RP 33-1986.

Department of Law and Order 1987. Annual Report of the Commissioner of the South African Police for the period 1 July 1985–30 June 1986. RP 91-1987.

Department of Law and Order 1988. Annual Report of the Commissioner of the South African Police for the period 1 July 1986–31 December 1987. RP 73-1988.

Department of Law and Order 1989. Annual Report of the Commissioner of the South African Police for the period 1 January 1988–31 December 1988. RP 57-1989.

Department of Law and Order 1990. Annual Report of the Commissioner of the South African Police for the period 1 January 1989–31 December 1990. RP-1990

Department of Law and Order 1991. Annual Report of the Commissioner of the South African Police 1990. RP 68-1991.

Department of Law and Order 1992. Annual Report of the Commissioner of the South African Police 1991. RP 68-1992.

Department of Law and Order 1993. Annual Report of the Commissioner of the South African Police 1992. RP 67-1993.

Department of Law and Order 1994. Annual Report of the Commissioner of the South African Police 1 January 1993–31 December 1993. RP 5-1994.

Department of Police and Prisons 1980. Report of Commissioner of Prisons, 1 July 1977–30 June 1978. RP 36-1980. Parliamentary Annexures, 82–101, 1980.

Department of Police 1981. Annual Report of the Commissioner of the South African Police for the period 1 July 1980–30 June 1981. RP 35-1981.

Department of Safety and Security 1996a. National Crime Prevention Strategy. May.

Department of Safety and Security 1996b. Annual Plan of the South African Police Service 1996–1997.

Department of Safety and Security 1997. Policing Priorities and Objectives for 1997/1998, South African Police Service, April.

Department of Safety and Security, 1998. White Paper on Safety and Security. In the Service of Safety, 1998–2003, September.

Department of Safety and Security 1999. Policing Priorities and Objectives for 1999/2000.

Department of Safety and Security 2001. Annual Report of the Department of Safety and Security, SAPS, 2000–2001. RP 129-2001.

Department of Safety and Security 2002. Annual Report of the National Commissioner of the South African Police Service 2001–2002. RP 172-2002.

Department of Safety and Security 2003. Annual Report of the National Commissioner of the South African Police Service 1 April 2002–31 March 2003.

Department of Safety and Security 2004a. Annual Report of the National Commissioner of the South African Police Service 1 April 2003–31 March 2004.

Department of Social Development 2002. Annual Report April 2001–March 2002.

Department of Welfare 1996a. White Paper on Welfare.

Department of Welfare 1996b. Annual Report 1996.
Department of Welfare 1999. Annual Report 1998–1999.
Department of Welfare 2001. Annual Report for the Department of Welfare, 1 April 2000–31 March 2001.
Government of South Africa 2000. A Report on the Moral Regeneration Workshops I and II, July 2000. http://www.info.gov.za/issues/mrm/index.html (accessed on 12 April 2007).
Republic of South Africa 2011. Judicial Inspectorate for Correctional Services. Annual Report for 2010/2011. Treatment of inmates and conditions in correctional centres. http://judicialinsp.pwv.gov.za/Annualreports/JUDICIAL_INSPECTORATE_ANNUAL%20%20REPORT_2010–2011.pdf (accessed on 20 September 2012).

Commissions of Inquiry

Report of Penal and Prison Reform Commission 1947. Pretoria: Government Printer.
Report of the Commission of Inquiry into the Penal System of the Republic of South Africa 1976. Pretoria: Government Printer.
Report of the Commission of Inquiry into Labour Legislation 1979. Pretoria: Government Printer.
Report of the Commission of Inquiry into Legislation Affecting the Utilisation of Manpower 1979. Pretoria: Government Printer.
Final Report of the Commission of Inquiry into Unrest in Prisons appointed by The President on 27 June 1994, Pretoria, February 1995.

ANC Documents

African National Congress 1985. Report of the Commission on National Structures, Constitutional Guidelines and Codes of Conduct, National Structures, Constitutional Guidelines, Code of Conduct, Umkhonto we Sizwe Military Code. National Consultative Conference. June 1985.
African National Congress 1990a. National Consultative Congress 1990: Programme of Action: Guidelines for Discussion. Centre for Applied Legal Studies, A1 ANC A1.1–4. South African History Archives, University of the Witwatersrand.
African National Congress Department of Political Education 1990b. The Road To Peace, resource Material on Negotiations, June, Marshaltown, Johannesburg, AK215 Centre for Applied Legal Studies N2 Negotiations N2 a–b N2 a, South African History Archives, University of the Witwatersrand.
African National Congress 1991. Open Letter to State President de Klerk and His Cabinet from the National Executive Committee of the ANC, Star 9 April

1991, Centre for Applied Legal Studies, File Negotiations, 1993 N2b. South African History Archives, University of the Witwatersrand.
African National Congress 1992a. Ready to Govern. ANC policy guidelines for a democratic South Africa adopted at the National Conference, 28–31 May 1992. http://www.anc.org.za/ancdocs/history/readyto.html (accessed on 5 January 2008).
African National Congress 1992b. Discussion Document: Crime and Crime Control. What Role Should the Police Play? Centre for Applied Legal Studies, File AK 2195, P2 Police, South African History Archives, University of the Witwatersrand.
African National Congress 1992c. The Security Situation in South Africa. December, Centre for Applied Legal Studies, File Negotiations, 1993 N2b. South African History Archives, University of the Witwatersrand.
African National Congress 1993. Policing in the New South Africa. ANC Department of Information and Publicity, Marshaltown, 1993 AK2915, Centre for Applied Legal Studies, P2 Police File P 2.5 b. South African History Archives, University of the Witwatersrand.
African National Congress, 1994. The Reconstruction and Development Programme, A Policy Framework. http://www.anc.org.za/rdp/rdp.html (accessed on 19 November 2008).
African National Congress 1998. The Moral Renewal of the Nation: Issued as a contribution to the Moral Summit by the National Executive Committee of the ANC, 17 October 1998, http://www.anc.org.za/ancdocs/misc/moralrenewal.html (accessed on 9 March 2007).
African National Congress 1999. Election Manifesto: Together, Fighting for Change, http://www.anc.org.za/elections/manifesto/ (accessed on 9 March 2007).
African National Congress 2001. Social development must be accompanied by moral renewal. *ANC Today*, 1 (10): 30 March–5 April, http://www.anc.org.za/ancdocs/anctoday/2001/at10.htm#art3 (accessed on 5 January 2007).
African National Congress 2004. Manifesto 2004. A People's Contract to Create Work and Fight Poverty. http://www.anc.org.za/elections/2004/manifesto/manifesto.html (accessed on 9 March 2007).

Newspaper Articles

Cape Argus, 2 August 1989, 63683, National Archives of South Africa (NASA), Cape Town Records Centre.
Cape Argus, January–July 1993, 63690 (NASA).
Cape Times, 19 March 1976, "Crackdown on gangs", file x14746 (NASA).
Cape Times, 5 April 1976, "Crime in the townships", file x14746 (NASA).
Cape Times, 19 June 1976, "Crime Rate Causes Concern", file x14746 (NASA).
Cape Times, 18 October 1976, file x14746 (NASA).

Cape Times, 29 December 1976, "46 Blacks die in Natal violence", file x14746 (NASA).
Cape Times, 30 December 1976, file x14746 (NASA).
Cape Times, 1 February 1977, file x147471977 (NASA).
Cape Times, 29 July 1977, "Prevention of crime is the responsibility of all citizens" (NASA).
Cape Times, 25 September 1977, "Crime Soars as Politics, Poverty Gnaw at Morale", file x14747 (NASA).
Cape Times, 29 April 1978, file x147471977 (NASA).
Cape Times, 18 August 1978, file X14748 (NASA).
Cape Times, 18 September 1978, "Gang attacks couple in city", file x14750 (NASA).
Cape Times, 29 July 1981, file x14749, (NASA).
Cape Times, 3 March 1983, "Come Clean on Crime", file x14749 (NASA).
Cape Times, 30 May 1983, file x14751 (NASA).
Cape Times, 27 September 1983, file x14752 (NASA).
Cape Times, 14 May 1986, "Teargas Fired into Homes", file x14756 (NASA).
Cape Times, 22 September 1986, file x14756, (NASA).
Cape Times, 1 November 1986, "The Peninsula Crime Wave", file x14756 (NASA).
Cape Times, 4 April 1987, "Fighting Crime", file x14757 (NASA).
Cape Times, 7 July 1987, file x14757 (NASA).
Cape Times, 2 August 1989, *The Argus*, file 63683 (NASA).
Cape Times, 23 March 1991, "Crime result of quality of life", *The Argus*, January–April 1991, file 63686 (NASA).
Cape Times, 30 November 1991, May–December 1991, file 6387 (NASA).
Cape Times, 19 September 1994, June–October 1994, file 69880 (NASA).
Cape Times, 2 November 1994, November–December, file 69881, (NASA).
Cape Times, 12 August 1996, file 69885 (NASA).
Cape Times, 19 August 1996, "Government Failure Lead to PAGAD", file 69885 (NASA).
Cape Times, 5 September 1997, "Police hail broke window approach" (NASA).
Cape Times, 21 November 2000, "Crime at an All-Time High", microfilm (NASA).
Cape Times, 6 April 2009 (NASA).
Cape Times, 21 September 2012, "Protests divert police resources" (NASA).
Financial Mail, 26 May 1978, "Bring Back the Bobby" (NASA).

Court Cases

S v Makwanyane and Another (CCT3/94) [1995] ZACC 3; 1995 (6) BCLR 665; 1995 (3) SA 391; [1996] 2 CHRLD 164; 1995 (2) SACR 1 (6 June 1995).

Shabalala and Others v Attorney-General of the Transvaal and Another (CCT23/94) [1995] ZACC 12; 1995 (12) BCLR 1593; 1996 (1) SA 725 (29 November 1995).

S v Williams and Others (CCT20/94) [1995] ZACC 6; 1995 (3) SA 632; 1995 (7) BCLR 861 (CC) (9 June 1995).

Index

Advances in Criminology

Full series list

Transitional Justice
Images and Memories
Edited by Chrisje Brants, Ton Hol and Dina Siegel

Racialized Correctional Governance
The Mutual Constructions of Race and Criminal Justice
Claire Spivakovsky

The Arts of Imprisonment
Control, Resistance and Empowerment
Edited by Leonidas K. Cheliotis

The Hidden Order of Corruption
An Institutional Approach
Donatella della Porta and Alberto Vannucci

Comparative Criminal Justice and Globalization
Edited by David Nelken

Racial Criminalization of Migrants in the 21st Century
Edited by Salvatore Palidda

Pervasive Prevention
A Feminist Reading of the Rise of the Security Society
Tamar Pitch

Children's Rights and the Minimum Age of Criminal Responsibility
A Global Perspective
Don Cipriani

Hate on the Net:
Extremist Sites, Neo-fascism On-line, Electronic Jihad
Antonio Roversi

Decisions to Imprison:
Court Decision-Making Inside and Outside the Law
Rasmus H. Wandall

The Policing of Transnational Protest
Edited by Donatella della Porta, Abby Peterson and Herbert Reiter

Migration, Culture Conflict, Crime and Terrorism
Edited by Joshua D. Freilich and Rob T. Guerette

Re-Thinking the Political Economy of Punishment:
Perspectives on Post-Fordism and Penal Politics
Alessandro De Giorgi

Deleuze and Environmental Damage:
Violence of the Text
Mark Halsey

Globalization and Regulatory Character:
Regulatory Reform after the Kader Toy Factory Fire
Fiona Haines

Family Violence and Police Response:
Learning From Research, Policy and Practice in European Countries
Edited by Wilma Smeenk and Marijke Malsch

Crime and Culture:
An Historical Perspective
Edited by Amy Gilman Srebnick and René Lévy

Power, Discourse and Resistance:
A Genealogy of the Strangeways Prison Riot
Eamonn Carrabine

Hard Lessons:
Reflections on Governance and Crime Control in Late Modernity
Richard Hil and Gordon Tait

Becoming Delinquent: British and European Youth, 1650–1950
Edited by Pamela Cox and Heather Shore

Migration, Culture Conflict and Crime
Edited by Joshua D. Freilich, Graeme Newman, S. Giora Shoham and Moshe Addad

Critique and Radical Discourses on Crime
George Pavlich

Blood in the Bank
Social and Legal Aspects of Death at Work
Gary Slapper

Engendering Resistance: Agency and Power in Women's Prisons
Mary Bosworth

Governable Places
Readings on Governmentality and Crime Control
Edited by Russell Smandych

Integrating a Victim Perspective within Criminal Justice
International Debates
Edited by Adam Crawford and Jo Goodey

For Product Safety Concerns and Information please contact our EU representative GPSR@taylorandfrancis.com
Taylor & Francis Verlag GmbH, Kaufingerstraße 24, 80331 München, Germany

www.ingramcontent.com/pod-product-compliance
Ingram Content Group UK Ltd.
Pitfield, Milton Keynes, MK11 3LW, UK
UKHW011014180926
475701UK00004B/739

* 9 7 8 1 1 3 8 2 6 6 9 6 4 *